Wild Neighbors

Wild Neighbors

The Humane Approach to Living with Wildlife

The Humane Society of the United States
Washington, D.C.

Edited by

John Hadidian
Guy R. Hodge
John W. Grandy

Fulcrum Publishing
Golden, Colorado

This book challenges people to enjoy wildlife in its natural beauty and live with it as humanely as possible. Nonetheless, there is always a possibility of injury, even serious injury, when people try to solve wildlife problems. Wild animals can be dangerous if improperly contacted or handled, and the procedures and even products used to humanely control wildlife problems can be dangerous if the individual does not take proper precautions.

The information provided in this book with regard to consumer products should be used with caution. Your use of this book expressly indicates your assumption of risk of serious injury as a result of risks inherently dangerous in interacting with wild animals or using any products or procedures described in this book.

The information and opinions expressed in this book represent the views of the authors and The Humane Society of the United States, and do not necessarily represent the views of Fulcrum Publishing. Neither Fulcrum Publishing, the authors, nor The Humane Society of the United States assume any liability for any injury or property damage that may result from the use of this book.

For information on membership in The Humane Society of the United States, see page 238.

Library of Congress Cataloging-in-Publication Data

Wild neighbors : the humane approach to living with wildlife / The
    Humane Society of the United States ; edited by John Hadidian, Guy
    R. Hodge, and John W. Grandy.
        p.   cm.
    Includes bibliographical references (p.   ) and index.
    ISBN 1-55591-309-1 (pbk.)
    1. Urban pests—Control.   2. Wildlife pests—Control.   3. Animal
welfare.   4. Urban animals—Identification.   I. Hadidian, John.
II. Hodge, Guy R.   III. Grandy, John W.   IV. Humane Society of the
United States.
SB603.3.W45   1997
628.9'69'091732—dc21   96-47459
                        CIP

Printed in the United States of America

0   9   8   7   6   5   4   3   2   1

Fulcrum Publishing
350 Indiana Street, Suite 350
Golden, Colorado 80401-5093
(800) 992-2908 • (303) 277-1623

Contributors
(in alphabetical order)

William Bridgeland, M.S.,
is a wildlife biologist who runs an
urban wildlife management business in Maryland.

Donald L. Burton, M.S., D.V.M.,
is the founder and director of the
Ohio Wildlife Center in Columbus, Ohio.

John W. Grandy, Ph.D.,
is the vice president of Wildlife and Habitat Protection for
The Humane Society of the United States.

John Hadidian, Ph.D.,
is the director of the Urban/Suburban Wildlife Protection Program for
The Humane Society of the United States.

Guy R. Hodge
is the director of Data and Information Services for
The Humane Society of the United States.

Dave Pauli
is the regional director for the Northern Rockies office of
The Humane Society of the United States.

Jill Valenstein, Esq.,
is the program coordinator for the Wildlife and Habitat Protection section of
The Humane Society of the United States.

Contents

Foreword

Dear Friend,

As we approach the new millennium, the United States is completing the most far-reaching transition in its history—from being a rural society to becoming an urbanized society. Eight out of every ten Americans now live in municipalities of fifty thousand residents or more. Every other American lives in one of our thirty-nine largest cities. More than 70 million acres of land have been taken to build cities and suburbs, while an urban "shadow"—an area reflecting the effects of urbanization—spreads over the countryside. Yet, even with this urbanization, we can be thankful that one element of our natural environment—wildlife—continues to share our world.

Wild animals are a blessing that enrich our lives. They provide a source of awe, wonder and learning for us and our children. As we become more urban, wild animals provide a link to our natural world of vital and special importance. Yet where animals and people coexist, problems may occur.

Our responsibility, as humane and caring individuals, is to solve those problems with understanding, compassion and tolerance. Not just for the animals involved, but for our own selves as well. What we need for the future is a kinder, gentler, more compassionate world. We must work to create this world in every aspect of our lives, including particularly how we solve conflicts with the wild creatures with whom we share

our lives. This book, I am pleased to say, offers us the best, most humane means of solving these problems. I commend it to you.

In the same vein, I hope you will also give special attention to the discussion concerning The Humane Society of the United States Wildlife Land Trust. As much as it is important to provide the most humane solutions to problems between wildlife and people, we must also take action to preserve the habitat base on which so much wildlife depends. In short, it is vitally important to provide wildlife with a natural home—permanently protected habitat that is a true shelter without walls. For this reason we have begun The HSUS Wildlife Land Trust, and with it we are offering this organization as a vehicle to permanently protect land and its wildlife throughout America, where our children and our children's children will be able to appreciate and enjoy the animals for which we care so deeply.

I urge you to join with The Humane Society of the United States in these and other programs to create a truly Humane Society.

Sincerely,

Paul G. Irwin, President

Preface:
Resolving Conflicts—The Humane Approach

This book has been written because many people are both thrilled and concerned about contact with wildlife in the city and suburbs. Thrilled because wild animals are a vital part of our lives. Concerned because where people and animals coexist, there are bound to be conflicts. When there are conflicts, people need solutions. For far too long, the so-called "solutions" have been simply to kill offending animals. Invariably, this approach only leads to a cycle of continued destruction. Yet now a world that is awakening to the need for environmental responsibility and appreciation for the diversity of life is demanding rational, realistic and harmonious solutions to conflicts with wildlife. Solutions that keep wildlife alive, but solve the problem. That is the subject of this book.

In our view, there are three integral principles that underlie the resolution of human-wildlife conflicts in urban and suburban settings:

- Respect for the environment

- Tolerance and understanding of living things

- Willingness to resolve conflicts using nonlethal means

A healthy environment is one of the most important components of conflict resolution. This is because healthy environments have many interacting components that keep potentially negative factors in balance. Thus, in many instances the first defense in solving problem situations involving wildlife is to let natural forces solve the problem without human intervention.

Human tolerance and understanding are necessary in creating a healthy environment. Many so-called wildlife problems arise out of the irrational fears that people sometimes have. For example, if we understand that a raccoon in our yard is not a threat, but a member of a natural community in which we also live, we may have removed the need to remove the raccoon. Education concerning the way of the natural world increases our understanding and tolerance, and, in fact, our appreciation for wildlife.

The last principle, and the focus of this book, is nonlethal conflict resolution. We have only just begun to investigate and understand the considerable arsenal of tools and techniques at our disposal that can be used to nonlethally resolve conflicts with wild animals. The future is bright in promising new and better techniques that emphasize solving problems without killing and without injury or insult to the animal or the natural environment.

It is our most sincere wish that this approach will lead both to more humane treatment of wildlife and greater appreciation for the wild animals that share our lives—our wild neighbors.

John Hadidian
Guy R. Hodge
John W. Grandy

Acknowledgments

This book would have been impossible to write without the direct and indirect contributions of many different individuals from many different fields of specialization. By teaching and advocating awareness of urban ecosystems and the role of wildlife as part of those systems, a small but growing group of individuals has fostered the hope that we will focus our attention as a society upon this subject. By their doing so, they prompt, stimulate and reinforce our own commitment to this field. We thank all of those listed below and the others we neglect to mention, but who also work to encourage awareness.

Initial enthusiastic support for commercial publication of this type of work was provided by Bill Schneider. We thank him. Funding for an earlier version of this book (*The Humane Control of Wildlife in Cities and Towns*) as well as support for the ongoing Humane Society of the United States urban wildlife seminar series were provided by The Geraldine R. Dodge Foundation. Their support and encouragement has been very helpful.

We are indebted to our friends and colleagues in research, state and federal agencies, nonprofit organizations and private business for information shared and ideas compared over a span of many years. We thank the following people for their professional advice, opinions and shared thoughts over the years: Lowell Adams, John Adcock, Rex Baker, Tom Barnes, Elizabeth Borden, Allan and Shirley Casey, Michael Conover, Scott Craven, Paul Curtis, Carol DiSalvo, Richard Dolbeer, Richard Farinato, Steve Fairaizl, Vagn Flyger, Tom Franklain, Steve Frantz, Tom French, Al Geis, John Hench, Jonathan Hoeldtke, Martha Hoopes, Craig Huegel, Scott Hyngstrom, Dianne Ingram, Suzanne Jenkins, Ron Johnson, Bill Kern, Jay Kirkpatrick, Pat Klein, Paul and Georgean Kyle, Dan Leedy, Randy Lockwood, Martin Lowny, David Manski, Rex Marsh, Frank Mazzotti, Charlie Nilon, Dick Randall, Seth Riley, Allen Rutberg, Terry Salmon, Joe Schaefer, Robert Schmidt, Tom Seamans, Bill Shaw, Stephanie Sheperd, Laura Simon, Arthur Slater, Faye Sorhage, Merlin Tuttle and Larry VanDruff.

Wild Neighbors

One

Living with
Wild Neighbors

Figure 1. *The typical dwelling and yard can provide abundant resources for wild animals. Backyard ponds (a) attract many species of birds and mammals to drink or search for food, while flower (b) and vegetable (c) gardens and fruit trees (d) often tempt animals with promises of meals. More tempting may be spilled seed from bird feeders (e) or unsecured trash cans (f).*

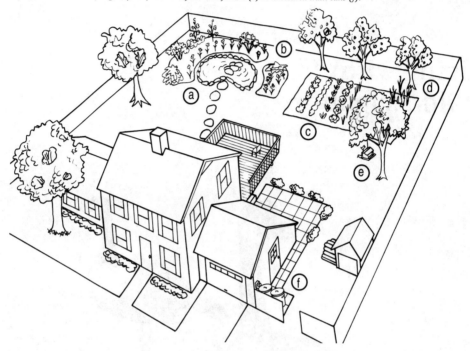

Figure 2. *The house and yard can also provide homes for wild animals in the form of shelter and cover. An overhanging branch (a) can provide access to a roof, while the tree itself may be used as a refuge. An uncapped chimney (b) or broken vent (c) can provide access to warm, dry living quarters. Entry for small animals can occur where wiring enters the house (d and e), vents are uncapped (f), doors are improperly fitted (g), ground-level windowsills (h) and bulkhead doors (i) have gaps. Shelter can be found under decks (j), and burrowing animals may tunnel beneath patios (k) or woodpiles (l).*

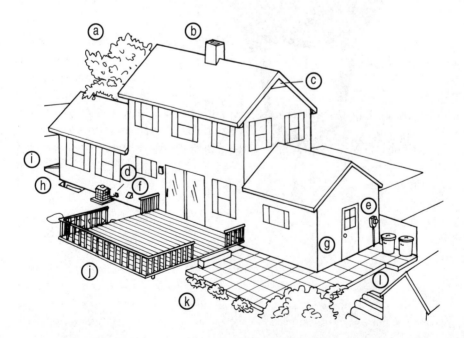

1

The Strategy of Conflict Resolution

CONFLICTS WITH WILDLIFE can occur at many different levels and in many different contexts. This book is primarily about encounters between homeowners and wild animals that establish themselves in yards, gardens and sometimes even our houses. It is important to approach human-wildlife conflict resolution situations with a practical, rational sense of purpose and planning. The following discussion describes this approach.

Determining the Problem

The first step for anyone who experiences a conflict situation with a wild animal in or around their home is to ask the question, Do I really have a problem? Many times the "problem" is really not a problem at all. A fox walks through a yard one afternoon. A bat flies overhead at dusk. Do they have rabies? Will they attack me or my pets? Flocks of starlings are landing on my lawn. Are they damaging it?

A little knowledge concerning these animals can yield simple answers. And the answers will often tell us that a problem doesn't really exist at all. If one does, the next step is to learn more about it.

Damage Identification

Suppose there *is* a problem. What animal is causing it? How long has it been occurring? Where and when is the damage occurring?

Before anything else occurs in a wildlife damage situation, it is absolutely necessary to collect a few simple bits of information: the species involved, the extent of damage, whether or not there are young animals present and what can be done to resolve the issue in a humane and permanent fashion.

Figures 1 and 2 on the preceding page illustrate some of the more common places where conflicts with wild animals are likely to occur. These are areas where routine inspection and monitoring can pay big benefits in heading off problems before they occur.

Assessment

How serious is the problem? (Are there safety or health concerns to people or pets?) How extensive is the problem? (Is the amount of damage insignificant? Real, but acceptable? Beyond acceptance? Likely to reoccur, or passing?) Noticeable damage often literally takes years to develop. Does sudden attention to the fact that damage is occurring justify taking the drastic action of trapping and moving or even killing animals? Even if an animal is causing some damage, is there enough to be classified as a problem or demand a solution? Timing also is a key component to damage assessment. Many problems with animals are of short duration, or occur only during certain seasons. Assessing the damage and the circumstances surrounding it is critical in determining the action that is taken, or even whether action need be taken at all.

Action

Only *after* the facts have been collected and evaluated should the need for action, the type of action necessary and the timing of that action be considered. People often take direct action immediately after discovering a problem. Taking action is one of the *last* steps. Action to resolve conflicts with wildlife does not have to be lethal. Exclusion, repellents, changing human cultural practices and habitat modification are all examples of nonlethal action described in this book. If lethal action must occur, or has happened because people acted before they stopped to think, then *nonlethal actions are still crucial.* As tragic as lethal responses often are, they are far worse when not followed by strategies intended to prevent them from being used repeatedly.

Evaluation

Will the action taken permanently resolve the problem? How can the problem be prevented from reoccurring? Frequently, whether or not action has been taken, the *cause* of the problem has remained untouched, making it necessary to deal with its symptoms time and time again. If lethal action has been taken, evaluation of the determining cause of the problem and ways to correct it *must* take place to prevent reoccurrence (of the lethal action and the problem itself).

Seeking Help

The homeowner faced with a wildlife problem often has no idea where to turn and, all too frequently, in seeking help enters a bureaucratic labyrinth that leads from one agency to another until they give up in frustration. Often there *is* no place to turn for good answers. Animal shelters, with their traditional emphasis on companion animals (cats and dogs), frequently lack the resources to respond to wildlife calls. State game and wildlife departments often do not have urban biologists or programs to support the suburban and urban communities in getting answers. Even when resources can be found at the local and state levels, there is often inadequate funding and support to meet all of the needs the community—especially during peak times of the year such as spring.

On the other hand, the homeowner may feel overwhelmed by the number of available services that address conflicts with wildlife. The relevant local, state and federal agencies all deal with different aspects of wildlife control, and there also are university cooperative extension services, wildlife rehabilitators, national organizations, such as The Humane Society of the United States, and private companies that deal with wildlife control issues. With so many places to turn, the homeowner can easily become swamped with conflicting advice and feel that with having to deal with so many agencies, it might be better to deal with none at all. To this, we offer our sympathies and some general guidelines to follow when choosing which agency to contact.

Local Agencies

In emergency situations, such as when a person has been bitten or an injured animal needs assistance, the homeowner should call their local animal control or police departments. In non-emergency situations the local animal shelter can be a good source of advice—even if they cannot or do not respond themselves. Most shelters have lists of local rehabilitators, wildlife specialists or nuisance wildlife control operators (NWCOs).

State Agencies

The individual states are responsibile for wildlife as a public resource and often regulate both the harvesting of "game" species and the control of "nuisance" wildlife. Contacting state offices is important when dealing with nuisance wildlife—and a must for anyone seeking a permit to stop animal damage. Many state Department of Natural Resources (DNR) or Department of Environmental Conservation (DEC) agencies also have specialists who can answer questions, and some states have toll-free numbers that citizens can use to get advice. Although the endangered species in this country are the responsibility of the federal government, they are of special concern to the individual states as well.

Federal Agencies

The United States Fish and Wildlife Service (USFWS) can provide timely information on a variety of wildlife issues and is primarily responsible for migratory birds and all endangered species. The United States Department of Agriculture's Animal and Plant Health Inspection Service (APHIS) has an Animal Damage Control (ADC) division that specializes in animal damage. Both of these organizations provide advice and information to the public. Most birds, excluding pigeons, house sparrows, starlings and a few native species that are considered agricultural pests, may only be captured or killed under special depredation permits issued by the USFWS upon the recommendation of APHIS-ADC. In recent years the USFWS has tightened the rules for obtain-ing depredation permits. Currently, a property owner must demonstrate that they are sustaining significant economic loss or damage and that nonlethal approaches have been seriously attempted and have failed to resolve the conflict. There is an application fee of about $25 and it takes about thirty days to get the permit. (Addresses and phone numbers for the regional offices of the federal agencies involved in animal control are given in Appendix 1.)

Nuisance Wildlife Control Operators

Increasingly, homeowners pay private companies to resolve wildlife conflicts. The nuisance wildlife control operator (NWCO), sometimes also referred to as a pest control operator (PCO), can serve a valuable function when municipal or state resources are not enough to meet all needs. This is a fledgling industry, however, and companies vary widely in expertise and professionalism. Some NWCOs are highly professional and some are no more than fly-by-night operators whose business practices are intolerable. How is the client to tell which NWCO they're dealing with? We suggest the following guidelines as a start:

- Does the NWCO listen to the description of the problem and ask relevant questions without first launching into a discussion of fees and responsibilities?

- Does the person appear to care about their work, the animals involved and the concerns of the homeowner? Are they willing to come to the scene, examine the problem and give an estimate in writing?

- Do they appear to be professional in approach and willingness to discuss the problem and in their manner of giving advice?

- Does the person appear knowledge-able and take the time to explain not only what the source of the problem is but its causes and potential solutions?

- Are they licensed by the state and bonded against any incidental damage that might be caused?

- Do they try to scare the homeowner with talk about wildlife disease or dangerous animals?

- Are the procedures to be used simply and concisely explained, with clear indication as to whether anything could harm the animal?

- Do they have more than one recom-mendation to resolve the problem—especially recommendations that involve nonlethal solutions?

- Does the recommendation include fixing the problem so that it does not reoccur? (This includes a discussion of needed structural repairs or changes [such as chimney caps], alteration of habits [e.g., bird feeding or trash maintenance] or exclusion to prevent animals from getting into areas where they are not wanted.)

- Is the work guaranteed for at least a year?

- Do they offer a written contract that protects both parties and stipulates that nonlethal methods will be used before any lethal methods are

considered *and* that the homeowner will be advised and consulted if lethal control is necessary?

Wildlife Rehabilitators

People who care for injured wildlife with the objective of returning animals to the wild are called *rehabilitators*. In growing numbers, these people are a valuable re-source in dealing with wildlife problems. Not only do they accept orphaned animals resulting from control actions, but many provide advice and counsel for people with wildlife problems. Usually, rehabilitators are licensed by the state. The code of the reha-bilitator is to minimize human contact with injured or orphaned wildlife while restor-ing or raising the animal so that it can be released into the wild. This gives the ani-mal the best chance to survive and to func-tion normally as a member of its species.

Not every locality has a rehabilitator within a convenient distance. State wildlife departments, as the licensing agency, keep lists of rehabilitators and can tell you which ones serve your area. In a situation in which an animal has been abandoned, home-owners should seek the help of a rehabili-tator before contacting another agency. Rehabilitators can also provide important information on local animal control ser-vices and private companies. Because most rehabilitators are swamped with injured and orphaned animals during spring and summer months, they sometimes cannot help. Homeowners can help by consulting the rehabilitator, delaying action if possible and working toward a solution that does not necessitate the handling of the animal.

Wildlife Law

When resolving human-wildlife conflicts, the homeowner must be aware of and comply with all federal, state and local laws that apply to a particular conflict-resolving activity. Even many of the nonlethal solutions emphasized in this book may have legal implications. For instance, under state law it may be illegal for a homeowner to live trap (trapping an animal without causing any bodily harm) and relocate a problem animal. Even constructing a fence intended to exclude wildlife from a yard may be prohibited by a local ordinance or neighborhood covenant.

This section provides an overview of some of the laws in the United States concerning wildlife control. Although this chapter discusses laws and regulations that relate to lethal control methods, this is done primarily to alert the reader that certain control activities may be unlawful. Nonlethal methods often provide the most long-lasting solution to human-wildlife conflicts and are less likely to be subject to regulation.

The HSUS recommends that homeowners also consult local sources, such as extension agents or humane society representatives, district game wardens or state wildlife agency personnel, for information on applicable statutes and regulations that may restrict the manner of control. Request copies of the laws and regulations when you call, and familiarize yourself with them. Local wildlife rehabilitators are an excellent source of information on laws and regulations. Ultimately, it is your responsibility to know the law; unintentional violations of the law are still violations nonetheless. These agencies should also be contacted if you believe anyone is controlling wildlife in a manner that may be unlawful.

Federal Law

THE MIGRATORY BIRD TREATY ACT

Perhaps the law that is easiest to inadvertently violate when dealing with human-wildlife conflicts is the Migratory Bird Treaty Act (MBTA). The MBTA makes it unlawful for persons to pursue, hunt, take, capture or kill migratory birds or to destroy any migratory bird nest or egg, unless otherwise permitted. For example, it is technically a violation of the MBTA to capture (or remove) a chimney swift, or its nest, from your chimney unless authorized by the United States Fish and Wildlife Service (USFWS). Persons who violate the MBTA or fail to comply with regulations made pursuant to it are guilty of a misdemeanor and may be fined up to $500 or imprisoned for up to six months, or both. It is important to note that a person need not know they are violating the MBTA to be guilty of a misdemeanor violation.

The "migratory" birds protected by the MBTA include hundreds of native bird species that nest in or migrate through the United States. Only introduced, or exotic, bird species such as house sparrows, pigeons and starlings are unprotected by the MBTA. These birds, however, may be protected by state wildlife and other state laws. The MBTA designates certain other birds as "migratory game birds." These birds may be hunted or trapped, but only during specified "open" seasons.

A homeowner has no constitutional right to control federally protected migratory birds (or other wildlife) to protect property. Instead, a property owner seeking relief from bird damage must apply to the USFWS for a federal depredation permit, even to employ certain nonlethal controls like relocation. The application must contain a description of the damaged area, the nature and extent of the harm and the bird species causing the injury. The USFWS will only issue a depredation permit upon the recommendation of the United States Department of Agriculture (USDA) Animal Damage Control (ADC) office. (These contacts are listed under Federal Agency Offices in

Appendix 1.) The ADC state office generally only recommends a permit to kill birds after the homeowner demonstrates that nonlethal methods have failed to resolve the conflict. Some states may also require a state depredation permit before certain nonlethal and lethal controls are applied.

A commercial animal control company is also required to have a federal permit to control migratory birds. If you plan to seek assistance from a commercial operator, make certain they have any necessary state licenses and the required federal and state permits. A federal permit is not required simply to herd or frighten migratory birds, except for endangered and threatened species and golden and bald eagles. Similarly, many of the humane solutions offered in this book, like bird exclusion, do not involve the MBTA.

Crows, yellow-headed, red-winged, rusty and Brewer's blackbirds, cowbirds, grackles and magpies are protected by the MBTA but may be "controlled" without a federal permit. These controls, however, may not be applied unless these birds are committing or are about to commit property damage or are constituting a health hazard or nuisance. A landowner's opinion that these conditions are met is all that is required under the law. It is still a good idea, however, to contact your state wildlife agency for assistance. Although no federal permit may be required to control these birds, a state control permit may be required or the methods of control may otherwise be limited by state law. To avoid inadvertent violations of the MBTA, as well as state and local laws, consult with the appropriate agency to determine the legal status of the bird species involved in the conflict.

THE FEDERAL INSECTICIDE, FUNGICIDE AND RODENTICIDE ACT

An important federal law that relates to wildlife control and that homeowners should also be aware of is the Federal Insecticide, Fungicide and Rodenticide Act (FIFRA). As the name implies, FIFRA regulates pesticide safety and use. FIFRA not only regulates pesticides that kill problem wildlife (a solution that The HSUS does not recommend), but also regulates repellents and other nonlethal control methods. FIFRA defines a "pesticide" as any substance "intended for preventing, destroying, repelling or mitigating any pest." FIFRA also regulates pesticidal devices (e.g., glueboards for mice). These devices, however, are not subject to the full registration process imposed upon chemical products.

If a product is sold as a pesticide it must be registered in accordance with FIFRA by the Environmental Protection Agency (EPA), the agency authorized to carry out FIFRA. EPA registration certifies that the product is legal for use in the United States. It is important to note, however, that states may limit or outright ban any federally certified pesticide for use in the state. States may also require a manufacturer to obtain state registration for a particular pesticide. Therefore, if you have any doubts about using a particular product in your state, check with your state environmental or agricultural agency.

The EPA may also classify a pesticide product for "restricted" use if it warrants special handling due to its toxicity. A "restricted use" classification means that the pesticide may only be used by or under the direct supervision of a certified applicator. When hiring a commercial pesticide company, a homeowner should make certain that the applicator is properly certified if applying restricted-use pesticides.

Finally, the EPA further regulates pesticide use through labeling restrictions. It is a violation of the law to "use any registered pesticide in a manner inconsistent with its labeling." Label restrictions set the concentration and amount of pesticide that can be applied, specify the general locations where the product can be used (e.g., certain pesticides may not be used near streams or other environmentally sensitive areas), identify the species that may be controlled and stipulate other conditions. It is important to note that it is illegal to poison certain animals such as beaver, cottontail rabbits, deer, opossum, porcupine and shrews, among others.

State and Local Law

Although federal and state laws protect most birds, endangered species and other select groups (e.g., marine mammals), individual state laws provide for the protection of virtually every resident animal species. Also, as noted previously in this chapter, where state law duplicates federal law, state law standards are often more restrictive than their federal counterparts. And local laws are sometimes more restrictive than state laws.

STATE ANIMAL CONTROL LAWS
State animal damage control schemes can be very complicated and may involve several different agencies. State agencies responsible for overseeing human-wildlife conflicts include state fish and wildlife, conservation, health and agricultural departments. Also, because no two states regulate the control of wildlife in the same way, it is a necessary first step to contact the proper agency—before taking any action—as a precaution to inadvertent violations of the law. These agencies can also be extremely helpful. Some states will provide a homeowner with technical assistance to nonlethally control wildlife. If your state does not provide this assistance, ask them who you may contact regarding nonlethal control methods. They may be able to direct you to a local control agent who can help.

Certain state laws illustrate just how varied this area of the law is and accordingly how important it is to contact your state agency when conflicts arise, especially for the wildlife involved. For instance, in recent years several states have passed laws and regulations concerning species thought to carry rabies and other disease. Generally, these laws and regulations prohibit homeowners and licensed animal control agents alike from live trapping and relocating certain rabies vector or other designated species. Some states require that a live trapped "nuisance" raccoon, for example, be euthanized upon capture. Other states allow a trapped rabies vector species to be kept under quarantine for a specified number of days before relocating the animal elsewhere. These laws, and the regulations made pursuant to them, are constantly being amended and still other states are in the process of passing similar laws. So before live trapping any problem animal be certain that it is legal to release and relocate the animal. It is extremely important to note here that avoiding encounters before they occur can save the lives of these species.

Also states differ in how they regulate animal damage control businesses. Although many states do not regulate commercial animal damage control operators, some states require that wildlife control businesses be state certified or licensed. Additionally, even licensed control operators need permits for certain wildlife control activities.

STATE HUNTING AND TRAPPING LAWS
State hunting and trapping laws may also determine how and when certain animals can be controlled. For example, in many states beaver are classified as a furbearer or as a game animal and may only be trapped or hunted with a license valid during the

state's trapping and hunting seasons. At all other times, beaver and other furbearers, as well as game animals, like deer, may be protected and only be killed or removed from property under conditions set by the game department or other authority. Similarly, states have jurisdiction over resident, nonmigratory birds and may designate species like pheasant, quail and grouse as game species. Game birds may only be killed during the state designated hunting season. Again, because hunting and trapping laws vary from state to state, it is important to contact the state wildlife agency or game department to determine the legal status of a particular animal before applying control measures.

Other wildlife species may be classified as protected nongame species. In most states bats are protected and may not be harmed except under specified conditions set by the state wildlife department. Unprotected animals, like Norway and roof rats, mice, gophers and moles, sometimes referred to as "vermin" or "pests," can usually be killed, captured or otherwise controlled without special authorization from the state wildlife department. But even though these species are totally unprotected, safe and humane methods are available and should be employed for their control.

STATE ANTI-CRUELTY LAWS

State anti-cruelty statutes arguably give some protection to otherwise unprotected species, like rats and mice, depending on the statute. Generally these laws state that no person may intentionally kill, mutilate, torment, torture or cruelly beat any animal. All fifty states, and the District of Columbia, have anti-cruelty statutes. In most states, all animals, including wildlife, are protected. Most statutes exempt certain activities from the definition of cruelty. For example, hunting, trapping, accepted animal husbandry practices, the use of animals in laboratory research and even "pest" control are sometimes specifically exempted under cruelty statutes, or are generally exempted as either necessary or are legal because other laws authorize them.

Although anti-cruelty statutes do not generally prohibit landowners from controlling wildlife, some "control" methods have been found to constitute cruelty. Cruelty prosecutions involving wildlife damage control are a relatively new occurrence, however, and this area of the law is still evolving.

LOCAL AND MUNICIPAL LAW

Finally, some local and municipal laws or ordinances may further restrict the methods of animal control permitted in a certain area. For example, in many places it is illegal to discharge a firearm in residential areas. Also, some places have prohibited the use of poisons and traps or have strictly limited their use. Acoustical repellents (noise-making devices used to scare animals) may be prohibited by local ordinance or neighborhood covenant. Even putting up a fence may not be allowed in some locales or neighborhoods.

The best way to ensure that you are complying with all applicable laws and regulations is to consult your local humane society, university extension service, district game warden or state wildlife department. For the most part, safe and humane controls—especially ones that exclude wildlife, change human cultural practices or modify the habitat—are not only the least expensive and most long-lasting solutions, but also the best defense against inadvertent violations of the law.

2

Health Concerns in Dealing with Wildlife

THIS CHAPTER DEALS WITH THE consequences of direct—and sometimes indirect—contact with wildlife for human health and safety. People naturally have concerns, whether real or imagined, about what might happen when they come into contact with a wild animal or have had one living in or under their house. Can they be bitten or scratched? Will they be exposed to disease? Is it dangerous? This section was written to answer some of the many questions people might have. In the individual species profile chapters in the second part of this book, we have included separate information regarding the public health issues associated with each. Issues that arise with more than one species are referred back to this chapter.

Animals and humans share approximately 175 known communicable diseases. The term *zoonosis* is used to identify any disease transmitted from vertebrate animals to humans. Wild animals can serve as primary or secondary reservoirs for many zoonoses. Many diseases that are readily controllable with preventative health programs in domestic species (canine distemper, for example) go largely unchecked in wild free-ranging populations. Transmission of zoonotic diseases can occur by direct means (via contact with the animal, its urine or feces) or indirectly (by air, soil and water contaminated with the infectious agent). Domestic animals may also become infected

through contact with wildlife and serve as the immediate reservoir for human exposure. *Vectors,* such as ticks and mosquitoes, also play an important role in the transmission of diseases from wildlife to humans.

The average person need have little concern about exposure to wildlife diseases in their daily life. Avoiding direct contact with wild animals is always recommended, and when they must be handled, it is best to rely on experienced and properly equipped people to do this job. Indirect contact with wildlife disease agents is likely to be much more frequent than direct contact.

Most of our attention in this chapter focuses on the practical means of prevention and *cleanup* that provide the front line of defense against common zoonotic diseases. The following presentation is not intended to alarm or frighten but to cultivate an understanding and respect for potential means of transmission and the preventative actions that can be taken to avoid transmission. Some very uncommon but potentially life-threatening diseases are reviewed to emphasize the importance of their prevention. *In any situation where exposure to a zoonotic disease is suspected, consult your private physician and public health officials.*

Physical Injuries

When a wild animal is held against its will, it will use all available defenses to resist restraint. Without proper restraint techniques and equipment, bites, scratches and other trauma injuries can occur.

If a person is bitten or scratched, immediately clean the wound by thoroughly scrubbing it with soap and water. Flush or irrigate the wound liberally, using clean tap water if sterile solutions are unavailable. Proper and early wound scrubbing and irrigation has been shown to significantly reduce the incidence of wound infections. Irrigation provides for the mechanical removal of potentially infectious microorganisms. Wounds should be cleaned again with iodine-based solutions and copiously irrigated under medical supervision.

All wounds caused by a wild animal should be examined by a physician. Puncture wounds can be serious no matter how minor they may appear. When you get medical help for a bite wound, your health care provider should discuss your tetanus immunization history and recommend treatment based on your age and vaccination history. Immediate medical care helps to reduce wound infections.

The risk of infection from a penetrating animal bite has been reported in the range of 5 to 15 percent. Predisposing factors increasing the risk of infection include being more than fifty years old, a delay in the delivery of treatment and puncture wounds in general. Any preexisting illness such as immune compromise, diabetes mellitus or organ dysfunction can further complicate wound infections.

Bites of certain species of animals are more likely to produce infections than others. Numerous bacteria can cause wound infections from bites and scratches. Among the most common are *Staphylococcus* spp., *Streptococcus* spp., *Corynebacterium* spp. and *Pasturella multocida*. Bacteria more common in wild animals than domestic animals (but less commonly reported) that are known to cause clinical wound infections include *Leptospira icterohemorrhagiae*, *Francisella tularensis* and *Brucella suis*. Two agents, *Streptobacillus moniliformis* and *Spirillium minus*, are associated with rat-bite fever of humans and can lead to fatality in 10 percent of untreated cases.

Evaluations of the wound in consideration of the offending species can determine the potential for rabies infection. Bites from known rabies vector species should be regarded as rabid unless proven negative by laboratory testing. If the animal is not available for testing, post-exposure (to rabies) treatment should be administered. Bites from squirrels, chipmunks, rats, mice, other rodents and lagomorphs (rabbits, hares) should be considered on an individual basis, but almost never call for post-exposure treatment.

Brucellosis (Undulant Fever, Bang's Disease)

Hosts

Feral swine, bison, caribou, elk.

Background

Brucellosis is primarily centered in domestic agricultural species but may also be found in populations of bison, elk and caribou in the western states and feral pigs in the southeastern United States. Brucella infections are usually transmitted by contamination of mucus membranes, especially by oral ingestion or through broken skin having contact with an animal's infected body fluids such as blood, urine, vaginal discharges, aborted fetuses, placentas or feces. Aerosol transmission also has been documented.

Clinical Disease

Incubation time is variable, ranging from one week to several months. In humans, onset of the disease can be characterized by fever with accompanying headache, chills, profuse sweating, prostration, insomnia, sexual impotence or arthralgia. Clinical disease can progress to encephalitis, meningitis, spondylitis, arthritis or cardiac disease. Chronic arthritis may persist for life.

Prevention

Protective gear such as coveralls, boots, masks and gloves should be used when handling potential carriers or reservoirs.

Bubonic Plague
(Yersinia pestis)

Hosts

Prairie dogs and ground squirrels.

Background

Plague is very rarely reported in most parts of the United States. Ninety percent of the reported cases are found in New Mexico, Arizona, California and Colorado. When rodent numbers are great and are accompanied by dense flea populations, periodic epizootics occur. These result in high mortality to the rodents, which then can increase the possibility of exposure of domestic pets and humans as fleas look for alternate hosts. Bubonic plague is primarily a flea-transmitted disease but can be acquired through direct contact with infected animals and their tissues, or by inhalation. Domestic pets, especially cats, have been a source of infected fleas.

Clinical Disease

After a two- to six-day incubation period, the infection emanates from the site of the flea bite. Characteristic symptoms include fever, headache, chills, muscle pain, weakness, fatigue and upset stomach. In bubonic plague, lymph nodes enlarge, forming "buboes" (enlarged and inflamed lymphs) especially in the region of first exposure. Pneumonia can be spread through the blood as well as by inhalation of infectious respiratory droplets. Case fatality rates reach 50 to 60 percent in untreated cases of bubonic plague and nearly 100 percent in pneumonic cases.

Prevention

It is important to educate the public in plague areas about the nature of the disease and its transmission. Control of rodent populations, through exclusion and habitat management, should begin before populations have a chance to increase to high levels. People should be aware that rodent die-offs may signal the start of a period of special concern and take appropriate steps to protect themselves and their pets. Pet protection is achieved by controlling fleas. Finally, people judged to be at high risk and people who live in plague endemic areas should consider immunization.

Chlamydiosis
(Chlamydia psittaci)

Hosts

Birds. More than 100 free-living species are potential vectors, especially pigeons and mallard ducks.

Background

Chlamydiosis (Psittacosis, ornithosis, parrot fever) has worldwide distribution and has long been described as a bird-to-human zoonosis. Though the majority of reported cases are associated with captive psittacine (parrotlike) birds, direct contact with birds of any origin can result in increased risk for contracting the disease. The primary modes of transmission involve fecal shedding and contact with infected excretions. Upon drying, *Chlamydia psittaci* becomes aerosolized and can be easily inhaled. This can initiate infection in the respiratory tract.

Clinical Disease

The incubation period varies but is usually ten days. The mild form of psittacosis can be easily discounted as a mild upper respiratory virus. Headaches, fever, chills and upper respiratory infections are found in 90 percent of the cases. Some patients, especially the very young, old or those with immune system problems, display an entire range of clinical symptoms. In the most serious form of the disease, symptoms include enlargement of the spleen and liver, vomiting, diarrhea, disorientation, depression and delirium.

Prevention

Educating people about potential exposure and modes of transmission is important, especially for those who frequently come into contact with or handle birds. Good personal hygiene, use of protective clothing and limiting exposure to exudates and feces from birds are important means of prevention. For those who clean bird feces and contaminated environments, rebreathing high-efficiency particulate air filter (HEPA) masks are recommended. Quaternary ammonium compounds (see Appendix 2) are recommended for disinfection.

Cutaneous, Visceral and Ocular Larval Migrans (*Baylisascaris procyonis*)

Hosts

Primarily raccoons.

Background

Larval migrans is a disease process started by the ingestion of the eggs of the raccoon roundworm, *Baylisascaris procyonis*. It involves the prolonged migration and persistence of the larval parasite in internal organs and tissues. Different syndromes are named for the primary tissue involved: cutaneous (skin), ocular (eyes), cerebral nematodiasis (brain) or visceral (organs).

Baylisascaris adults reside in the small intestine of raccoons, causing disease primarily in heavily parasitized young raccoons. The adult worms produce and shed eggs in the feces. Adults are known to shed up to six million eggs per day. These become infective in three to four weeks under most environmental conditions. In the Midwest, studies indicate that 70 to 85 percent of the raccoons are infected. Due to high population densities of raccoons, particularly in urban environments, the high incidence of *B. procyonis* among raccoons and the persistence of eggs in the environment for months to years, the potential increases for human exposure to eggs and consequently to infection. People who have increased contact with raccoons and their feces have the highest risk of exposure.

Clinical Disease

The most common manifestation of *Baylisascaris* in humans is minor tissue damage and ultimate encapsulation of the parasite in noncritical sites such as skeletal muscle. Large numbers of the parasite, however, can lead to more serious symptoms, including fever, blood disorders and lung conditions similar to pneumonia. Most seriously, central nervous system (CNS) disease is possible: *B. procyonis* can likely develop in the tissues of the nervous system, in particular, the brain. CNS disease depends on the number of larvae entering the brain, the location, extent of migration and size of the brain. Progressive CNS disease has resulted in the deaths of at least two children who ingested large numbers of larvae. Ocular larva migrans results when larvae are delivered to the eye by the systemic circulation. Migration of larvae in the retina can cause loss of vision or acute sensitivity to light.

Prevention

The key to preventing exposure to raccoon roundworm is to avoid contact with feces or areas where fecal matter has lain. The eggs are highly resistant to environmental and chemical disinfectants and can remain adhering to interior surfaces and dormant in soil for long periods of time. Old wood piles that have been used as latrine sites by raccoons particularly need to be recognized as outdoor sources of contamination and should be removed using protective clothing (e.g., coveralls) and gloves to handle logs or any exposed material. Indoors, cages in which raccoons have been housed or areas in buildings where they have deposited scats should be cleaned and disinfected. A 1:30 solution of household bleach, while not destroying eggs, will help to remove the protein coat on them that makes them sticky enough to adhere to most surfaces. After that, mechanical removal through washing or flushing should be easier.

Echinococcosis/ Hydatidosis (*Echinococcus* spp.)

Hosts

Wild canids (red foxes, coyotes) and dogs are the definitive hosts. Rodents are intermediate hosts.

Background

Echinococcosis is characterized by infection of the larval cystic stage of tapeworms. Immature stages of these parasites produce cysts that commonly develop in the liver, but can also develop in the lungs, kidney, spleen, bone or nervous tissue. Initially these cysts are well tolerated by the patient. After a while, though, they grow to occupy more and more area, compromising surrounding organs. Cysts may rupture, producing severe anaphylactoid (shock) immune responses.

E. granulosis depends on a predator-prey relationship to continue its life cycle. The predator-prey relationship in the domestic realm is the dog-sheep relationship. In the sylvatic realm, it is the wolf-moose.

E. multilocularis is the second North American species that produces human disease. *E. multilocularis* produces alveolar hydatid disease (AHD), a highly invasive and destructive form causing tumorlike solid masses. Normally, red foxes are the definitive hosts, and rodents serve as the intermediate hosts. Historically, the range of *E. multilocularis* has been the north-central states, including North Dakota, Minnesota, Iowa, Nebraska, Wyoming and western Alaska. Range extension in the last decade has been made into Wisconsin and Illinois and more recently into Indiana and Ohio. Adult echinococcus tapeworms shed eggs in their host's feces. The eggs are immediately infective and the disease begins in humans upon accidental ingestion of them.

Clinical Disease

Once infected, it can take months or even years before disease symptoms occur. It depends on the number and location of cysts and how quickly they grow. The clinical signs of cystic hydatid disease (CHD) result from the mass effect from the slow-growing cyst. Patients often display allergic reactions in response to antigens leaked from the cyst or acute anaphylaxis following cyst rupture. Other complications may involve the formation of abscesses or secondary cysts.

AHD is associated with a higher mortality rate than CHD. The insidious onset and progressive nature of AHD usually delays diagnosis until the lesions have advanced beyond the operable phase. Surgical intervention is possible in only 20 to 40 percent of all diagnosed cases. Of the inoperable cases, 90 percent of patients die within ten years.

Prevention

Public education concerning the risks of exposure, mode of transmission and characteristic history of these diseases is critical. Dogs and other definitive hosts should be controlled from feeding on slaughtered herbivorous animals, which are the intermediate hosts. Dogs in areas where this parasite is endemic should be treated to prevent infection. The risk of exposure to feces, especially from red foxes and coyotes, must be acknowledged and minimized by individuals in contact with those species. The sale or transport of foxes between different areas of the country for gaming or sporting purposes must be recognized as a major threat to spread disease into areas from which it may currently be absent.

Giardiasis (*Giardia* spp.)

Hosts

Widespread among many mammals, avian and reptile species, especially aquatic species. Often associated with raccoons and beavers.

Background

Giardiasis is caused by a one-celled flagellated organism *(G. lamblia)* and is the most common parasite infecting people in the United States. Its overall prevalence in the general population has been estimated at 3.8 percent. Children, due to their common lack of good personal hygiene, are approximately three times more likely to be infected than adults. There remains some debate over the significance of *Giardia*'s disease-causing abilities, even in the face of a number of reports implicating it as a cause of diarrhea.

Cross-infectivity studies have shown that the giardia of human origin can be transmitted to several wildlife species. It is currently accepted that humans, who reportedly pass 900 million infective cysts per day, are the single most common reservoir. *Giardia* seems to be widespread in surface waters, having the ability to live for at least two months in cool waters. Water treatment with chlorine alone does not alter the presence of *Giardia*. Humans become infected by accidental ingestion of the cysts or through water contaminated with fecal material. More research is needed to determine the role wildlife plays in transmitting giardia to humans. Currently, exposure to wildlife sources is not regarded as likely a source as is exposure from human sources.

Clinical Disease

After a nine- to twelve-day incubation period, giardia can often remain as a subclinical infection—meaning that, while present, the infection does not cause any noticeable symptoms. When clinical disease does result, it is characterized by a variety of intestinal symptoms: chronic diarrhea with fatty, floating stools, increased flatulence and abdominal discomfort. In chronic cases, the organism can completely cover the intestinal lining, giving rise to signs often attributed to irritable bowel syndrome, food allergy or lactose intolerance.

Prevention

As with other diseases discussed here, it is essential that people practice good personal hygiene, including frequent hand-washing. Gloves should be used when handling potential reservoirs. Water supplies should be protected from human, companion animal (cats and dogs) and wildlife contamination. Untreated or unprocessed water should not be drunk, even if the source is assumed to be pure. Carrying water on camping trips or processing ground water through approved filtering devices that will remove giardia cysts is mandatory. Surfaces known to be contaminated can be disinfected with quaternary ammonium compounds and followed by mechanical removal (washing) of cysts.

Hantaviruses (Sin Nombre Virus [Western and Midwestern United States]; Blackwater Creek Canal Virus [Southeastern United States]; Hantavirus-7 and Other Serologically Distinct Types)

Hosts

Many different types of rodents. Deer mice *(Peromyscus maniculatus)* are primarily associated with Sin Nombre virus; cotton rats *(Sigmodon hispidus)* with the Blackwater Creek Canal virus. Norway rats *(Rattus norvegicus)* and black rats *(Rattus rattus)* are associated with the Seoul virus.

Background

Hantaviruses (rodent-borne hemorrhagic fever viruses) have been known as important agents of human disease throughout Europe and Asia. These viruses collectively cause several diseases termed hemorrhagic fever with renal syndrome (HFRS). The typical course of the disease leads to hemorrhage and acute shock, frequently accompanied by kidney failure. In the severe form of the disease, there is a 5 to 10 percent chance of death.

Dating back to the 1980s, hantaviruses were isolated from rodents in the United States and were not associated with human disease. However, in 1993 the first outbreak of human disease associated with hantavirus was diagnosed in the Four Corners area in the Southwest United States. This form of hantavirus was characterized initially by fever, myalgia, headaches, nausea and a cough. These signs led to difficulty in breathing and eventually to dramatic respiratory distress syndrome. Mortality rates exceeded 50 percent, despite aggressive treatment. To date, 131 cases have been diagnosed in twenty-four states with approximately a 50 percent mortality rate resulting.

As the nature of this group of viruses becomes better known, it seems certain that they will be found to be widespread across the United States. Hantavirus is maintained in the rodent as a persistent infection characterized by long-term shedding in the urine, feces or saliva. Humans become infected by inhalation of small particle aerosols (dust) of virus-contaminated feces, urine or saliva. Rodent bites could be another avenue of virus transmission.

Clinical Disease

After the initial exposure, hantavirus undertakes a two- to four-week incubation period before disease ensues. Previously healthy individuals suddenly develop symptoms of headache, fever, myalgia and dry cough. The first symptoms mimic a typical upper respiratory virus. These flulike symptoms progress to acute pulmonary (lungs) insufficiency, indistinguishable from adult respiratory distress syndrome. Within days of onset, death from respiratory failure can occur.

Prevention

Again, the first step in prevention is educating our communities in hantavirus transmission and taking the necessary measures to ensure personal safety. In the long term it is necessary to develop strategies aimed at rodent habitat modification (e.g., preventing access to human dwellings, reducing rodent shelter and food sources). Controlling rodent populations near buildings by trapping or using lethal baiting programs will only temporarily address the problem; habitat modification and exclusion must be the principal line of defense.

For individuals working in places infested by rodents, protective clothing, including thick rubber gloves, should be worn. Work should be done in well-ventilated areas when possible, and a respirator fitted with a high-efficiency particulate air filter (HEPA) is recommended. Negative-pressure or a powered air-purifying respirator may be necessary, and current advice should always be sought to establish a respiratory protective program that conforms to the most recent OSHA Respiratory Protection Standard. Disinfect working surfaces or old areas of contact with a 1:30 solution of household bleach or any Environmental Protection Agency (EPA)–approved hospital-grade disinfectant used according to manufacturer's instructions.

Histoplasmosis (Histoplasma capsulatum)

Hosts

Soil enriched with bird or bat droppings, especially those established for at least three to five years.

Background

Histoplasmosis cannot technically be considered a true zoonosis but must be designated as a saprozoonosis (environmentally acquired disease). The soil, a nonanimal site, is its reservoir. The Mississippi and Ohio River Valleys have historically been considered endemic areas for histoplasmosis, as most reported cases arise from this region. Histoplasmosis also occurs outside this area whenever the environmental conditions meet the optimum growth requirements for fungal growth. Health officials have estimated that, if tested, fifty million people across the central United States would give a positive histoplasmin skin test reaction.

Histoplasmosis has frequently been linked to roosting sites of birds and bats. Winter assemblages of blackbirds, nesting gull colonies, pigeon roosts and bat roosting areas such as caves, mines or bridges have all been documented as point sources of environmental histoplasmosis. In all these instances, the animals' excrement enriches the soil, thus promoting the growth of *Histoplasma*. Birds display a remarkable resistance to infection but do act as mechanical transport hosts of the fungus. Bats, on the contrary, can become clinically infected as well as serve as transport hosts. Transmission occurs mechanically, usually through inhalation of spores produced by the mycelial free-living branching form of *Histoplasma capsulatum*.

Clinical Disease

After inhalation of the spores, *H. capsulatum* usually causes inapparent disease. While infection is common in endemic areas, overt disease is not. When the infecting inoculum is large enough or if the individual's immune system is weak, clinical disease can result. At least five forms of histoplasmosis are clinically recognizable, ranging from a mild hypersensitivity to a disease mimicking chronic pulmonary tuberculosis. Children are especially susceptible to severe disease and, without aggressive therapy, may die.

Prevention

The first line of defense in preventing exposure is to minimize potential contact by avoiding soil contaminated with either bird or bat droppings. If it is necessary to be in such areas, wear boots and use a mask or self-containing breathing apparatus. Properly bag clothing for washing, block places where a bat may be able to enter your home and, when deemed as a necessary pubic health measure, use humane dispersion strategies on urban bird roosting sites. As a last resort, treat contaminated soil with 3 percent formalin solution on three consecutive days to kill the fungal spores.

Leptospirosis (*Leptospira interrogans*)

Hosts

Raccoons, opossums, Norway rats, mice, white-tailed deer and striped skunks.

Background

Striped skunks are a significant reservoir, with some populations demonstrating a greater than 50 percent prevalence. Skunks can shed leptospires in their urine for up to 300 days. Transmission occurs by direct contamination of mucus membranes or broken skin by urine. Indirectly, it can be acquired through contaminated soil and water.

Clinical Disease

The incubation period may be as short as four days or may extend for three weeks (in humans it is usually ten days). Fever, headache, chills, weakness, vomiting, muscle pain and conjunctivitis (inflammation of the eyelids), or a combination of these signs, are noted early in the disease. In the more severe infections, jaundice, kidney damage, blood disorders and hemorrhages of the skin and mucus membranes occur.

Prevention

Avoiding exposure to the urine of wild animals, either in handling them or coming into contact with places where they have urinated, is the primary course of protection. Protective clothes, boots and gloves are recommended. Good personal hygiene following any potential exposure is important.

Lyme Disease (*Borrelia burgdorferi*)

Hosts

White-footed mouse (larvae, nymphal stages) and white-tailed deer (adult stage).

Background

Lyme disease gained national attention in the 1980s when the infectious agent was first isolated, named and made a reportable disease. Throughout the 1980s, more cases were reported each year. Now more than ten thousand cases are diagnosed yearly. Lyme disease has quickly gained the distinction of being the most common tick-borne disease in the United States. The majority of cases occur in the northeastern seaboard states, the upper Midwest and California. Most cases of Lyme disease are acquired in the early summer months when peak activity of nymphal ticks corresponds with increased human activity in wilderness areas. Because white-tailed deer are increasing in numbers, it is probable that the geographic distribution of tick populations and, consequently, Lyme disease cases will increase in the United States. Two species of Ixodid ticks are the primary vectors: *Ixodes scapularis* (formally *Ixodes damini*) in the East and Midwest and *Ixodes pacificus* in California.

Clinical Disease

When a nymph feeds on a human, it must be attached for at least twenty-four to forty-eight hours before infection can occur. The borrelia, residing in the tick's midgut, migrate to the salivary gland and enter the human's blood as the tick feeds. Upon inoculation of borrelia into the host's skin, an incubation period of three to thirty-two days follows before clinical disease develops.

In 90 percent of cases, initial symptoms include fever, muscle pain, lethargy and the development of a characteristic skin lesion known as an "erythema migrans." Erythema migrans is a characteristic red annular "bulls-eye" lesion, which clears centrally as it expands. This lesion will spontaneously resolve, even without treatment. Untreated cases progress by being carried through the blood to many body sites: heart, muscles, bones, joints, liver, spleen, eyes and brain. Signs usually involve the skin, musculo-skeletal and nervous systems. Headaches, muscle pain and transient joint pains often occur. The majority of cases manifest as arthritis primarily of the large joints, especially the knee. Bouts of subtle nervous system disease such as memory loss, drowsiness or behavioral abnormalities are characteristic. Case fatalities are rare but patients experience a life-changing morbidity.

Prevention

Procedures to avoid exposure to Lyme disease begin with avoiding contact with ticks. One way to do this is simply to avoid tick-infested areas, especially between May and July. Where that cannot be done, wearing light-colored long-sleeved shirts and pants, tucking pant legs into socks and conducting frequent inspections of clothing and body (every three to four hours) are recommended. Tick repellents used on clothing may also be effective. When attached, remove ticks without crushing them and thoroughly scrub the wound. Put flea collars and use pet-safe insecticides on companion animals to minimize the risk of secondary exposure to ticks.

Rabies *(Lyssavirus)*

Hosts

Any warmed-blooded mammal can carry rabies, but the primary carriers in North America are raccoons, striped skunks, bats, foxes and coyotes.

Background

Rabies (bite wound disease) has seven distinct variants or *strains* that affect land mammals as well as an unknown number of strains that affect bats. This helps to explain why different species are responsible for being primary carriers or vectors of the disease in different geographic areas. Since 1960, rabies in the United States has been more frequently reported in wild than in domestic animals. Wildlife now account for more than 90 percent of all reported rabies cases. Geographically, the dominant types of carriers vary between different regions. Other species within those regions usually become infected as a result of a "spillover" from the dominant carrier, and often tend to be "dead-end" hosts that do not transmit the virus to other members of their or different species.

Raccoons account for the greatest number of cases along the East Coast of the United States. Skunks are the dominant reservoir in the north-central and south-central states and California. Three fox strains have been identified as long-standing reservoirs. An Arctic and red fox strain occurs from western Alaska, throughout all of Canada and into adjacent New England states. Two other small but persistent areas of fox rabies include central Texas and southeastern Arizona. Coyote rabies has reached epizootic proportions in the southern eighteen counties of Texas. The Mexican dog strain is responsible for coyote-to-dog and dog-to-dog transmission cycles. Bats, like terrestrial mammals, have distinct rabies strains and comprise the third most frequently reported wild reservoir. Bat rabies does not conform to the geographic patterns of terrestrial mammal rabies. Cases are scattered widely across the United States and are reported sporadically from forty-five of the lower forty-eight states.

Human rabies continues to be reported in small numbers; twenty-four cases were reported from 1980 to 1994. Fourteen individuals were diagnosed with strains known from animal reservoirs in the United States. Eleven cases can be traced to strains associated with bats. Though the overall numbers are small, these statistics emphasize the possibility of humans becoming infected by bats. Treatment should be considered in any situation when a bat was physically present and the individual cannot rule out a possible bite (e.g., was asleep and awoke to find a bat in the room) unless prompt testing of the bat results in a negative rabies test. Most cases of rabies are a result of a bite from an infected animal.

The majority of diagnosed human rabies cases (eighteen out of twenty-four) have been after death and so cannot be traced to a known animal bite or animal contact. Therefore, changes are being made by the Centers for Disease Control and Prevention (CDC) in recommending rabies post-exposure treatment.

Clinical Disease

Humans are relatively resistant to rabies. Reports indicate only 15 percent of humans bitten by a known rabid animal become infected with rabies. Reliable incubation periods range from fewer than ten days to more than six years. After initiation of clinical signs, the virus is almost always fatal. Early signs are characterized by apprehension, headache and low-grade fever accompanied by vague sensory changes such as discomfort and irritation or pain in the area of the bite. Visual and auditory sensitivities are reported. As the disease progresses, changes in the mental status may occur, causing disorientation, agitation, hallucination and (rarely) aggression. Difficulty swallowing due to muscle spasms and hypersalivation lead to hydrophobia in approximately 50 percent of the cases. Partial paralysis and, eventually, complete paralysis ensues. Death usually results from respiratory failure one week after the onset of the disease.

Responding to Exposure

As with any other potential zoonotic disease exposure, prompt consultation with a physician is extremely important. (Immediate medical response to a bite from any wild animal is necessary.) Scrub any bite wound immediately and aggressively with soap and water. If an antiseptic soap such as betadine or Nolvasan (Fort Dodge) is available, use that. Flush thoroughly with water to facilitate organism removal. If the animal that caused the bite can be safely captured, it should be held until animal control agents can take it to the local health department.

Prevention

Vaccination of companion animals such as dogs and cats is imperative—even in areas without one of the dominant terrestrial carriers—because the potential of exposure to bats always exists. Where rabies outbreaks are occurring or the disease is prevalent in animals such as skunks, the vaccination of horses and other livestock may be recommended by local veterinarians. In cases of potential or known human exposure, the treatment series has been greatly modified from former procedures to one in which a few (three to five) shots are given in the upper arm.

Rocky Mountain Spotted Fever *(Rickettsia rickettsii)*

Hosts

Rabbits, rodents, Virginia opossum.

Background

Rocky Mountain spotted fever (RMSF) is not confined to the western mountain states, as its name suggests, but is in fact more commonly reported from the south-central states. It is the second most common tick-borne disease in the continental United States. The American dog tick *(Dermacentor variabilis)* in the east and the American wood tick *(D. andersoni)* in the west are the regional primary vectors.

Clinical Disease

After a human is bitten, there is a delay in the actual transmission of the rickettsia (the disease-causing microorganism) from the tick to the host. A reactivation process occurs leading to a four- to twenty-hour delay of infection. (People often do not realize this.) Human infection is characterized by a three- to fourteen-day incubation period followed by nonspecific signs of disease such as lethargy and weakness, rapidly progressing to fever, chills, headaches, muscle pain and pain in the joints. Fever is the most predictable and persistent sign. In 88 percent of the cases, generalized spotting or blotchiness starts first on the extremities, next on the palms and soles and then rapidly spreads to the trunk. Petechial (pinpoint) hemorrhages are common.

In the absence of a diagnosis and specific therapy, a 15 to 20 percent mortality rate results. Even with effective antimicrobial therapy, a 2 percent mortality on an annual basis results in the United States. Nationally, approximately fifty people die each year from RMSF. Persons over forty years of age experience an increased chance of mortality. In cases in which there is no tick bite or no display of the typical spotted fever skin lesions, a diagnosis may be delayed, resulting in increased mortality chances. Early diagnosis and initiation of therapy, before serologic or isolation evidence, leads to a rapid uneventful recovery in most cases.

Prevention

Procedures to avoid contact with ticks are the primary recommendation. One way to do this is simply to avoid tick-infested areas, especially between May and July. When that cannot be done, wearing light-colored long-sleeved shirts and pants, tucking pant legs into socks and conducting frequent inspections of clothing and body (every three to four hours) are recommended. Tick repellents used on clothing may also be effective. When attached, remove ticks without crushing them and thoroughly scrub the wound. Put flea collars and use pet-safe insecticides on companion animals to minimize the risk of secondary exposure to ticks.

Salmonellosis
(*Salmonella enteriditis*)

Hosts

Reptiles, birds (pigeons, house sparrows, mallard ducks) and mammals (rodents, opossums, white-tailed deer).

Background

Salmonellosis is possibly the world's most common zoonotic disease, closely associated with poultry and swine industries. Humans comprise the next most important reservoir. Our immediate environment, such as landfills, sewage treatment facilities and meat-processing plants supply ready access to wildlife for contamination. Transmission occurs by ingestion of salmonellae shed in feces, and animal handling without using good personal hygiene.

Clinical Disease

The disease is commonly manifested, after a short incubation period of six to seventy-two hours, as an enterocolitis (inflammation of the intestines) with sudden onset of headache, abdominal pain, diarrhea, nausea and vomiting. The signs can vary from very severe to inapparent, depending on the infecting dose, the patient's age, immune status and stomach acidity. Dehydration, especially in the young, can be life-threatening. Fever is almost always high. Diarrhea can persist for several days. The organism can develop into a bacterial septicemia, localizing in any tissue, causing abscesses with numerous secondary complications. Salmonellae can be shed in the feces for days or weeks. Antibiotics tend to increase the length of shedding.

Prevention

Good personal hygiene and proper environmental disinfection are important steps in prevention of this disease. Currently, nonwildlife sources make up the bulk of human exposures.

Tularemia
(*Francisella tularensis*)

Hosts

Rabbits (*Lepus* spp., *Sylvilagus* spp.) and approximately 100 other rodent and rabbit species.

Background

The two types of tularemia (rabbit fever) include Type A, which is the more virulent form carried by a vector species, and Type B, a milder form that can be carried by water. There are approximately 200 cases of tularemia reported in humans each year, but under-reporting is suspected. Most cases occur in Missouri and Arkansas. In these states, tularemia is endemic as a tick-borne disease. In western states, biting flies, ticks and direct contact with infected animals are equally responsible as sources of infection. In the Midwest, direct contact is the most frequent source. Water-borne tularemia predominates in northern regions where muskrat and beavers contaminate surface waters. Transmission generally follows direct contact while skinning rabbits, tick bites, biting flies and contact with contaminated water.

Clinical Disease

After an incubation time of two to ten days, tularemia can take at least four different forms, depending on the method of infection. The most common clinical course is the ulcero-glandular form. At the site of entry, usually the hands, or at the site of an arthropod bite, a necrotic ulcer develops and the organism spreads to the regional lymph node. When the organism contaminates the eye, an ulcer often forms on the lower lid. Other forms of the disease include glandular (of the glands; without a skin lesion), typhoidal (post-ingestion) and oropharyngeal. The case fatality rate in untreated cases is 5 to 7 percent.

Prevention

Where tularemia can be transmitted by tick or insect vectors, insecticides and repellents can help avoid bites. Anyone handling potentially infected animals, especially rabbits, should wear impervious gloves and otherwise practice good hygiene. In areas with known occurrences people are cautioned to avoid drinking, swimming or bathing in surface waters.

3

Tools and Tactics

THIS CHAPTER DESCRIBES some of the specific tactics and individual tools that can be used to resolve human-wildlife conflicts without resorting to lethal means. Many of these techniques can be employed *before* any problem occurs. Others will be useful *after* a problem is diagnosed (following the steps outlined in Chapter 1). Most of the procedures in this chapter can be used for more than a single species. *(Consult the individual species accounts before using any of the products or strategies described in this chapter.)* Special techniques and approaches are described there, and information on the biology and behavior of the problem species can often lead to homeowners deciding *not* to take action, finding that the wildlife "problem" is not a problem at all.

The *first* and *best* approach to dealing with wildlife in urban and suburban environments is to practice tolerance—understanding and acceptance of the natural patterns of animal life and respect and appreciation for wild animals as they are. As useful as the resources and procedures described below may be, they all create inconvenience (at least) and displacement or even death (at worst) for the species treated and perhaps nontarget species as well. This fact is paramount when considering their use.

Next to tolerance and coexistence, by far the most humane economical and environmentally sound procedures to deal with actual or potential animal damage in or

around the home are to prevent access to the area or the resource to be protected. You can do this by (1) physically excluding animals from places where they might be a problem, (2) negatively conditioning or repelling animals with scare devices, (3) deterring animals with bad-tasting or bad-smelling chemical repellents or (4) simply removing sources of attraction.

Consider the perennial problem that many homeowners face with raccoons getting into the trash. Prevention strategies to solve this problem could include (1) using a strong garbage can with a locking lid that can defeat break-in (but not hamper trash collection), (2) rigging the can or area around it with an alarm that uses light, noise or even water to chase raccoons away, (3) using a repellent on or inside the can or (4) keeping the trash in the garage or shed until the morning of collection and putting it at the curb *after* the raccoons have gone to bed. In this case the most sensible approach would be to use either of the last two strategies mentioned, but all might work well enough to solve the problem.

Figures 3 and 4 on page 26 illustrate how problems in houses can begin with structural breakdowns that invite wild animals to move in. These common points of entry at ground level and above are areas that need frequent checking. The following information describes some of the more commonly used techniques to prevent wild animals

Figure 3. *A close-up of our house at ground level shows common entry points occurring around gaps where window wells or bulkheads enter the foundation (a), where windows are improperly fitted or left ajar (b), where doors have gaps (c) and where electrical lines enter buildings and are not properly sealed (d).*

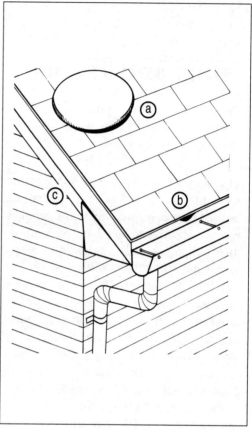

Figure 4. *The house at roof level shows other common entry points, such as underneath exhaust fans or ventilator caps where screening may be may be worn out (a), where holes occur in soffits or gutter lines (b) and where any framing pieces have loosened and present even small gaps that animals such as squirrels can work on (c).*

from moving into buildings where they are not wanted or from causing damage to buildings or grounds.

In the text that follows, we discuss common methods of *exclusion, scare devices* and *chemical repellents*. We include some information on *live trapping*, a resolution strategy that, while sounding humane, has many problems that deserve careful consideration. Finally, we have also identified and described some of the more common lethal control chemicals or toxicants that are currently marketed. This is *not* because we are recommending these products, but because they frequently are suggested in approaches to dealing with wildlife conflicts to home-

owners who may *not* realize they are dangerous, deadly chemicals.

Exclusion

A lid placed on a garbage can is a form of exclusion. A cap on a chimney prevents any animal from gaining access. A simple fence can keep wild animals out of a yard or garden. Below we describe some of the most effective and useful exclusion methods.

Animal-Proof Trash Containers

In most cases simple latching or holding devices (bungee cords, rope tie-downs or weights) will adequately secure cans.

Commercial lockout systems (see Appendix 2) are available for those who face unusually difficult problems, extremely persistent animals or special problem species, such as bears. While expensive, the commercial animal-proof systems may be the only solution for municipal parks or open-space areas and are probably worth the price in the long run.

Bafflers

At least one commercially patented device is sold to keep beavers from plugging culverts (see Appendix 2), and several useful publications describe others that can be built from easily obtained materials (see Chapter 6). These devices are generically know as "bafflers."

Another type of baffler is intended to keep squirrels away from bird feeders. It can be a tube that is weighted so that it throws a climbing squirrel down before it can gain access, or a circular ring that attaches to the feeder pole and prevents squirrels from

climbing. There also are bafflers designed to prevent predators such as raccoons from reaching in to snatch baby birds. These are widely available at the specialty bird supply stores, which are becoming increasingly popular in many urban areas and in large hardware stores.

Bird Wires

A variety of devices using single-strand or more complex wiring (see Figure 5) can be used to keep birds off buildings or other places where they are considered a problem. In many situations, a single strand of galvanized or stainless steel wire (18 to 20 gauge) strung 3 to 4 inches above a railing or ledge can be highly effective in preventing birds such as pigeons, house sparrows and starlings from landing. The lines are anchored to eyelet screws (or the like) and are kept taut by support posts placed every few feet or so. Small springs can be used to help maintain tension (the same way larger devices of

Figure 5. *Devices used to keep birds from landing on buildings include single-strand wire (a), wire coils (b), "porcupine" wire (c) and new devices such as this spiderlike coil mounted on a swivel base (d).*

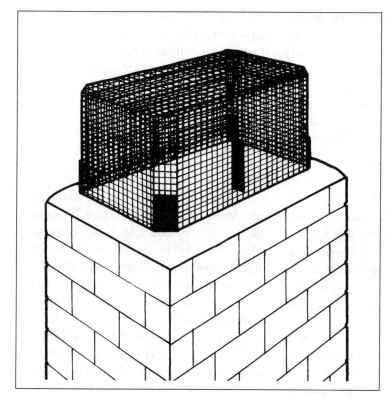

Figure 6. *A properly fitted chimney cap provides a permanent solution to the problem of animals getting caught in chimneys or making them homes. When installing such a device it is essential that the chimney be checked carefully to insure that it is not in use.*

this sort are used in high-tensile fencing). Either homemade or commercial systems can be used.

A variation on single-strand wire is the bird coil. A bird coil looks a lot like the toy called Slinky®; it's wound around a balcony railing or fixed on a ledge to keep birds from landing. In fact, the toy itself can serve in a pinch, or for temporary purposes, as a bird coil, but we suggest the commercial product for greater durability and longevity.

More involved than the single-strand wires and coils are the commercially available products known generally as "porcupine wire." These are glued or fastened to ledges and other areas where birds perch, and generally are used at difficult sites where problems have been long-standing. The repellent properties of these devices are considerable, although some claim that frequent minor and occasional serious injury to birds occurs. Porcupine wire also re-

quires some upkeep; wind-blown debris can easily accumulate on it and must be removed. Some users have even reported situations in which pigeons have learned to drop nesting material onto the wires—they then build nests and raise young on them! Several companies that manufacture this product are listed in Appendix 2; they can give more information and advice to guide users.

A new generation bird wire device is being marketed to protect rooftops and light poles from nesting or perching birds. These cast long stainless wire legs out as much as 8 feet from a swivel base that is fixed to the surface to be protected. The legs move and flex up and down in any breeze at all and repel birds attempting to land. While only just coming on the market, these devices appear to have good potential for use in difficult situations, such as the repelling of nesting birds from building rooftops. A smaller version of this device is made to affix to the top of lampposts or streetlights and prevent birds from landing on these sites.

For information on these products, see "Bird Wires" in Appendix 2.

Caulking and Foam Sealants

Caulking materials range from silicone-based fillers to the expanding-foam products sold at most hardware stores. These are used to both finish off jobs in which wire mesh is used or alone to fill entry holes up to several inches in size. For those who might have a big job or need to repeatedly use foam, commercial grade systems are available (see "Caulking and Foam Sealants" in Appendix 2).

Chimney Caps

Chimney caps come in many sizes and designs. Most hardware outlet stores carry them. (See Figure 6.) (We have listed a couple manufacturers in Appendix 2 under "Chimney Caps.") The commercial caps are made of painted heavy-gauge steel or stainless steel and generally will withstand many seasons of exposure to weather. Some people make their own caps to save money. We feel, however, that in the long run commercial caps end up costing less because they will probably last much longer. Another advantage with commercial caps is that they are appropriately sized and engineered to conduct gases out of the chimney under all weather conditions, whereas homemade caps could, if inappropriately sized or placed, ice up in bad weather and back dangerous—possibly lethal—gases up into your home.

Door Curtains

In warehouses or open buildings that have a lot of vehicle or foot traffic, keeping birds such as house sparrows or pigeons from entering is often a problem. Plastic strips, 12 to 18 inches in width, are often used in these situations to keep both intruding birds and weather out (see "Door Curtains" in Appendix 2).

Fencing

Fencing may be the most effective way of excluding wild animals from larger areas. Although it initially costs more, in the long run a fence may be the most cost-effective procedure in cases in which damage is likely to reoccur or in which the thing being protected is valuable. Usually, letting professionals put up a fence is your best bet. We always recommend that homeowners collect as much information as possible from local sources (extension agents are usually a good place to start) before installing a fence because successful designs and installations vary from one situation to another.

Electric fencing can be used to protect areas as large as fields or as small as the space needed to enclose a beehive. Electric fencing works on the principle of delivering a high voltage but low amperage jolt that does not physically harm the animal. It does deliver a shock unpleasant enough to give strong negative conditioning. Because of the great differences in size and susceptibility to shock among species (deer, for example, are quite resistant to shock because their hooves are relatively good insulators), the exact requirements for electric fencing will vary greatly.

It is also important to recognize that, even if not deadly, these fences are potentially dangerous, and their use must be in accordance not only with any local restrictions or ordinances, but with common sense as well. Electric fences should not be used in places where small children or pets could be shocked, and must always be well marked with signs. All electric fences

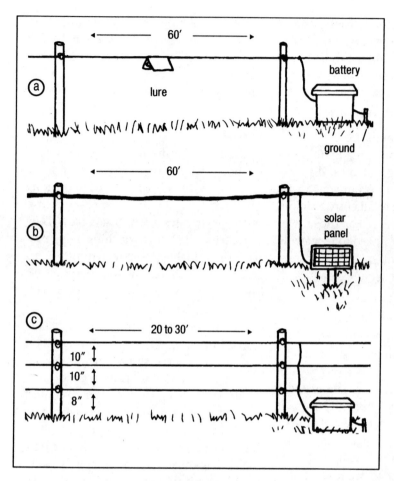

Figure 7. *There are several kinds of electric fencing. Single-strand fences can be effective in repelling animals as large as deer from yards and gardens (7a). They work best when used with a baited lure (peanut butter works well) that draws the animal into contact with the wire. Polytape fences are more noticeable and durable than single-strand (7b). Multiwire fences may be used in areas where valuable resources need to be protected or damage is particularly high (7c). Homeowners should collect as much information as possible on various types of fences and seek advice and assistance from professionals.*

require frequent inspection and maintenance; it is important to keep surrounding areas clear to prevent plants from shorting them out. Three basic designs (see Figure 7) are commonly used as described below.

Single-strand fences can be used to deter species ranging from woodchucks and raccoons to deer and bear. Sometimes the fences work best by attracting the animal rather than by repelling it. The theory is that by baiting the animal in to investigate the fence, it is much more likely to be shocked in a way that effectively conditions it to avoid the area in general. For deer (or raccoons) this can be done by using tinfoil strips (Figure 7a) to hold a lure (peanut butter for deer, jelly or licorice for raccoons) that draws the animal to investigate the wire.

Sometimes animals do not need to be attracted, as anyone using an electric fence to protect beehives from bears can vouch to. For smaller animals, such as raccoons and woodchucks, single-strand electric fences can be installed in front of nonelectrified fences or other obstacles. The shock is then delivered before the animal is able to climb the larger fence.

Polytape electric fencing (Figure 7b) is also single-strand, but this much wider and more highly visible tape strip is meant to work as a visual repellent as well as a shocking device. Once an animal has been shocked by a polytape fence, it is likely to both remember and recognize the brightly colored tape and avoid going near it again. The tape is also more visible to people. There is less maintenance required for a polytape than for single-strand fences simply because the greater visibility of the tape prevents it from being knocked down as often.

High-tensile multi-strand electric fences (Figure 7c) are the most costly and complicated of the electric fences used as wildlife deterrents, but in areas where heavy damage is likely they work better than other designs. Because of their special design characteristics and greater difficulty in installation, these fences should be installed by professionals. Spacing of the wires is important in the design of effective multi-strand fences, and wires must be low enough to prevent animals from crawling underneath (see Table 1 on page 34). Several manufacturers (see "Electric Fencing" in Appendix 2) provide fencing of different styles and types.

Non-electric woven wire and other perimeter fences are made of a wide variety of materials and come in various designs and sizes (see Figure 8). The most common is vertical fencing made of metal or wood and surrounds the area to be protected (Figure 8a). With deer, an 8- (preferably 10-) foot-high chain-link fence is usually the most effective design; where browsing pressure is slight, lower fences may be adequate deterrents. Decorative wrought-iron fences are fine, but they must be designed so that the spacing between bars does not tempt deer to try to squeeze through. No more than a 6-inch gap (preferably 4 inches) between rails is recommended.

A split rail fence with the area from the ground to the first rail covered with chicken wire will keep rabbits at bay. Solid wood palisade fences will keep most animals out of a yard, although those adept at climbing may find their way over. Few fences keep climbers like raccoons and squirrels out if they want in; these animals can get in by climbing on tree limbs that bridge over fences.

High-tensile multi-strand fences of the sort used to confine livestock may be used to exclude animals such as deer, although if

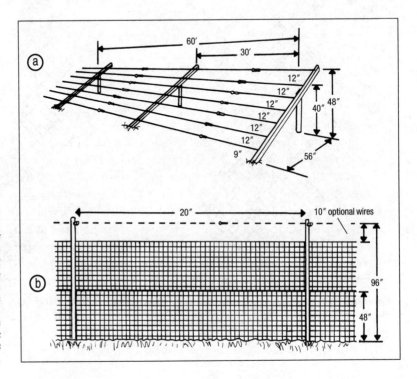

Figure 8. *Slanted and vertical nonelectric fences. Two of the many designs of fencing used to exclude animals from yards and gardens. The slanted fence design is more common surrounding large areas such as crop fields (8a), due to its lower cost than the woven wire fence that should ideally be at least 8 to 10 feet high (8b).*

motivated, deer can jump those lower than 8 feet. An effective design of multi-strand fencing relies on a slanted design (see Figure 8b). The slant works on the notion that deer will approach a fence closely and try to find a way under it before considering jumping. By the time they are close enough to find out this cannot be done, the upper part of the fence is above them and inhibits their even trying to jump. Whatever the design, all perimeter fences require maintenance, not only to ensure they remain structurally intact, but to keep them clear of vegetation as well. Virtually all forms of non-electric fences are available locally, and we recommend the yellow pages or university extension services for local sources.

Netting, Hardware Cloth and Welded Wire

These are among the most widely used and versatile exclusion materials available. Of the three, only netting may need to be purchased from a specialty supplier. Hardware cloth and welded wire are available in many different sizes at virtually any hardware outlet. Hardware cloth (see Figure 9) is used to

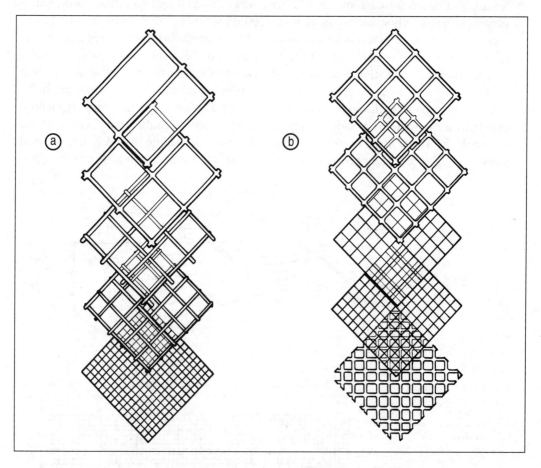

Figure 9. Hardware cloth comes in a variety of sizes and is the perfect material to seal holes in and entrances to buildings that provide access for wild animals. Both plastic (9a) and metal (9b) cloth can be used.

make or repair window screening and is available in a range of fiberglass or galvanized metal styles with sizes that range from very fine ($1/32$ inch) to larger ($1/2$ inch) mesh.

Generally $1/4$-inch hot-dipped galvanized screening is most useful in wildlife exclusion work. This screening can be used as a temporary seal to keep an animal from returning to the attic or other place where it is not wanted, as an excluder when it is fastened so that an animal can exit but cannot return through a hole or as a permanent form of exclusion.

Larger stronger animals may have to be excluded with welded wire, which also is readily available at most hardware or construction supply outlets. This is simply a heavier gauge and larger mesh of screening. Welded wire can be installed over window screening, and it will keep small animals and insects out as well. The size of the opening, location and other factors depend on the type of animal and the site itself.

Commercial netting (see "Netting" in Appendix 2) is increasingly being used to solve many wildlife problems—from the unwanted perching of sparrows and pigeons on buildings to the temporary protection of fruit trees until harvest. Netting is sometimes used in very large-scale commercial operations, such as the protection of entire vineyards from depredating birds. Homeowners can often find netting for their fruit trees at the local nursery or garden supply store. Netting is also used to protect ornamental shrubs from deer damage in the winter, when plants are most susceptible. It's also the material used in "checkvalves" to allow bats to leave, but not return, to buildings (see Chapter 5).

Table 1 gives some general recommendations regarding the more common type of structural invaders.

There are some general considerations that should be taken into account when ex-

cluding animals from attics, crawl spaces, under decks or other places they might seek refuge. Above everything else, it is important to recognize that the animal is not willfully threatening or trying to harm either people or their property. It simply is trying to survive by using any of the opportunities provided to it either by natural or by human-created means.

It is quite important that the homeowner actually identify the species involved before making plans to exclude it. Misidentification is common and can lead to ineffective or injurious attempts at exclusion. It is *critical* to determine whether or not young animals are present. We do *not* recommend trapping and removal or exclusion of families except in extremely urgent or necessary cases. Families of animals should be tolerated with the understanding that they will eventually move on their own, and exclusion can wait until after the move has taken place. Even in an emergency, females can often be persuaded to move their young, thus avoiding the need to trap, relocate or euthanize families.

Netting or hardware cloth is good as a temporary excluder, and commercially available or homemade one-way doors (see Figure 10) can also be used. Entries *must* be

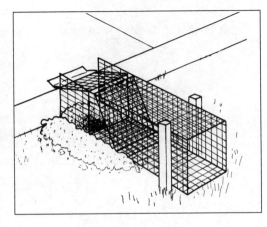

Figure 10. *A one-way door allows an animal to exit but not return to its burrow or den.*

Table 1
Minimum access area needed by common wild animal species found around homes

Species	Opening (in inches)	Comments
Bats (most species)	$1/4$ x $1/2$	Usually gain access through gaps where materials join, such as siding and soffit.
Foxes (red and gray)	4 x 4	Both climb well; gray foxes can even scale small trees.
House sparrows	$3/4$ x $3/4$	Can climb fairly well to gain access to dryer, range and bathroom vents, among other places.
Mice	$1/4$ x $1/2$	Can fit through openings the size of a dime.
Raccoons	$2\,1/2$ x 4	Can fit through surprisingly small openings. Heavier material required to exclude because of greater strength.
Rats	$1/4$ x $1/2$	Can fit through openings the size of a quarter.
Snakes	$1/4$ x $1/2$	Some snakes will even fit through openings as small as $1/8$ x $1/4$.
Starlings	1 x 1	Dryer and exhaust fan vents are a favorite; starlings can lift their flaps and get in.
Tree squirrels	2 x 2	Entry often occurs through screening behind attic vents and deteriorated louvers. May require very heavy exclusion materials because of gnawing ability.
White-tailed deer	12 x 12	Deer prefer to crawl under obstructions rather than jump over. A 9-inch lower wire is recommended on either electric or non-electric fencing because the animals may push through higher sets.
Woodchucks	3 x 4	Under decks and porches; the characteristic mound of earth in front is an indicator.

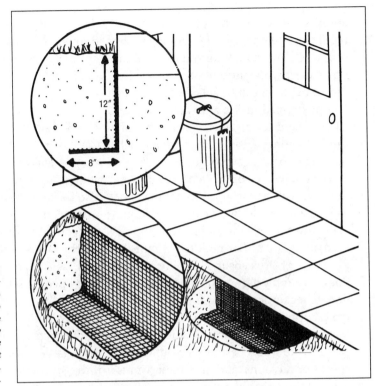

Figure 11. *An L-shaped footer under a patio, deck or walkway can prevent access to burrowing animals or keep them from returning once they have been evicted by other means. Also shown are tie-downs used to prevent animals, such as raccoons, from opening trash cans.*

permanently sealed after making sure the problem animals are gone. Take advantage of the natural behavior patterns of the species causing the problem. Squirrels are active by day, raccoons by night. Where young are not involved, exclude them when they are out looking for food.

Usually, attics are too large for odor repellents to work, but increased human activity, turning lights on or leaving a portable radio on for a day or two will often disturb the animal enough to leave. You may find that a tree limb overhanging the roof is providing access. It is advisable to trim limbs back from the house to a distance of at least 6 to 8 feet, but only after the animal is off the roof, out of your yard, away from homes.

Hardware cloth or welded wire used to exclude animals from underneath decks should be buried a foot deep in an L shape at least 8 inches out to keep animals from burrowing under it (see Figure 11). If vegetation is in the way, a tight fit to the ground

and an L extension that runs out on the surface instead of under the ground should do the trick.

Finally, the screened-off area should be examined periodically. And make frequent inspections during the first week or two to make sure that animals have not tried to get back in.

One-Way Doors

As the name implies, these devices let animals out of their dens or burrows but do not let them back in. Not too long ago one-way doors had to be homemade; now you can get them from at least one manufacturer, which carries several different sizes (see "One-Way Doors" in Appendix 2). These devices can be used in a variety of settings: above ground on buildings where squirrels or raccoons have gained access to attics or along the surface of the ground where woodchucks, skunks, foxes, raccoons or other animals are getting under decks or patios (see Figure 10 on page 33). Although they may take a bit more time and effort to install correctly, and must be used only when the homeowner can be sure that no young will be trapped inside after adults are excluded, these devices offer what is probably the best approach to dealing with animals residing in or under a house.

The one-way door is often used in conjunction with an L-shaped footer made of welded wire or hardware cloth. The footer is usually needed when a one-way door is used along a patio or deck (see Figure 11 on page 35). This ensures that the animal does not simply dig around the sides of the door to regain access. Figure 11 illustrates a typical application of an L-shaped footer. Materials depend on the situation: larger welded wire works best to keep out woodchucks or raccoons, and finer mesh works best to keep out animals as small as rats or mice. It's important to use material that will withstand the weather. Metal that is hot-

dipped or galvanized after welding is recommended, and putting on two or three coats of rust-proof paint before the material is laid down is a really good idea.

Plant Covers

Cloche is a French word that describes a bell-shaped glass cover that's used to protect young plants from frost. These covers can also be used to keep hungry wildlife at bay when plants are most vulnerable (during the first couple of weeks of the growing season). Cloches are available in garden supply catalogs (see "Plant Covers" in Appendix 2). Many people settle for cutting the bottom out of a 1-gallon plastic milk jug (Figure 12). Larger plantings can be protected by fabric plant covers and tents that are available in local garden centers, hardware stores and through garden supply catalogs. Both covers and cloches are especially useful where protection is only necessary during the early spring. This is the time before natural foods

Figure 12. *Plant covers can be used to deter animals as small as voles or as large as deer from attacking seedlings and tender young plants that have just been set in the garden. Covers can be made from readily available materials such as plastic milk jugs, or they can be purchased from garden centers or garden supply catalogs.*

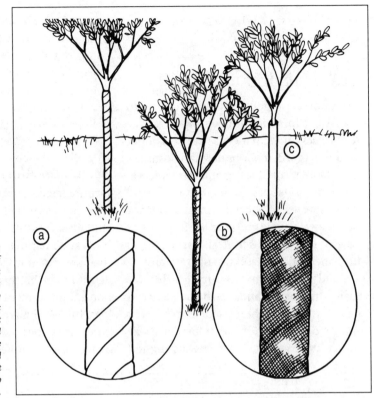

Figure 13. *Tree wraps are available in a variety of materials and can protect trunks from damage by animals ranging from voles and rabbits to those as large as deer. Plastic wrap is easy to install (13a) but does not hold up as well as metal mesh (13b). Tree "tubes" are made of rigid, solid plastic and provide a level of protection that falls between plastic wrap and metal mesh (13c).*

are readily available, and damage from deer, rabbits or woodchucks can be intense but temporary. Covering may be all the protection a garden needs.

Tree Protectors

Most garden supply stores and commercial nurseries sell products to protect tree trunks. They range from heavy plastic wrap and tubing to stainless steel mesh (see Figure 13). Homemade wire cages made from material ranging from hardware cloth to welded wire (Figure 14 on page 38) can also protect trees from animal damage. The material depends on who's causing damage, the number and sizes of trees to be protected and whether the protection is meant to be permanent or removed once the tree has gone through a growing season or is large enough not to be damaged. Plastic wrap is often adequate for protecting trees from deer and rodents, but

a beaver can quickly break through it. And the size of welded wire mesh needed to keep beavers away easily allows rodents in to attack trees. Commercial manufacturers offer a variety of products if you can't find them locally or if you need them in bulk (see "Tree Protectors" in Appendix 2).

Wire Stuffing

The copper or stainless steel mesh scouring pads sold in hardware and grocery stores are perfect for small jobs—sealing openings in houses to exclude rats, mice, bats or other animals. Plaster, caulking or other filler can be used to finish the job, and it provides the final weather seal for energy conservation as well as helping to keep out insects. We do not recommend standard steel wool for this work because it can quickly corrode after becoming wet. High-quality and reasonably priced bulk material is available for larger jobs (see "Wire Mesh" in Appendix 2).

Scare Devices

Common sense tells us there is a limit to the extent in which frightening or scaring techniques can humanely be used to control wildlife. Legal definitions of what constitutes acceptable techniques or unacceptable harassment are set for migratory birds and some species of special concern, but for other species the limits are set in terms of cruelty statutes, if set at all. In regard to humane standards it is usually inappropriate and unnecessary to pursue wild animals—frightening and even harassment can be appropriate when used to achieve a specific objective and *not* employed in a way that creates excessive stress. Frightening and

harassment are *not* ends or solutions to problems themselves and must *always* be coupled with other strategies whose objective is the elimination of the immediate circumstances that caused the problem in the first place. Some of the strategies and devices used in this regard are described below.

Acoustical Alarms

Commercially manufactured alarms rely on loud noises (usually combined with other stimuli such as bright lights) to frighten both birds and mammals away from areas where they are not wanted. Hand-sized motion detectors and alarms are advertised in many home improvement and garden supply catalogs. Intended mainly for indoor use, these products can be used in attics or crawl spaces or, with proper protection from the weather,

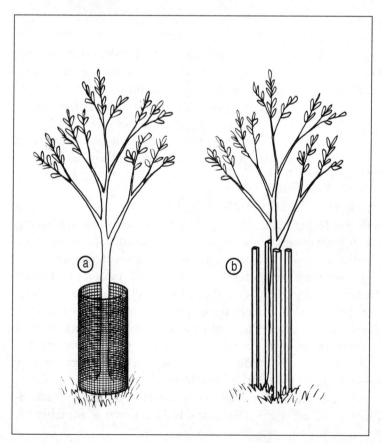

Figure 14. *Trees also can be protected by using hardware cloth or mesh fencing and sometimes even by such simple devices as wooden stakes. The hardware cloth barrier (14a) affords good protection from attacks by beaver, as long as it is at least 30 to 40 inches high and secured so that it does not move. Where deer are a problem and "buck-rubbing" leads to stripped or damaged bark, wooden stakes may be used during the summer and fall to protect vulnerable trees (14b).*

in some outdoor situations. Triggered by motion, they set off a loud alarm to frighten intruding animals. These alarms might also frighten or waken nearby humans, so they should only be used when they are not likely to alarm people (or just bother them). See also "Acoustical Alarms" in Appendix 2.

Bird Distress Calls

For a long time prerecorded distress calls have been used to keep in selected wildlife species away from certain areas. Often intended for agricultural settings, these calls may be successful in dispersing roosting birds as well. As is the case with pyrotechnics, distress calls are rarely usable in neighborhoods where people could be bothered or inconvenienced. Also distress calls are most likely to be effective when used in combination with other techniques. Therefore, before going to the effort of using this strategy, we suggest you contact your local extension or federal Animal Damage Control (ADC) offices.

Effigies and Scarecrows

Scarecrows are one of the oldest, simplest and most effective methods of frightening birds and even some mammals. Homemade scarecrows can be as simple as plastic garbage bags or strips of lightweight material on a stake in the ground, or as complex as the Scarecrow in *The Wizard of Oz*. Movement is an important element in any scarecrow design, and those that can catch breezes, or are motorized, are generally more effective than stationary ones.

Lifelike replicas of hawks, snakes and owls are widely marketed as deterrents to problem birds. The effectiveness of these devices varies with the target species, the type of model, placement and the extent to which

the device resembles a real predator. Again, effigies that move are likely to be more effective than stationary ones. Regardless of the combination used, however, over time most target birds become acclimated to these devices and cease to fear them. In some cases this habituation can occur in only a few hours. See "Effigies and Scarecrows" in Appendix 2.

Lights

Many hardware stores now sell outdoor lighting kits that are motion sensitive. These *might* be effective in situations where nocturnal raids on trash cans or gardens are occurring and the lights are positioned to go on when the culprit arrives on the scene. They certainly could be used to alert any humans inside a house that something was afoot outside, from which point other forms of deterrence, such as simply stepping outside and making a noise, could frighten animals away.

More expensive and elaborate power strobe lights can be purchased in the form of commercially designed bird repellers or can be modified from the devices sold to mount on vehicles. Set to go on and off periodically, lights such as these have been used in agricultural settings to scare birds away from crops and might work in some situations on mammals such as deer. A modified version of these devices coupled with an acoustical alarm is being tested as a coyote deterrent by federal Animal Damage Control researchers. At this writing the device appears to hold some promise, principally in situations where livestock need to be protected.

Pyrotechnic Devices

Pyrotechnic devices use an explosive charge or substance to create loud noises to frighten

Figure 15. *Eye-spot balloons have proven effective in repelling many different kinds of birds from areas where they are not wanted. They also are claimed by some to be effective on certain mammals, such as foxes, when mounted 12 to 18 inches above the ground and placed near the entrance to a burrow dug under a patio or deck.*

and so negatively condition animals. These include gas exploders, modified firearms and their charges and ordinary fireworks. Usually, pyrotechnics can only be used outside of urban and suburban areas because the loud noises are very disruptive and because many of these products are technically firearms and banned by local ordinance. Protection of agricultural fields and dispersion of roosting birds are two major uses for pyrotechnics.

Gas exploders or cannons give off a loud bang by igniting small quantities of propane or acetylene. The cannon has a barrel that amplifies the noise to at least the level created by a shotgun. These cannons are relatively expensive, ranging in price from around $150 to as much as $300, and are usually only cost-effective in agricultural settings. They will protect areas up to several acres in size, depending on the depredating species, nature of area in which they are used and other factors. Standard fireworks, firearms using special ammunition

and devices that require their own launching apparatus are available from commercial manufacturers (see "Pyrotechnic Devices" in Appendix 2). Boat flares that do not make noise are being tested in some urban areas. Again, the use of any of these must comply with local restrictions on firearms and fireworks. Take into account the effect of disturbances on other people in settled areas and follow all recommendations by the manufacturers for safe and proper use, including eye and ear protection for the user.

Scare Balloons

Eye-spot balloons (see Figure 15) have been used for a number of years to repel depredating birds from fields and open lawn areas, and work really well in many different settings. The balloons rely on what is called a "supernormal" stimulus—in this case a highly enhanced "eye" that menacingly occupies the center of the balloon. Yellow, black and white styles are made (yellow seems to be the most effective). Suspended from a support or sometimes even filled with helium, these balloons move in the slightest wind and are effective on waterfowl such as geese, and may be at least temporarily effective on animals such as deer.

Less expensive and readily available in many places are Mylar party balloons. With their bright silvery finish, these balloons may provide equally effective deterrents on a short-term or emergency basis. The species on which these might be used include any of the variety of birds (waterfowl, starlings and pigeons being the most common) and deer, foxes and (perhaps) raccoons.

Scare Tape

Mylar tape is a strong laminated metal and plastic material that was originally developed for use in the space program. It is highly reflective and creates a dazzling pattern of light when in motion, which has led to its adoption as a wildlife scaring tool. A holographically imprinted version of scare tape has even greater light-reflecting properties, while another variant, called the "hummer," resonates in the wind and combines visual and auditory stimuli (see Figure 16, page 42). Cut into strips of varying lengths and widths, this tape can be suspended from posts, wires, gutters on houses or anywhere else the homeowner wishes to repel not only birds but mammals as well. It may be most effective when used in combination with other strategies, and it, of course, is less effective on cloudy days and at night. However, any time it can be set up to catch occasional flashes of light it should work.

Although little tested as yet, this tape might be effective in combination with motion-sensitive lights to repel animals such as deer from yards and garden areas. This tape is available in many hardware and garden supply stores. A number of commercial manufacturers and distributors carry it too (see "Scare Tape" in Appendix 2). In gardens or in open lawn areas, the tape can be strung between posts made of simple lath material or anything handy, twisting it to enhance the reflective properties.

Sprinklers

The ordinary garden hose with a power nozzle attachment has long been used to scare or frighten away unwelcome animals. The difficulty in using water sprays as a deterrent is that the homeowner typically has to actually see the animal and the animal has to be pretty close. A second generation device (see Figure 17 on page 43) combines a motion sensor with an oscillating sprinkler. This sentinel can sit quietly in a yard or garden for hours waiting for an offending creature to draw near before coming to life with an energized blast of water. The main drawback appears to be its somewhat hefty price as well as the possibility that individuals given to forgetfulness may be in for a bit of a shock when setting forth on their own property with one of these devices armed and waiting.

Ultrasonic Devices

Numerous products designed to produce sounds that are inaudible to humans but claiming to be highly aversive to wildlife species have appeared on the market over the years. Often heavily advertised in garden and home improvement catalogs, these products, in our opinion, remain completely unproven. The studies that have been conducted on animals such as deer suggest that devices marketed with the claim that they will work against these animals *do not*. Until they have been demonstrated to be effective in real-life situations, The HSUS does not suggest ultrasonic devices be considered for use in wildlife control.

Chemical Repellents

There are several dozen products on the market that are registered by the Environmental Protection Agency (EPA) for use as repellents to control animal damage. Natural products such as garlic, common household supplies such as soap and ammonia and even materials such as human hair are often recommended for their repellent properties. Because they are not registered for use as repellents by the EPA, they cannot be commercially manufactured or distributed. Their use by individual homeowners falls into a gray area, however. We suggest that anyone with concerns for how, when and where any product or substance can or should be used as a wildlife repellent contact the EPA (see Appendix 1).

The role the EPA plays in registering repellents is that of protecting people, nontarget animals and, to some extent, the target animals themselves. Common sense should apply in any use of a product or substance

to repel wildlife, and the EPA is currently trying to speed up approval of many natural products that are believed to be effective in animal damage control.

Where we all might feel it is overkill to worry about putting an ammonia dampened rag in a fireplace damper to repel an unwanted resident, it is obvious that genuine safety and health concerns would apply to anyone doing the same with gasoline, and we all should recognize the very difficult role that any regulatory agency is asked to serve in doing what they do—drawing the line. Common sense combined with understanding and compassion are important guides—even when registered products are used according to label instructions. No one should assume that just because the label recommends it, a product can safely and humanely be used from the *animal's point of view*.

Chemical repellents are intended to deter, but not harm, wildlife. There are two general types: area and contact. As implied

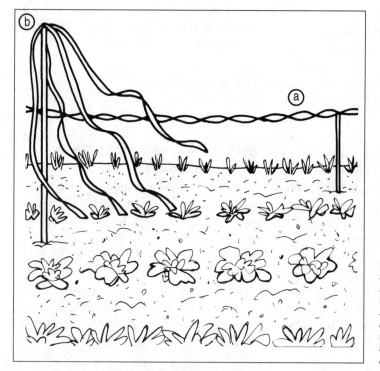

Figure 16. *Scare tape is made of shiny metallic material and can be set out in the garden or yard in any number of ways, two of which are shown here. The reflective properties are enhanced by twisting the tape as it is mounted between posts (a) or by using multiple streamers attached to a central post (b).*

Figure 17. *This device combines a motion sensor with an oscillating sprinkler that detects movement and then sprays a blast of water on an animal trying to get into the garden. Sensors can be set to detect movement farther than 30 feet away and will operate night or day. While fairly expensive, devices such as these demonstrate the potential for using new technologies to humanely resolve conflicts with wild animals.*

in the name, area repellents broadcast alarming or unpleasant odors or other sensations to deter animals. Contact repellents are placed directly on the plant or material that is to be protected (e.g., corn plants or bags full of garbage) and work best when the animal comes into direct contact with them.

Bittering Agents

Thiram is a fungicide that was discovered some time ago to have strong taste-repellent properties to certain animals. It is the active ingredient in repellents such as Nott's Chew-Nott® and Gustafson's Thiram 42-S™ (see "Repellents" in Appendix 2). Thiram is for use on plants that are not intended for human consumption. It can be used to soak the bulbs of flowering plants susceptible to rodent damage before they're planted. Thiram can protect plants for up to six months but must be periodically reapplied to new growth that might be damaged.

Ro-Pel® (denatonium saccharide) comes as a liquid preparation in a variety of container sizes, including quart spray bottles. It contains both a bittering agent (ammonium saccharide) and a penetrating agent (thymol) to allow it to better absorb into plant tissue or other material to be protected. It works by imparting an extremely bitter taste to anything it contacts. It is registered for use on deer, rabbits, raccoons, rats, mice, beaver, squirrels and birds. It, too, is not for use on plants that will be eaten by humans.

Ziram (zinc dimethyl dithiocarbamate) is the active ingredient in a rabbit repellent that is registered for use on ornamentals as well as vegetables up to about a week before they are harvested and eaten. This product is a strong taste-repellent that must be thoroughly washed off any treated plant before it is consumed. (See "Earl May Seed & Nursery" under "Repellents" in Appendix 2.)

Capsaicin (Hot Sauce)

There are several products on the market that contain capsaicin. Capsaicin is an extract derived from peppers, the fruits of plants found in the genus *Capsicum*. Both powder and liquid forms are available. Hot sauces can be used on edible fruits and vegetables before the edible parts begin to develop. Effectiveness may be extended by using a sticker-extender product (see page 46).

> Capsaicin is an extreme irritant and should not be used where pets are free-roaming. Your animals can experience the effects just as much as the target animal.

Miller's Hot Sauce® is approved for use on deer and elk, rabbits, meadow and pine voles and squirrels. Under special permits, it has been used for porcupine that are damaging maple syrup collection equipment.

Deer-Away® Deer and Rabbit Repellent uses extracts of oil of mustard and capsaicin as both an odor and taste repellent to repel rabbits and deer. The label indicates that it can be used on lawns, gardens, trees and shrubs. The label needs to be carefully read by the user: the product is not intended for use *on* an edible food; it's to be used in bands *around* lawns and gardens.

A product with the identical active ingredient component of Deer-Away® is sold by the manufacturer under the label GET-AWAY™ and is registered for use in repelling squirrels from bird feeders, raccoons from garbage and gardens and both squirrels and raccoons from lawns.

Castor Oil

Castor oil is the active ingredient in one product, Mole-Med®, that is registered for use in repelling moles. The plant from which this material is derived has often been claimed by gardeners to have wildlife repellent values and is now getting its first broad commercial test for that.

Cat and Dog Repellents

Methyl nonyl ketone is a chemical used in more than thirty registered dog and cat repellent products to keep these animals away from areas of yards in which their defecation or urination is a problem. Although not registered as such, it is likely that it will work to deter some wildlife species. Taxonomically similar animals, such as foxes, would undoubtedly be affected in much the same way companion animals are.

Egg Solids

Deer-Away® Big Game Repellent (putrescent whole egg solids) is available as both a powder or liquid preparation. It is for use on plants that are not going to be eaten (ornamentals, shrubs, trees, seedlings, etc.), and can be used on dormant fruit trees as well. It is registered for use on white-tailed and black-tailed deer and elk.

Garlic

Increasingly recognized for its insecticide activity, many home gardeners use garlic in mesh bags to repel deer and rabbits from specific plants (see Figure 18). Some put garlic in mole tunnels to force them out. You can also use garlic in a puree as a spray on plants to keep almost any herbivore from eating them. We can't tell you with 100 percent certainty that it works, but it is worth trying.

Hair

A very popular home remedy to repel deer, and sometimes rabbits, from gardens and orchards is human hair. Usually available in abundance from local barber shops, the hair is hung in $^1/_4$- to $^1/_2$-pound quantities in open mesh bags (nylon stockings are sometimes used). Bags should be used on *each* tree or shrub to be protected (see Figure 18). Early response to damage and frequent (monthly) changes are also important if this material is to be effective. While human hair is usually the most available material, experimentation with other types, including the family dog's, is encouraged.

Methyl Anthranilate

Methyl anthranilate is a naturally occurring substance found in a variety of different flower blossoms (gardenias, for example) as well as in Concord grapes. It has long been used in the food industry as an additive to grape soda, candy and gum. Surprisingly, methyl anthranilate has been proven to highly repel birds, and in different formulations it is registered to repel waterfowl such as Canada geese and ducks from lawns, or even from ponds (without fish in them) when applied directly in the water. A third is made to spray on landfills to repel birds such as gulls, starlings and brown-headed cowbirds and a fourth has been used to spray a fog into bird roosts to displace large aggregations of some species. Two manufacturers currently market this product (see Appendix 2), one primarily for agricultural use and the other for the sorts of urban/suburban applications described in Chapter 33. This is a fairly new product and testing and field experience with it are still needed to determine when and where it will be most effective. It does hold great promise, however, as one of several tools necessary to begin to deal with urban waterfowl issues.

Figure 18. *Mesh bags filled with hair or garlic may be suspended from individual trees or shrubs for protection from deer or rabbits. Materials should be replenished frequently to enhance effectiveness.*

Napthalene

Napthalene is an insecticidal repellent and fumigant that is sometimes used to repel animals because of its highly potent smell. It is currently registered for use on squirrels, rabbits and bats, as well as on birds that are found inside buildings (in areas enclosed enough to allow the smell to act in a repellent manner).

Mothballs are composed of the active ingredient *paradichlorobenzene.* Although paradichlorobenzene is less toxic than Napthalene it is not registered for use as a wildlife repellent. Napthalene is also sometimes compressed into balls, but we recommend against using these. Flakes will dissipate faster and cannot be picked up and carried away by inquisitive animals or children.

Napthalene may be the most overused and overprescribed animal repellent on the market. In enclosed areas, such as attics and crawl spaces, it may work adequately to humanely displace an animal and allow permanent exclusion to take place. Many times, however, it seems to have little or no effect. There are human health concerns associated with prolonged exposure to Napthalene, and some individuals may be highly sensitive to it. Even for those without high sensitivity the inadvertent use of Napthalene around central heating or air conditioning units can lead to the dissipation of strong enough odors to force a temporary building evacuation. For these reasons we urge that careful consideration be given to any situation calling for the use of this product, even though the repertoire of nonlethal techniques certainly needs all the tools that can be found.

Soap

Simple bar soap is often used to repel deer by setting it out the same way that hair can be. Drill a hole in the bar, run a string through it and suspend it from the tree or shrub to be protected. As with hair, this broadcast repellent is best used one per plant (unless the plants are very closely spaced) and altered with other repellents or strategies to keep the animals from becoming accustomed to it. It's OK to leave the wrapper on the bar (this will allow it to hold up much better in rain).

Hinder® is a commercial repellent made from ammonium soaps of higher fatty acids and is registered for use in repelling deer and rabbits. This product can be used on fruit and vegetables as well as ornamental plants and is one of only a few repellents that can be used on plants that will be eaten by people.

Sticker-Extenders

These are waxy adhesive formulations of different chemicals that are widely used by gardeners and nursery professionals to protect plants from dehydration. Adhering to leaves when applied in a spray the sticker-extender slows down the transpiration of water through leaves (it also repels the effects of rain as a leaf wash). This means that any chemical mixed with it is likely to adhere to the plant longer. Popular brands widely stocked by garden centers are Wilt-Pruf®, Vapor-Gard® and Nu-film-17®. Some, such as Vapor-Gard®, are recommended for long-term use (such as protection of dormant trees in winter), while others (e.g., Nu-film-17®) are intended for use on crops or fruit for shorter-term repellency. Not all repellents can be used with extenders, so it is important to consult the label or seek advice from the manufacturers if in doubt about how to use the product.

Live Trapping

Often, homeowners try to solve a wildlife problem by trapping a problem animal and transporting it to the "country" or to a local park, thinking that its release will give it a better, more "natural" habitat while solving their problem at the same time. We wish we could say this was always going to be true, and that trapping and moving animals *(translocation)* is a safe, benign and humane procedure. Unfortunately, translocation is one of the least understood and most problematic wildlife "control" practices we know of. Not only might the trapping and movement of the animal cause it harm or even bring it death, but the activity might adversely affect other wild animals as well. There is currently an extensive debate among wildlife professionals about this procedure, suggesting that each proposal for transloca-tion should be rigorously evaluated. Cer-tainly under some circumstances, and with some species, it might be far preferable to death, but in other cases it could be quite stressful and result in suffering or death.

Our advice, at this time (and acknowl-edging first what is not legally permitted in any given jurisdiction), is to use transloca-tion as the *next-to-last* resort in dealing with human-wildlife conflicts. Live trapping and euthanizing the animal is the last resort. Neither of these should ever happen with-out making every effort to deal with the cause of the problem, to ensure that it will not reoccur. It is the position of The HSUS that the vast majority of wildlife conflict situations can be resolved by simpler, more humane means than by removing an animal from its natural home area or by destroying it.

Toxicants

Toxicants are chemicals registered for use in the lethal control of wildlife. We identify and describe some of the more commonly used kinds of toxicants here because we feel a re-sponsibility to you—the homeowner—to make sure you are aware of the possibility that they might be recommended or used in "solving" problems with animals that involve you. The HSUS does not consider the use of these products appropriate for resolving human-wildlife conflicts in urban and suburban settings except perhaps un-der the most urgent conditions, such as when a critical public health and safety con-cern arises or when the problem animal threatens the survival of an endangered spe-cies. The use of toxicants is *never* justified unless it is part of an integrated plan that has a strong commitment to employing nonlethal methods before, during and after

any lethal measures take place, and with the committed objective that lethal control will not repeatedly have to be used.

The HSUS feels that it is important that homeowners be aware that some products, even when used in accordance with the manufacturer's instructions, can be harm-ful to wildlife. Accordingly, we also include in this section substances and products whose use might not be immediately lethal, but in which the likelihood of injury or dis-abling side effects to both target and non-target species is sufficiently great that we regard them as unacceptable.

Avitrol®

Avitrol® (4-aminopyridine) is a chemical used to control bird problems and is regis-tered for use as a flock repellent device, even though it has lethal properties. The product is supposedly applied to only a small pro-portion of the bait that is set out for prob-lem birds (pigeons, starlings and house sparrows). Birds who ingest treated bait ex-perience acute distress and engage in behav-iors (vocalizations, fluttering of wings, staggering and struggling) that alarm other members of the flocks and lead to flock dis-persal. Any bird ingesting the chemical can consume a lethal dose. Thus, all birds that consume treated bait will be at risk, and unless extremely careful bait placement and

Table 2

List of chemical repellents and species for which products are registered. Company addresses and phone numbers are listed in Appendix 2.

Species/Use	Product Name	Manufacturer	Active Ingredient
Bats	Chaperone® Squirrel and Bat Repellent	Sudbury Laboratory, Inc.	Napthalene
Beavers	Ro-Pel®	Burlington BioMedical & Scientific Corp.	Dentonium saccharide
Birds			
Fruit-eating	Bird Shield®	Bird Shield® Repellent Corp.	Methyl anthranilate
	ReJeX-iT® AG-145	RJ Advantage, Inc.	Methyl anthranilate
Canada geese from lawns & turf areas	ReJeX-iT® AG-36	RJ Advantage, Inc.	Methyl anthranilate
Misc. birds from ponds (without fish)	ReJeX-iT® TP40	RJ Advantage, Inc.	Methyl anthranilate
Misc. birds from landfills	ReJeX-iT® TP40	RJ Advantage, Inc.	Methyl anthranilate
Roosting birds	ReJeX-iT® F6=40	RJ Advantage, Inc.	Methyl anthranilate
Deer	Thiram 42-S	Gustafson, Inc.	Thiram (42%)
	Deer-Off®	Deer-Off, Inc.	Putrescent egg solids, capsaicin and garlic
	Deer-Away®	IntAgra, Inc.	Putrescent egg solids
	GET-AWAY™	IntAgra, Inc.	Putrescent egg solids, capsaicin and oil of mustard
	Miller's Hot Sauce®	Miller Chemical and Fertilizer Corp.	Capsaicin
	Chew-Nott (20%)	Nott Manufacturing	Thiram
	Hinder®	Uniroyal Chemical Corp.	Ammonium soaps of higher fatty acids

Animal	Product	Manufacturer	Active Ingredient
Moles	Mole-Med®	Mole-Med, Inc.	Castor oil
Porcupines	Miller's Hot Sauce®	Miller Chemical and Fertilizer Corp.	Capsaicin
Rabbits (*Sylvilagus* spp.)	Shotgun®	Bonide Chemical Co.	Napthalene, dried blood and tobacco dust
	Rabbit Scat	Earl May Seed & Nursery Co.	Ziram
	Thiram 42-S	Gustafson, Inc.	Thiram (42%)
	GET-AWAY™	IntAgra, Inc.	Thiram (42%)
	Miller's Hot Sauce®	Miller Chemical and Fertilizer Corp.	Capsaicin
	Chew-Nott	Nott Manufacturing	Thiram (20%)
Raccoons	GET-AWAY™	IntAgra, Inc.	Capsaicin and oil of mustard
Rats (*Rattus* spp.) and **House Mice** (*Mus musculus*)	Ro-Pel®	Burlington BioMedical & Scientific Corp.	Dentonium saccharide
Squirrels, Chipmunks (*Sciurus* spp.)	Thiram 42-S	Gustafson, Inc.	Thiram (42%)
	Ro-Pel®	Burlington BioMedical & Scientific Corp.	Dentonium saccharide
(*Tamiasciurus* spp.),	GET-AWAY™	IntAgra, Inc.	Capsaicin and oil of mustard
Flying Squirrels (*Glaucomys* spp.)	Miller's Hot Sauce®	Miller Chemical and Fertilizer Corp.	Capsaicin
	Chaperone® Squirrel and Bat Repellent	Sudbury Laboratory, Inc.	Napthalene
Voles (*Microtus* spp.)	Miller's Hot Sauce®	Miller Chemical and Fertilizer Corp.	Capsaicin
	Chew-Nott	Nott Manufacturing	Thiram (20%)

monitoring occurs, nontarget species can also ingest the chemical and die. The HSUS does not consider this product appropriate for control of bird problems and considers its use to be inhumane.

DRC-1339

This poison (3-chloro-4-methylbenze-namine hydrochloride) is manufactured in different forms to kill starlings, gulls, pigeons, magpies, crows and ravens. It is a very dangerous toxicant that is to be used only by certified personnel, but even that restriction does not seem, to us, adequate to control its potential misuse and the danger of accidental exposures. One common use of this product is to control birds in cattle feedlots. The HSUS considers this product inappropriate for use in animal control and considers its use to be inhumane.

Fenthion

Fenthion is a toxicant, or poison, that is used in Rid-a-Bird® perches to lethally control starlings, house sparrows and pigeons. The toxic material is put in perches that are set out in fields or farm lots where birds congregate. Any bird that just lands on one of these perches absorbs enough of the toxicant to kill it in a very short period of time. Nontarget species are susceptible as well, and Fenthion will also kill animals that scavenge poisoned birds. The HSUS considers this material to be extremely hazardous and inappropriate in animal control.

Gas Cartridges

Several toxicants, including sodium nitrate, sulfur and red phosphorus, are formulated into cartridges that are made to be ignited and placed into animal burrows to kill anything inside. Aside from dangers to operators and bystanders through accidents or careless handling, the discharge from these devices kills any animal in the burrow, whether the problem species or not. All too frequently those who use this method of animal control do nothing to remove the cause of the problem, but simply reapply it in burrows that are then left as open invitations for other animals to move in to. The HSUS considers the use of these devices to be inhumane and generally inappropriate for solving wildlife problems.

Glueboards

These devices are made from sticky substances that trap small mammals, usually mice or rats, and slowly kill with a combination of stress, exhaustion and (eventually) dehydration or inanition as victims give up the struggle to free themselves. Any nontarget animal encountering the traps will face the same fate. The HSUS considers these devices to be inappropriate for solving wildlife problems and their use to be grossly inhumane under any circumstances or conditions.

Polybutenes

These are highly dense sticky substances (e.g., Tanglefoot®, Eaton's® 4 The Squirrel™) that are marketed in different formulations to discourage both birds and squirrels from climbing, sitting or roosting on surfaces treated. Animals exposed to these materials have been treated in wildlife rehabilitation clinics, and claims that polybutenes do not cause injury need to be examined critically. The product may disfigure buildings or tree surfaces, especially in hot weather when it becomes much more fluid. The HSUS considers this material to be inappropriate and inhumane for solving wildlife problems.

Rodenticides

Most of the recent battles between humans and rats have been fought using one generation after another of rodent poison, or rodenticide, to which the rats, in their typically adaptable manner, have developed increasing levels of immunity. After ill-advised and environmentally unsound experimentation with fast-killing and indiscriminate poisons such as zinc phosphide, the development of anticoagulant poisons was hailed with high hope and enthusiasm. Most of the current generation of anticoagulants depend upon repeated ingestion over time to build up fatal dosages, to take advantage of the fact that rats are samplers—they will eat a little bit of new food at a time to see if it is palatable. This increases the poison's efficiency because the rat does not associate eating it with pain or discomfort. There should be a great concern for the potential exposure of nontarget animals or humans to poison baits. This can occur either through direct ingestion of baits that have been improperly placed on the ground or were rejected from burrows by the rats and not removed, or exposure of predatory species through ingestion of poisoned rats themselves.

Two

Our Wild Neighbors

4

Armadillos

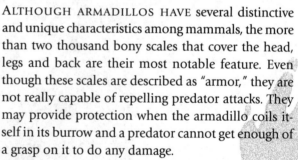

Armadillos range throughout the south-central and southeastern parts of the United States, but are slowly making their way north.

The armadillo will construct burrows in any loose soil, but around homes under patios and decks is usually where they are a problem.

It's not a myth: this animal does hold its breath and walk along the bottom when crossing streams.

ALTHOUGH ARMADILLOS HAVE several distinctive and unique characteristics among mammals, the more than two thousand bony scales that cover the head, legs and back are their most notable feature. Even though these scales are described as "armor," they are not really capable of repelling predator attacks. They may provide protection when the armadillo coils itself in its burrow and a predator cannot get enough of a grasp on it to do any damage.

A very long time ago the North and South American continents were separated by a sea wide enough to isolate their animal inhabitants sending them along quite different evolutionary paths. When the continents later joined, the more advanced predators in the north swept down into the south, and many fascinating and unusual South American life-forms disappeared. Three that not only managed to survive but actually moved north are animals we are familiar with today—sloths, anteaters and armadillos. Only the armadillo, however, remains within the boundaries of the United States. The name *armadillo* comes from the Spanish and means "little armored one."

Unique among mammals, this armored "shell" is composed of hard bony plates covered by a leathery skin. The armadillo has adapted very well to the southern United States and is still expanding its range. In this it has been aided sometimes by humans, who seem delighted to transport the animals from one part of the country to another. The full biological and ecological impact of human-aided movements of different animal species from one part of the United States to another has never been estimated, but it is certainly much greater than commonly recognized.

Having aided in their moving about, we then encounter many species we label as nuisances. We should remember that it got this way because of us. It is also important to recognize that when a species moves into new habitat it usually undergoes a period of adjustment, during which it may prove to be more of a problem than it is later. Control programs launched during these periods may make no difference at all, although the natural adjustment and stabilization of populations makes it appear as if they do.

Natural History

Classification and Range

The armadillo *(Dasypus novemcinctus)* found in the United States is called the nine-banded because of the nine bands that run across the armor plating on the back (they allow it to flex). This number actually varies somewhat, but this does not change the actual taxonomy of the animals found throughout much of the south-central and southeastern parts of the country. One population of these animals in Florida started with the introduction of a pair that escaped from a zoo in 1922. They later met up with animals that, over generations, came from Texas, where they first entered the country. All armadillo colonization of the United States seems to have taken place within the last 150 years. Now, populations are found as far north as Oklahoma and Arkansas, and only winter severity seems to prevent the species from further expanding its range.

Habitat

Armadillos live in a variety of habitats, including thorn scrub, mixed grasslands and wooded bottomlands. Their preferred habitat may be wetlands with dense shade and sandy soils that are easy to dig. River valleys, creek drainages and areas around stock ponds or reservoirs are choice habitats. Usually nocturnal, armadillos dig numerous emergency and temporary burrows. The burrows range in depth from 20 inches to 20 feet. Most have a single entrance with a southern exposure. Other more permanent abodes may include a network of tunnels with three to four entrances. Birthing chambers tend to be located at least 3 to 5 feet below the surface and at sharp angles off a main tunnel. The chamber is usually lined with leaves and grass.

Diet

Nearly all of the armadillo's diet consists of insects and other invertebrates. Some plant food is ingested, mostly incidental to capturing insects. Small animals, baby birds and eggs and carrion may occasionally be eaten.

Reproduction

Armadillos reach maturity at about nine months. Mating occurs between July and August, but implantation is delayed until November. In fact, under some conditions it is thought that mated armadillo females may delay implantation for as much as two years. Once implantation has occurred, gestation takes about 120 days. The normal litter size is four, all of the same sex and all genetically identical because all are derived from a single egg. The kits are born fully developed, but it takes several weeks for the pink leathery skin to harden into its lifelong protective covering.

Behavior

The armadillo is generally a solitary forager, although it may share its den with other armadillos of the same sex. Armadillos are almost constantly active when foraging—poking and probing into crevices and under litter for the insects and small animals that make up its diet. They continuously grunt while foraging and appear not to be particularly attentive to their surroundings. In fact, if a person holds still it may be possible to have a foraging armadillo actually bump into them before recognizing they are there.

Armadillos have few natural enemies other than people: domestic dogs and perhaps larger predators such as coyotes and bobcats. Vehicle collisions and weather are the biggest population control factors. Unlike some of its relatives, the nine-banded armadillo is not able to roll up in a ball. Its defense is to either dig or enter an existing burrow, or to press its unprotected belly against the ground with its legs tucked under its shields. The nine-banded is the only armadillo that can swim.

Public Health

Armadillos are not implicated in the transmission of any zoonotic disease to humans. They can be infected with the bacterium that causes human leprosy, but do not naturally carry or transmit this disease.

Problems and Their Solutions

Problems

Two types of problems with armadillos generally occur. The first comes during opportunistic feeding activities when a passing armadillo roots around in a landscaped area or garden and disturbs plantings. The second type of problem occurs in the digging of semipermanent tunnel networks or birthing tunnels.

Solutions

TOLERANCE

The disturbance of vegetable or flower gardens is generally temporary and may not require any damage control measures because the armadillo may simply move on after exploiting a locally abundant food source. In some cases the armadillo may even be providing a free service by feeding on destructive insects. Armadillos are one of the few animals that will take on fire ants and can be highly beneficial when these insects are present. The damaging effects of tunneling and burrowing are also usually localized and should be addressed by a combination of habitat modification, exclusion, elimination of cover and acceptance of a temporary or limited presence these animals sometimes make.

HABITAT MODIFICATION

This can be accomplished by controlling access to food, water or shelter. Removing brush or weed cover can eliminate shelter and encourage armadillos to move elsewhere. Implementing an insect or other food-source control program may help, and, if it can be humanely accomplished, restricting access to sources of water can deter armadillo presence.

EXCLUSION

Fencing can be used to exclude armadillos from gardens, small yards or water sources. Armadillos are able climbers, and fences should be designed to provide a rigid overhang that extends outward for a foot or more at about a 45° angle to prevent "climb-overs." Alternatively, semirigid plastic fencing of the sort used at many construction sites to mark off areas where people should not be can work with armadillos on the principle that they would not provide enough support to climb. Ideally, a 4-foot section of this sort of fence should be used, forcing the animal to fully support its weight in climbing. Any fence intended to deter armadillos must take into account their digging skills and be securely fastened to the ground or, better still, buried a foot or more to deter tunneling.

One-way doors may prove useful in getting armadillos out of burrows but not allowing them back in. The digging abilities of these animals, however, are formidable, and attempts to exclude them from burrows must be persistent.

A Last Word

It wouldn't hurt us to be more aware of the consequences both of moving animals around the land as well as modifying that land to favor some species over others. The armadillo is a good example of a self-inflicted wound of sorts, as we have undoubtedly aided their settling the south and southeastern United States by transporting them there. Probably they would have gotten where they are today without our help, but this movement might have taken far longer and involved a better natural adaptation of both armadillos and native plant and animal communities to the new relationship.

Additional Sources

Galbreath, G. J. 1982. "Armadillo." In J. A. Chapman and G. A. Feldhamer (eds.), *Wild Mammals of North America.* Baltimore: Johns Hopkins University Press. 71–82.

Smith, L. L., and R. W. Doughty. 1984. *The Amazing Armadillo.* Austin: University of Texas Press. 134 pp.

5

Bats

There are more than forty different species of bats, found throughout virtually all of Canada and the United States.

Attics make excellent places for colonial bats to roost and raise young. Occasionally, individual bats fly into houses.

These are the only mammals capable of true flight.

BATS ARE ONE OF A SELECT GROUP of animals, including the wolf, whose public image has quite recently turned from a highly negative to a mostly positive one. Not long ago these diminutive creatures, typically weighing no more than a few ounces, inspired such universal dread in humans that many thousands were indiscriminately killed each year. They now enjoy better favor, in part due to an increasing ecological awareness by the public and in part due to their being championed, first by individuals and then organizations that have promoted our awareness of them. Individuals can, and do, make a very real difference in advancing animal welfare concerns. Sometimes that difference comes when animals are defended from unwarranted controls imposed by humans who know no better solution to conflicts with animals than to kill them. Sometimes it comes simply through a better understanding of species biology to recognize that the animal is not a threat. Thanks to the individuals and organizations that have taught us about bats, we now know that they rarely cause problems for humans and frequently serve a valuable role in controlling insect pests. When conflicts do occur, there are effective, efficient, safe and humane ways to deal with them that make lethal control unnecessary. Unhappily, this fact is not known everywhere, and it will take continued education and public involvement to reach the point where lethal control of bats becomes a thing of the past.

Natural History

Classification and Range

All bats belong to the order *Chiroptera*, the only group of mammals that are truly capable of flight. Most people would not distinguish one species of bat from another in the air (nor probably feel a need to do so). It is important to note, however, that a bat is not just a bat. Some are solitary, some live in groups. Some use houses to roost when they can, others never will. In fact, of the many species in North America only a few ever come into conflict with humans. These are typically house- or building-dwelling bats such as the little brown bat *(Myotis lucifugus)*, the big brown bat *(Eptesicus fuscus)*, the evening bat *(Nycticeius humeralis)*, the pallid bat *(Antrozous pallidus)* and the free-tailed bat *(Tadarida* and *Eumops* spp.). Many lesser-known species occur locally as well, and the best way to get to know them is to visit the library. In addition to mammal field guides, there are many excellent (and colorful) publications describing bats that show the amazing diversity and variety of this group of animals.

Habitat

All of the bats found in North America are nocturnal, although when they begin foraging just at dusk they may be quite visible. Bats tend to have specific habitat requirements. For example, big brown bats prefer that nursery colony temperatures not exceed 95°F, while little brown bats prefer temperatures in the 110 to 120°F range. Almost all bats migrate, and both the summer colonial and solitary species will collect in groups, often at caves used as hibernation sites or *hibernacula*.

Diet

All common North American bats feed on insects, which they usually catch in flight. They detect their prey by echolocation, which is the remarkable ability to emit high-frequency sounds (outside of human hearing) to discern objects by the sound reflected back to the bat. This sense is so acute that some species can detect objects no wider than a human hair. Different species specialize in eating different types of insects, but as a group all are considered beneficial because many of the insects eaten can be nuisance species.

Reproduction

Depending on the latitude, most species give birth to their single baby (occasionally twins) in early to late May, with the young unable to fly until sometime in July. The newborn of some species cling to the mother while she hunts, but all offspring are left behind as they grow too large to be carried. Attics are often used as nurseries because they maintain desired temperature regimes for raising young. Nursery colonies only contain breeding females and their young, as the adult males find elsewhere to roost at these times.

Public Health

Although bats are more commonly associated with the transmission of *rabies* to people than any other type of animal, the incidence of this disease in bat populations is estimated to be less than one-half of 1 percent. Rabid bats generally do not become aggressive and do not bite without provocation, but any bat may bite in self-defense if handled with bare hands. If a bat must be handled for any reason, leather work gloves provide adequate protection from their small teeth. Large accumulations of bat droppings may harbor *histoplasmosis* fungi spores and should be approached with the precautions that are described in Chapter 2.

Problems and Their Solutions

Problems

Bats rely on existing openings to enter buildings and so do not cause structural damage by making or enlarging entry holes. Small ($^1/_2$ inch or greater) openings high on houses, around chimneys, at the union of dormers with roofs or at loose siding can all provide access. Bats roosting in houses often go unnoticed for years. Then, they may first be noticed after an accumulation of feces and urine leach through attic spaces to stain the wall or ceiling on the living area below. It is under these conditions that homeowners often feel they have a crisis that must be dealt with immediately, when, in fact, they have been living with the bats for years.

A second type of problem occurs when an individual bat is found inside the house. Often the bat is first observed flying around a room early in the evening, landing on curtains or furniture and then taking flight again. In this case, getting the bat out of the house becomes a high priority.

Solutions

TOLERANCE
First, the sight of bats flying at dusk above the yard is absolutely no cause for alarm. This event is perfectly natural—the bats are foraging for flying insects. Their abilities in this regard are considerable. Little brown bats, tested in controlled indoor enclosures, have been documented eating upwards of 600 mosquitoes in one hour! Clearly, a few

of these creatures working the skies above our homes are performing a welcomed service. Even encounters with bats temporarily trapped inside a house or discovered in an attic should not lead to hasty or panicked responses. Trapped bats can be removed and

---

Bats and Bedrooms

The current recommendation of the National Centers for Disease Control in Atlanta is that any bat discovered to have been in a room with a sleeping person be captured and submitted to local or state health authorities for rabies testing. The reason for this is that the bite of these animals can be so insignificant it could be overlooked by an adult or unreported by a child. As we advise with any situation involving potential exposure to rabies, consultation with your physician and local health authorities is the recommended course of action. (See Chapter 2.)

---

attic colonies excluded in a humane and effective manner that will minimize stress to both humans and bats (see "Exclusion").

Accidental Encounters

Any direct encounter with a bat inside or outside can be termed accidental, because these animals will always try to avoid contact with humans and their pets if they can. The myth of bats becoming entangled in one's hair is exactly that—a myth. Bats found outside may be ill, may be temporarily stunned from flying into a window, exactly as birds sometimes do, or may in colder weather simply be torpid and unable to move or fly as well as when warmed. Bats indoors require essentially the same responses as for bats outdoors, except that the bat needs to be permitted to get out or be captured and taken out if necessary.

The rule in any encounter with a bat is to remain calm and keep pets and children away. Observe the bat and consider circumstances closely enough to formulate some understanding of what caused the bat to get into the situation it's in. If the bat is inside, remember that it will probably try to fly to an opening. Because of the confined space, however, it will have to follow a U-shaped path, gaining altitude near the walls and losing altitude in the center of the room. A person standing in the middle of the room may feel that they are being attacked when actually all that is happening is that the bat is trying to stay airborne.

Keep as near to a wall as possible when moving around the room. Close interior doors and give the bat an exit by opening an outside door or window. If the bat disappears before an exit has been provided, it probably has landed somewhere it can hang—behind curtains or upholstered furniture, on hanging clothes or in house plants. Search for it, and try to capture it using a net if one is available. If a net is not available and the bat is hanging on a curtain or other vertical surface, carefully place a jar or plastic tub over it (metal cans can quickly cool bats down to temperatures that are unsafe for them) and gently work a piece of cardboard or stiff paper between the opening and the surface of the wall, trapping the bat inside.

A thick towel is a good way to capture a bat on the floor or within reach. Roll the bat up gently, take the towel outside to a location safe from bystanders or domestic animals and unroll it. Leather (not cotton) work gloves are adequate protection from a bat's teeth and will allow a person to safely pick it up. *Never try to handle a bat with bare hands.* Be prepared for the bat to vocalize loudly in protest when picked up. Release the bat as soon as possible in a place where it will be out of harm's way if it does not fly immediately.

After the bat has been freed, it is important to find how it entered the house. Possible entry routes are through an open door or window, but if these can be ruled out then it is more likely the bat has been roosting somewhere within the outer walls of the house and accidentally found a route to the living space. Common entry points include gaps around window air conditioners, chimneys and openings in interior walls that lead to attics or cellars that may harbor even more bats. Inspect and seal these interior entrances immediately if it appears they could allow entry. The inspection must be thorough because bats can fit through openings as small as $1/2$ inch.

EXCLUSION

The most likely place for a bat colony to become established in a house is the attic. The key to excluding a bat colony from a building is to find any and all openings that the bats are using. A well-used opening will sometimes be discolored on the outside from the body oils that come from the bats rubbing against it when coming and going. Because this is not always observed, a "bat watch" just at dusk can reveal other entrances. Watch closely from before sunset until at least thirty minutes after sunset; it only takes a second or so for a bat to exit and take flight.

The best strategy for excluding a bat colony from a building is to allow the bats to leave on their own and then to deny them reentry. *Bats should be evicted from a building only when it is known that no young animals are present.* From May through August, then, is not a good time to try to solve bat colony problems. Waiting until they have left for the winter hibernation cave allows the exclusion to be done in a more careful and deliberate manner.

Bat Colonies

No lethal control of bat colonies is warranted or excused, and the potential for serious injury or illness to humans occupying a house treated with the toxicants that are used illegally to control bats is far greater than any possible harm or risk the animals themselves could pose.

If the bat colony must be excluded at once, all outside entrances should be located and noted. All except the largest or most obviously used should be sealed with appropriate building materials (hardware cloth, netting or sheet metal). The last opening can be sealed with netting after bats have exited at night to forage. Because not all members of the colony will leave to feed on a given night, this process will have to be repeated for as many nights as necessary to ensure all the bats are out of the building.

Alternatively, the last entrance can be fitted with a one-way bat checkvalve. There are several variations of these (see Figure 19), but in principle all work to let bats exit from the building but not return. Left in place for several nights, these devices should give all bats a chance to exit but frustrate their returning. If possible, check the attic to be sure there are no bats left, and watch the outside of the house in the evening again to make sure the bats have not found another way in. If they have, move the excluder to the new entrance. After the bats are gone, remove the excluder and seal the last opening.

BAT HOUSES

In the interest of promoting bat conservation, and (to be honest) because it is something of a fad, many people are putting up bat houses in their yards. The jury is out on whether or not these are effective as first- or even second-choice roosting sites. Currently, studies suggest that bat houses put up just prior to eviction of colonies from buildings are rarely chosen as an alternate residence. There are so many factors that go into correct construction and placement of bat houses that it is not advisable to assume that displaced bats will be fine because a house has been put up for them. Fortunately, the information needed to properly design and install bat houses is improving every year. We recommend consulting with the staff at Bat Conservation International in Austin, Texas, prior to undertaking the effort to build and install a house; their workbook cited at the end of this chapter is especially helpful. Prefabricated bat houses are available at many nature centers and retail outlets specializing in bird feeding and wildlife products.

Bat Information Resources

Bat Conservation International (BCI) is the best source of advice and information on bats, although some states have local bat conservation societies that can be helpful also. BCI can be reached at P.O. Box 162603, Austin, TX 78716; (512) 327-9721; (fax) (512) 327-9724.

A Last Word

There are dozens of other species of wildlife that need to join the bat and the wolf as deserving of public respect and understanding. Taken one at a time it might be some while before they will all be given these, but by using an ecosystem approach, we may make progress more rapidly toward accepting the positive value of all wild animals.

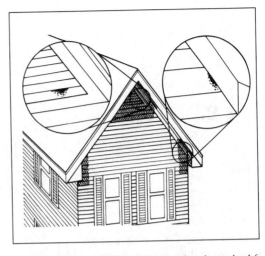

Figure 19. *Bat checkvalves consist of netting draped over—but left open at the bottom—an entrance being used by house-dwelling bats. Bats will exit, crawl down the side of the house and leave, but they will not be able to return.*

Additional Sources

Frantz, S. 1986. "Batproofing Structures with Birdnetting Checkvalves." Proceedings of the 12th Vertebrate Pest Conference, University of California at Davis. 260–68.

French, T. W., J. E. Cardoza, and G. S. Jones. 1986. *A Homeowner's Guide to Massachusetts Bats and Bat Problems.* Massachusetts Department of Fish and Wildlife, 100 Cambridge Street, Boston, MA 02202.

Kern, W. H., Jr., J. Belwood, and P. G. Koehler. 1993. "Bats in Buildings." Fact sheet ENY-272. Florida Cooperative Extension Service, University of Florida.

Lee, C., and F. R. Henderson. 1992. "Bats: Urban Wildlife Damage Control." Publication L-855. Cooperative Extension Service, Kansas State University, Manhattan, KS.

Tuttle, Merlin D. 1988. *America's Neighborhood Bats.* Austin: University of Texas Press.

Tuttle, Merlin D., and Donna L. Hensley. 1993. *The Bat House Builder's Handbook.* Bat Conservation International, P.O. Box 162603, Austin, TX 78716.

Bat House and Rabies

Bat houses and bats have such an incredibly small possibility of contributing to the potential for exposure to rabies that efforts to pass ordinances prohibiting them are entirely unnecessary. Not only do the species of bats that inhabit houses tend not to be the ones that are implicated in bat-to-human transmission of the disease, but the overall rate of rabies in bats is so low that their residence is of positive value—insect control.

6

Beavers

Distributed completely throughout Canada and most of the United States; absent only from the most arid regions.

Problems in yards when trees are cut down; flooding resulting from beaver dams is an issue in some areas.

Spend the entire winter with up to eight family members in a tiny enclosed chamber in the lodge—and without any bickering.

IT MAY SEEM FAR-FETCHED to suggest a relationship between North America's largest rodent and a statue that stands in the Kremlin's Red Square, but that's what we're about to do. The statue commemorates Lewis Henry Morgan, an American lawyer recognized as one of the founders of the field of cultural anthropology. His seminal work, *Ancient Society*, was published in 1877, fully nine years after his natural history study entitled *The American Beaver* appeared. Morgan's thinking about the evolution of human society was so highly admired by Karl Marx and Friedrich Engels that their praise of him led to the statue in Moscow. His monograph on beavers produced no statues but still came to be credited as a major influence on the thinking of the founders of Ethology, the science that focuses on the study of animal behavior under natural conditions.

Beavers are an example of a species nearly driven to extinction and making a comeback. At issue in that comeback is the fact that beavers and humans are in conflict over who gets to occupy floodplains. We are only just recognizing that while it is reasonable and environmentally appropriate for the beaver to build in these areas, it is far less so for humans to build or live there. One of the great challenges facing us as a society in the coming years will be to focus on how we deal with environmentally unsound decisions made in the past and now needing to be fixed. At issue is whether we begin to work with nature or to continue to employ brute force to "overcome" the natural world. How we deal with human-beaver conflicts is one chapter in that story.

Natural History

Classification and Range

The beaver *(Castor canadensis)* is the largest rodent found in North America. It has a very close relative in the Old World *(Castor fiber)* that some taxonomists regard as essentially the same species. In most of Europe and Asia, this Old World beaver is in critical trouble and may be close to following its cousin, a late-Pleistocene beaver that was about the size of a bear, into extinction. Our beaver can weigh more than 60 pounds, but an average adult is more likely to weigh about 35 to 40. Including the trademark flat tail used as a rudder, construction tool and communication device, the adults are about 30 inches long and a foot high. When standing on its hind legs an adult beaver can reach almost 3 feet.

Beavers are well adapted to the aquatic habitat that, for the most part, they design and maintain. A beaver can submerge for as much as fifteen minutes, during which time it can carry tree limbs under water in itss incisor teeth thanks to a special flap of skin designed to prevent water from being swallowed.

Their dense waterproof fur was so coveted by the colonists that beavers in the East were nearly trapped out of existence soon after European settlement. Viable popula-

tions persisted in the most inaccessible parts of the far West, and hence much of the romantic lore concerning the "mountain man" became associated with the continuing pursuit of the species. A good deal of the trade and commerce of the early colonial period was based on beavers—so much so that for a time their pelts were the standard currency. The economic viability of the early colonial period depended to a large extent not only on beaver fur, but on the rich soils that surfaced when beaver dams were broken and agricultural land was created. In a sense, these animals gave breath to early America twice: once through their lives and again through their land.

Habitat

Beavers live in and around water and constantly modify streams by building dams and impounding flows to create ponds, although they will also live by large rivers and lakes without building dams at all. Lewis Henry Morgan visited beaver impoundments just south of Lake Superior that had probably been in place for hundreds, if not thousands, of years. The beavers were mostly gone, but their lodges and dams remained as archaeological evidence. The dam at Grass Lake that Morgan describes was 260 feet long, over 6 feet tall and had obviously been the work of generations of beavers. Still, it would be dwarfed by the dam measured at an astounding 2,160 feet long by Enos Mills in what is now Rocky Mountain National Park in Colorado.

The beaver impoundment provides a rich environment for many animal and plant species. There is a regular cycle in land changes habitat created by beavers, providing different values at each stage. Early beaver ponds, for example, create conditions attractive to many species of waterfowl, including the threatened black duck *(Anas rubripes)*, a species of special concern all along the Atlantic Coast. Later development of beaver wetlands encourages many sensitive plant species to proliferate, and eventually many beaver ponds are abandoned and revert to rich meadows that support abundant plant and animal life.

Diet

Beaver are *herbivores*, feeding on the inner layer of the bark of woody plants (the *cambium*), leaves, shoots and aquatic herbs such as duckweed, water lilies and pond weed. Occasionally the fruits of terrestrial plants, some herbaceous forest plants and even crops such as soybeans and corn may be eaten. The favored woody species may vary from area to area, depending on what is locally available, but where they are found, aspen, birch, willow, cottonwood, poplars, maple, apple and even oak are preferred. A beaver's preferred food trees may also include popular ornamentals such as dogwood, hybrid poplar and fruit trees, for which they may travel long distances from the water. Evergreen trees are rarely eaten, and signs of beavers eating trees such as pine may be an indication that suitable food is lacking. In the fall, beavers sink large accumulations of branches into the mud close by the lodge. These food "caches" provide winter food supplies.

Most of the trees used for food or for other construction activities are felled within 100 feet of the main body of water the beavers are using. Damage up to 600 feet from water can occur, but usually only in places where beavers have built canals, straight waterways about 3 to 4 feet wide and equally deep that provide cover and access to inland areas. Beavers can cut down fairly large trees (preferring those 2 to 6 inches in diameter, but sometimes working on trees that are more than 24 inches in diameter) to eat the trunks and branches. Often, they partially or completely girdle trees, but leave them still standing.

Reproduction

Beavers produce one litter per year, usually between March and June. After weaning, parental duties are shared not only by the female and male, but in part by earlier young that remain with the family. A typical litter contains three or four kits. Interestingly, unless they are harvested very heavily, trapping appears to stimulate the production of more young than if the animals are not trapped. Beavers become sexually mature at about two years. A beaver colony commonly contains six to eight animals, including an adult pair and the kits from the last two litters. The older young usually leave the area of birth by their second birthday, a process referred to as *dispersion*. Dispersing beavers usually travel less than 6 miles in search of new homes, but movements of up to 150 miles have been documented.

Dens and Lodges

Beavers typically live in lodges built from branches, mud and other debris or in dens dug into the banks of streams or lakes. Lodges can be constructed along the edge of a canal or pond, or as mounded islands of interwoven branches that stand in the deeper parts of the pond. Both dams and lodges are packed solid with mud to make them weatherproof. All residences will have at least two openings and sometimes more.

Public Health

It has long been suggested that beavers may be responsible for outbreaks of giardiasis in humans. However, recent studies and examination of past outbreaks suggest that other factors, such as the contamination of drinking sources with human waste, may play a larger role in the spread of the disease than beavers do. Even domestic pets have been found to harbor *Giardia,* and the potential public health threat represented by beavers regarding this disease must be completely reexamined.

Giardia

Giardiasis is caused by the single-cell protozoan *Giardia lamblia,* which can be spread through contamination of water systems with the fecal matter of both aquatic and terrestrial mammals, including the beaver. Drinking untreated water is the most common way humans become infected.

Problems and Their Solutions

Problems

The two most common problems caused by beavers are the flooding that results from dam-building and the damage or destruction to trees used as food and building material. Flooding can suddenly become a crisis if beaver dams have not been monitored and unusually heavy rains inundate an area. Occasionally, bank dens dug by beavers contribute to erosion or undermining of earthen dams, a problem that also occurs where muskrats are active. Damage to trees in urban and suburban areas is likely to be no-

ticed before it becomes critical but perhaps not before one or more valuable trees have been lost. Much more substantial claims are made by operators of commercial forests in the Southeast, where beaver flooding is said to result in the loss of $100 million of timber annually.

Solutions

TOLERANCE

Recognizing that beavers play an important role in establishing and maintaining wetlands that provide critical environmental functions is a key to living with them. Among other things, beaver impoundments provide a habitat for other animals, provide a refuge for sensitive plant species, improve water quality by acting as a settling basin and provide flood control by slowing water movement. To these values can be added the considerable aesthetic and recreational benefits that we humans derive from the presence of beavers and the habitat they create. Clearly the primary influence of these animals, which is to create wetlands, provides a critical function in restoring an important ecological process.

FLOODING

Beavers are superb engineers, but still no competition for humans. This means that no matter what engineering problems they cause, humans can counter with solutions of our own that beavers cannot overcome. Where flooding or potential flooding from beaver dams is an issue, it is possible to install any of a variety of devices, variously called beaver "bafflers" or "levelers," that can control water level without the removal or destruction of beavers (see Figure 20, page 68). Beavers are thought to be stimulated by the sound and perhaps feel of flowing water to quickly repair any breach to their dam. Bafflers work by dispersing the flow of water

Figure 20. *Beaver bafflers are devices that allow for water-level regulation in beaver ponds or that let water flow unobstructed into culverts. Many different designs exist, and new ones are frequently being developed.*

into the devices so that the beaver is not obliged to plug them. Bafflers can be constructed with easily obtained materials, such as plastic or metal pipe, wooden troughs, tree trunks or heavy metal mesh fencing formed into box culverts.

Culvert pipes running under roads are often plugged by beavers. This can result in road flooding. Concentric semicircles of welded wire plugged into the upstream end of the culvert have been used to successfully stop beaver activity in such situations. One such device has even been patented and is currently being manufactured in a kit that can be shipped preassembled and ready to put up at the site (see Tools and Tactics—Bafflers). The design and installation of beaver leveling devices are sufficiently complex that technical assistance from experienced professionals is recommended. It is also important to be aware of local, state and federal regulations when planning to install these devices.

Organizations that can provide information on bafflers include Beaver, Wetlands & Wildlife, P.O. Box 591, Little Falls, NY 13365,

(518) 568-2077; Beaver Defenders, Unexpected Wildlife Refuge, P.O. Box 765, Newfield, NJ 08344, (609) 697-3541 and Wildlife 2000, P.O. Box 6428, Denver, CO 80206, (303) 935-4995.

Videos illustrating baffler installation can be obtained from

Maine Department of Inland Fisheries and Wildlife
284 State Street
Augusta, ME 04333
("Outwitting Maine's Busy Beavers")
$19.95, including postage

"Building a Beaver Baffler and Dam Flume"
Alliance for Animals
122 State Street, Room 309
Madison, WI 53703
$10, including postage

Publications that provide information on baffler design and installations include

The Beaver Handbook. 1995. Available from the Ontario Ministry of Natural Resources through Northeast Science & Technology, 60 Wilson Avenue, Timmins, Ontario, Canada, P4N 2S7.

How to Prevent Beaver Flooding. Available from Beaver, Wetlands & Wildlife, at the address given above.

The Clemson Beaver Pond Leveler. 1992. AFW Leaflet. Cooperative Extension Service, Clemson University.

Living with Beavers. Published by The Fund for Animals, 850 Sligo Avenue, Suite LL2, Silver Spring, MD 20910. $2, including postage.

See "Beaver Bafflers" in Appendix 2 for additional information.

EARTHEN DAMS

Beaver are occasionally responsible for breaching earthen dams. They sometimes extend bank dens far enough back into earthen dams that the dams become weak. It is generally older structures that pose problems. A well-built and properly maintained dam with an impermeable core of clay or other material should withstand beaver tunneling. Rock rip-rap used on the upstream slope for erosion control can inhibit both beavers and muskrats from attempting to build bank dens in the first place, and it's also the most expedient way to protect older structures. Habitat modification (e.g., removing cover or limiting access to food) is another method of dealing with this, as is exclusion through the use of simple fencing, as described below.

TREE PROTECTION

Either homemade or commercially available tree guards can prevent beaver damage to trees, especially where small (2- to 6-inch) ornamental or specimen trees need to be protected. Simple cylinders of galvanized welded (2-inch x 2-inch) wire placed out from the trunk and standing about 3 feet can be used to cage trees (see Figure 14 on page 38). Cylinders around larger trees may require staking, and mulching within the cylinders is a good idea to keep weeds from becoming a problem. Hardware cloth ($^1/_4$- to $^1/_2$-inch mesh) or chicken wire will do the job, although they will not hold up as well as heavier welded wire. In some situations simple corrugated plastic drainpipes can be used to protect small trees. The pipe is slit (allowing room for growth) and placed around the tree. Although beavers can and sometimes do easily gnaw through this material, they usually won't, thus providing a low-cost and easy-to-do protection. To prevent tree damage, frequently monitor them and put protective barriers in place upon the first signs of damage. Larger or more desirable trees (especially) should be protected before damage occurs.

FENCING

Beavers are not good climbers, and even a 3- to 4-foot fence can be a permanent deterrent. Where trees that need protection are grouped (for example, in an orchard), fencing may be the most practical way to do this. Often, it is not necessary to completely encircle the grove to protect it because the beaver may only be approaching from the water side of the property.

First, the landowner should try fencing off the water side and extend the fence a bit farther if beavers can find their way around it. It is sometimes recommended that fencing be buried about a foot into the ground, but if there is a tight fit to the ground, this isn't necessary. A newly installed fence should be monitored frequently, especially where established beaver trails cross. If a beaver does slip under or over the fence, immediately reinforce that section with more fence posts and stakes holding the bottom of the fence down or additional pieces of fencing attached to the fence bottom and buried at least 6 inches. Alternatively, the lower edge can be left trailing at least 18 inches toward the water (approach) side. An electrified wire strung approximately 4 inches off the ground can also prevent beavers from entering an area. This type of fence can be especially effective in a small garden or crop plot and set up to protect plants for a few weeks when they are most vulnerable (and taken down afterward).

REPELLENTS

One bittering agent, Ro-Pel® (see "Repellents" in Appendix 2) is registered for use as a repellent when painted or sprayed onto trees. A disadvantage to using repellents to deter beavers is the cost of the product and the need to reapply the repellent every couple of months during the period when these animals are most active (late summer to early spring).

A Last Word

It is estimated that on the arrival of the first European settlers the beaver population of North America was between 60 and 400 million. At the turn of the century, during the greatest period of exploitation, the beaver population is unknown, but we know that beavers were virtually extirpated from most parts of the eastern United States and greatly diminished in numbers throughout most of Canada and the western United States as well. Today, the United States has between six and twelve million beavers, as populations have begun a comeback. Because humans have so dramatically changed the landscape and destroyed significant parts of our wetlands, beaver populations can never return to any semblance of what they were. These animals will continue, however, to occupy every niche available to them, and they will reach and exceed carrying capacity throughout many parts of their former range by the turn of the next century.

Dispersing young as well as adults that have used all locally available food resources will be forced to move to marginal habitat and be at high risk for any number of mortality factors. The automobile will likely be the main regulator of beaver populations in many urban and suburban areas. A debate regarding the future of beaver-human relationships has already begun and will intensify within the next few years. The environmental benefits that come from beaver wetlands are just being realized and clearly need to be better understood. For a continent that has lost much of its former nontidal wetlands to development or agricultural conversion and that lately has come to realize the significant environmental damage done by this, the reurn of the beaver is a timely and welcome event.

Additional Sources

Novak, M. 1987. "Beaver." In M. Novak, J. A. Baker, M. E. Obbard, and B. Malloch (eds.), *Wild Furbearer Management and Conservation in North America*. Ontario: Ministry of Natural Resources. 282–313.

Ryden, H. 1989. *Lily Pond*. New York: William Morrow. 256 pp.

7

Black Bears

The black bear lives throughout most of Canada and is widely distributed in the eastern and western parts of the United States.

Human-bear encounters usually occur away from residential areas, in parks or other open spaces. Around homes, bears may pass through to inspect gardens, compost bins, beehives or outdoor barbecues.

The largest bears found in the United States come from Pennsylvania.

IN MANY PARTS OF THE COUNTRY bear sightings are increasing. Part of the reason for this is that the "suburbs" are increasingly encompassing wildlife habitat. We infringe on *their* homes and force the issue of encounters. Some inward migration also occurs, however, where habitat has returned to places previously made so unsuitable for animals that the human residents are unaware wildlife could (or should) even be there.

In New England, for example, forests are returning, as much of the farmland was abandoned after the colonists discovered they could reach far richer soils to the west. Now as much as 70 percent of the land previously cleared and worked for agriculture has reverted back to forest, some of it mature enough to support bears. Traditional conflicts between humans and bears involved agricultural depredation and such time-honored scenarios as bear raids on beehives. Assaults on garbage cans can now be added, as well as occasional attempts to establish winter dens under porches and decks and miscellaneous run-ins with domestic pets.

Because they are large and powerful animals, encounters with bears must be taken seriously. While contacts are potentially quite serious, the frequency with which these actually happen is remarkably low. Yet it seems like every encounter with bears receives headline attention in the press. No doubt, more people are bitten, stepped on or injured each year by horses than by bears, yet these events almost never make the news.

Natural History

Classification and Range

The black bear *(Ursus americanus)* is the most widespread and smallest of the three bears found in North America, with the larger polar *(Thalarctos maritimus)* and brown *(U. arctos* spp.*)* bears much more restricted in their distribution. The grizzly is the best known of a group of closely related brown bears that are among the most formidable carnivores in the world. Fortunately, they tend to shy away from places where people are, and remain more or less restricted to remote natural areas, where they rule. Black bears range completely throughout Canada, the eastern United States and throughout the West, excluding most of the Great Plains and Great Basin areas. In general, the range of black bears follows the range of the older, more mature forests wherever these are, or have been restored.

Reproduction

Bears are slow breeders. Cubs are born in late January or February and remain with the mother for the first two years of life. She does not breed again until they are old enough to survive on their own. Add to this the fact that females do not usually begin breeding until they are between three and five years of age, and it is clear that this animal's reproductive patterns keep its populations lower than many other animals.

Habitat

Bears occupy a variety of habitats in areas where large enough blocks of undisturbed (by humans) land is available to them. In the East, deciduous woodlands are favored; in the Southwest, chaparral and scrub forests may be used. That bears require fairly large areas to sustain themselves and that they have a general intolerance toward one another (outside of the mother-cub relationship) contribute to the low population densities typical of them. The movements of individuals within their range vary according to the seasonality of preferred foods.

Diet

Many people assume bears are exclusively meat-eaters while, in fact, plant foods make up the bulk of their diet. Ripening fruits, berries and nuts are eaten heavily, but when these are not available the average black bear can be found grazing on leafy or *herbaceous* vegetation (the way a cow would). The animal material eaten includes insects, occasional small live prey, such as deer fawns, and carrion.

Dens

Dens are occupied during the winter for hibernation. Even in the South most bears enter into some sort of period of dormancy, although it may not last as long nor be as profound as the winter sleep of bears farther north. Rock ledges, brush piles, hollow trees and occasional human-provided dens, such as areas under decks and patios or culvert pipes, are used to take refuge from winter snows.

Public Health

There are no significant diseases or parasites that afflict bears and can be transmitted to humans. *Rabies* does occur in these animals but is so rare that no confirmed exposures of humans are in the record.

Problems and Their Solutions

Problems

Fortunately, bears do *not* make dens in chimneys or attics. They *will* den occasionally under decks or porches, especially in summer houses or residences that are used sporadically. They raid gardens and get into trash with a facility that aptly demonstrates their size and power. They also occasionally cause significant damage to beehives.

Solutions

TOLERANCE

As with all of the animal issues discussed in this book, tolerance and understanding have a key role to play in how we approach resolving conflicts, even (or maybe especially) with animals as large and formidable as bears. Large animals tend to be potentially more dangerous to people than small ones, admittedly, but they also tend to be less common and tend to need a larger living area, or *home range*, to sustain them. Thus, for the individual homeowner, an encounter with a bear might be a once-in-a-lifetime event. The animal might be a youngster moving out of its mother's home range, or *dispersing* to look for a suitable home for itself, or it might be an adult that has come by the house to investigate a smell or sound that attracted its attention. Once it has figured out that the attraction is related to humans, it is likely to head over the mountain and not be seen or heard from again.

EXCLUSION

Where bears are a serious problem and repeatedly cause depredation on a specific resource (such as a set of beehives), electric fencing is the recommended tool for use as a deterrent (see Chapter 3). Such fencing can also be used to protect campsites, refuse sites and other areas that might attract curious bears.

HABITAT MANAGEMENT

Do not place trash cans outside at night. If trash *must* be placed out at night, then an investment in a "bear-proof" can is the way to go. A useful publication on this subject is *Animal Resistant Garbage Containers* (1995, USDA Forest Service publication 9523 1205-SDTDC by Lester Sinclair), published by the U.S. Forest Service and available from the Superintendent of Documents, Government Printing Office.

Stockade enclosures that will hold most bears at bay can also be built. It is important *not* to try to keep an open compost pile in bear country, especially one in which household refuse is dumped. Enclosed recycling bins are advised if refuse must be stored outside a secure outbuilding. Even ruggedly built bins may be broken into by determined bears, however. Burying compost is not advised because bears will easily dig it up if motivated by enticing odors. Keep grills that are on back decks or close to the house clean and as free of drippings as possible. Preferably, move the grill well away from the house when it is not being used.

MINIMIZING CONTACT

As with other large and potentially dangerous mammals, there are rules about encounters with bears that can help to minimize the possibility of people putting themselves in danger. The rules described here for black bears are, we caution, different from those for dealing with brown or polar bears. These bears are extremely dangerous in close encounters, while black bears are always more likely to withdraw than confront humans, even when surprised. People are usually afraid of bears, and sometimes in thinking that they might be attacked or even eaten, will react to encounters in ways that actually increase the likelihood of injury.

Never try to approach a bear to drive it off! Shouting, banging objects together, making as much noise as possible and looking as big as possible (by spreading your arms, or better, coat outward) are all effective responses. The key here is to let the bear know you are a human. Running away from a bear is not said to be dangerous, as it is with cougars, because the bear is usually turning in the opposite direction to run itself. Throwing things at the bear and even hitting it in the rump if you can are excellent ways to get it to move off. In the rare instance where a black bear *bluff charges*, the experts advise standing still. The bear does this only as a warning and invariably turns and moves off after the display.

ERRANT BEARS

Young bears dispersing from the area in which they were born and in search of a suitable home for themselves sometimes find themselves in suburbia without a good idea of how to get out. Frequently enough this leads to a perceived crisis, in which the bear climbs a tree, a telephone pole or anything it can reach to get away from people, who only gather in larger crowds as word spreads of the curiosity. Confusion and uncertainty, coupled with inexperience and a misconception of the threat such an animal poses, can often lead to fatal consequences for the bear. This does not have to happen if a little foresight and planning are applied to make sure that qualified and properly equipped wildlife professionals or veterinary assistance can be called upon. Leaving the bear alone and giving it the opportunity to move off by itself is always the preferred solution. Tranquilization and removal of the trespassing bear can save a life, or it can take one, because this procedure is always a high risk for the bear. In forced situations, however, removal may be the best solution to protect both humans and the bear.

Repellents

The pepper repellent that is marketed for repelling human attackers has also been used to repel bears. Much tested in parks where panhandling bears are a problem, the spray has been generally proven to work and to be effective at chasing bears from campgrounds. The smarter bears, however, learn the effective range (usually about 10 to 12 feet) and stand just beyond that when they encounter humans whom they suspect of intending to use the spray on them.

A Last Word

It is possible that human-bear encounters will become more frequent in the future. People are increasingly entering bear habitat, and bears are returning to places from which they had been previously displaced. As serious as encounters between people and bears might be, the solution to conflicts will *not* be to manage bear populations through hunting or deliberate actions intended to lower population density.

Additional Sources

Kolenosky, G. B., and S. M. Strathearn. 1987. "Black Bear." In M. Novak, J. A. Baker, M. E. Obbard, and B. Malloch (eds.), *Wild Furbearer Management and Conservation in North America*. Ontario: Ministry of Natural Resources. 443–54.

Pelton, M. E. 1982. "Black Bear." In J. A. Chapman and G. A. Feldhamer (eds.). *Wild Mammals of North America*. Baltimore: Johns Hopkins University Press. 504–14.

8

Bobcats

The bobcat ranges widely throughout most of the United States into southern Canada, but is mostly replaced by the lynx farther north.

Bobcats are rare visitors to yards, but generally shun developed areas.

One wildlife photographer waiting in a blind to get a photograph of a bobcat was about to take a picture when the cat startled and bolted off (*ten minutes* later a hiker passed on the nearby trail).

THE BOBCAT IS SMALLER than a cougar and larger than a house cat but often confused with both. Like its cousins, the bobcat exhibits sexual dimorphism. This means that one sex (in this case the male) is larger on average than the other. A large male bobcat can weigh as much as a small female cougar, and a small female bobcat can weigh less than many large house cats (hence the cause for confusion). With a little experience an observer can soon come to know the distinguishing characteristics of all of these cats and will see that the larger-boned and more muscular body structure of the bobcat readily distinguishes it from house cats, and that the short tail tipped with dark fur is quite distinguishable from the long sweeping rear appendage carried about by the cougar.

Bobcats cause very few problems for humans, the worst being their occasional predation on small animals. Generally, bobcats are so retiring and secretive that people never even know they are there.

Natural History

Classification and Range

The bobcat *(Felis rufus)* and its close cousin the lynx *(F. lynx)* are widely distributed throughout North America, with the lynx tending to have a more northerly distribution and the bobcat, a more southerly one. Bobcats are distributed widely throughout the United States but are absent from a large part of the Midwest. They are believed to have been extirpated from these areas soon after the first settlers arrived, but there is a debate as to how numerous they might ever have been there. A number of unique anatomical features of these animals indicate clearly that the lynx is a cold-climate specialist, while the bobcat is built around a more general feline model that does well under many different conditions. Male bobcats tend to be about a third larger than females within the same geographic area. Usually females are less than 20 pounds, while males average around 25 on a frame that is between 30 and 36 inches. Females as light as 10 to 11 pounds fall well within the house cat range.

Habitat

Bobcats are adapted to a wide variety of habitats as is obvious from their wide geographic distribution. They do well in even small forested areas and inhabit open grasslands as well as brushland and semiarid desert as long as some cover is available. The area used as a *home range* can vary enormously in these animals, from being less than a square mile to more than a hundred times that. Like many other mammalian carnivores, female home ranges tend to be exclusive, and those of males can overlap several female home ranges and sometimes even the ranges of other males.

Diet

Bobcats are opportunistic carnivores who will take prey that range in size from just about the smallest animals (shrews) up to the size of adult deer. The general preference for prey appears to fall within size categories ranging from that of the cottontail rabbit (about 2 pounds) up to raccoon (about 10 to 15 pounds). Where an abundance of rabbits occur, the best dietary conditions for bobcats are believed to exist also. Large prey may be partly hidden under leaves or other plant material and visited repeatedly if it cannot be consumed all at once.

Reproduction

Bobcats are seasonal breeders and become sexually active sometime in late winter or early spring. Male and female relationships generally last only for the brief period of courtship and mating, after which they go their separate ways. The gestation period is

Bobcat Tracks

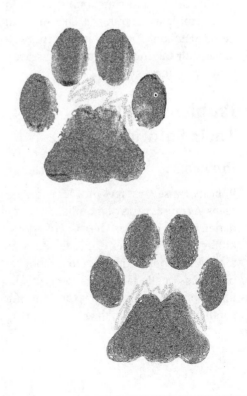

about sixty days, roughly the same as for the house cat. Litter size ranges from two to four on the average, and there is some speculation that females might have more than one litter a year under optimal conditions. The young are usually independent by late fall or early winter.

Dens

There is a general agreement that rocky ledges are critical habitat elements for these animals. These provide cover, shelter and den sites that are suitable for birthing and rearing young. The hollow trees and logs that are favored by other animals, such as raccoons, are also occasionally used, but not with the great preference given to rock ledges.

Public Health Concerns

Bobcats do not cause any public health or safety problems for humans. Like all warm-blooded animals, bobcats are susceptible to rabies, but the incidence of this disease is very low in these animals.

Problems and Their Solutions

Problems

Bobcats cause very few problems for humans. As rare as cases of mountain lion predation on livestock are, the cases of bobcats killing sheep or other domestic stock are rarer still. As opportunistic hunters, bobcats may occasionally take house pets, this being the one way in which they can come into conflict with people in developed areas.

Solutions

TOLERANCE

Traditions die hard, and in some places the bobcat still carries around the image of being a dangerous "varmint." Bounties on bobcats were established almost as soon as land was colonized and remained in place long after there was an economic concern to protect them. Clearly a better understanding and more tolerant approach to these animals is still needed.

HABITAT MANAGEMENT

Feeding house cats outdoors should be stopped—or never started. Elimination of the cover and food resources that might attract rodents or rabbits could help eliminate the attractiveness an area might have to bobcats. The typically large home range of a bobcat, however, more often means that sightings and visits by these animals will be relatively rare events. Only where rocky ledges are nearby and where the possibility of females using these to bear and raise young are permanent attractions likely to be an issue.

REPELLENTS

There are no repellents registered to control bobcats. The variety of products sold to deter house cats from using gardens or flower beds will undoubtedly have some effect on bobcats.

A Last Word

Bobcats can be an important, perhaps even a critical, part of the balance of nature, even in areas that are fairly densely settled by people. Their almost exclusively carnivorous habits and their preference for rabbits and rodents as prey mean that they can help to balance the populations of these animals. That process may be taking place already in the burgeoning feral cat populations found in many urban, and even suburban, areas, which is another issue entirely. The bobcat may eventually eliminate some of the arguments surrounding *that* by moving back into those places from which it has been driven.

Additional Sources

McCord, C. M., and J. E. Cardoza. 1982. "Bobcat and Lynx." In J. A. Chapman and G. A. Feldhamer (eds.), *Wild Mammals of North America*. Baltimore: The Johns Hopkins University Press. 728–66.

Ryden, H. 1981. *Bobcat Year*. New York: Lyons & Burford. 205 pp.

9

Chimney Swifts

Chimney swifts range in summer throughout the Midwest and eastern parts of the United States, north into southern Canada.

Will make nests in suitable chimneys, meaning uncapped clay-lined or mortared structures.

Voracious insect-eaters, these birds are always seen in the air, coming down to roost only at dusk.

ONE WHO KNOWS THESE BIRDS, with their cigar-shaped bodies almost constantly aloft, chattering, sweeping insects out of the sky, will wonder why they are mentioned in a work on humane control of animal problems. The reason for this is not because they cause any special problem for humans, but because we have caused a problem for them. Simply put, there is a conflict between the practice of chimney-capping that animal damage specialists advocate and the swifts' need for roosting and nesting sites. This again reminds us that everything is interconnected and part of a larger picture, our living environment, of which this work addresses but one small part.

There are several species of swifts in the United States, but the chimney swift (*Chaetura pelagica*) is the most common and widely distributed. Before Europeans arrived, these birds nested in the old giant hollow trees of the forest. These trees were lost when the land was cleared for agriculture. This might have had a devastating impact on swifts except for one thing: the building of houses with their stone and mortared brick chimneys that are almost exact replicas of the nesting trees. Today, many houses are built without chimneys or come with chimneys that use smaller metal flue pipes rather than clay liners. These metal flues are special problems—they can sometimes be a death trap for animals. Homeowners, increasingly aware that exclusion is the best practical method of dealing with unwanted intruders such as raccoons, are also capping chimneys in large numbers and thus denying nesting sites to swifts.

Chimney swifts migrate between North America and Peru, making a round-trip journey of 6,000 miles every year to be able to pursue their insect prey, which they take from the air in amazing quantities. They are easily recognized on the wing, with their gray cigar-shaped bodies, constant wing beats and distinctive vocalizations, but few people ever see them at rest. Chimney swifts are so specialized in their adaptation to clinging on vertical surfaces that they cannot perch or stand on their legs in the way that most other birds do. The feet of the chimney swift have four grappling hook-shaped toes with claws that can hold on a roughened surface and partly support the bird while the stiffened tail feathers with exposed spiny tips bolster it as well. These traits have served to allow swifts to make the adjustment from trees to chimneys.

Swifts not only roost in chimneys, but build nests in them. These nests are small cup-shaped structures constructed of small twigs and glued to the chimney wall with saliva. They are not a fire hazard, being far too small, but should always be removed after the birds have left in the fall. This also does the swifts a favor, both by removing bird parasites as well as the nest structure itself, which might be used by returning swifts, but could be unstable enough to collapse during the nesting period.

If swifts are in a chimney during spring or summer it is almost always a single breeding pair. Varying somewhat from north to south, brooding and raising of the young takes place between June and August. As they prepare to migrate south in the early fall, swifts congregate, sometimes in the hundreds, to use a single chimney as a roost. The nightly return of foraging birds is impressive, as they dart into the chimney at dusk with an uncanny synchronization that must be highly organized, even if it looks confused.

There are a few simple rules regarding swifts in chimneys. First, delay the annual cleaning until after young have left the nest.

Although you may hear the noises of young birds as they beg for food, these are only temporary and should be tolerated. If a chimney sweep has been hired and reports the birds present in the chimney, ask that they come back later in the fall to complete the work. Professional sweeps should be well aware that swifts are protected under the Migratory Bird Treaty Act, and that fines and penalties could be applied to anyone who knowingly destroys birds or nests that might contain eggs or young. Finally, chimneys lined with metal should always be capped, as birds that enter these can easily become trapped.

Resources

Anyone interested in swifts and seeking more information about them can contact the Driftwood Wildlife Association at the address listed in Appendix 1. The association publishes a newsletter (*Chateura*) that provides useful information on these birds and how to help conserve and protect them.

A Last Word

One approach to dealing with diminishing nesting habitat for swifts is being undertaken by the Driftwood Wildlife Association and the U.S. National Biological Survey. The North American Chimney Swift Nest Site Research Project designs and tests alternate nesting structures for swifts. The most elaborate of these is an extra-large birdhouse— really an artificial chimney, 12 to 20 feet high and 2 x 2 feet in dimension. Monitoring and testing efforts are still under way to perfect an efficient, inexpensive structure and to determine how best to place and maintain them. Plans illustrating this concept and further information on swifts are available through the Driftwood Wildlife Association.

10

Chipmunks

The one eastern and many western species of chipmunks are found almost anywhere there are woods or even scrub brushlands.

Usually in stone walls, under walkways or patios or in the flower garden.

The burrow of one chipmunk that lived to a venerable age of six was accessed by at least thirty different entrances over its lifetime.

PEOPLE WHO LIVE NEAR A WOODLOT of any size are likely to have chipmunks as neighbors. More obvious in the woods than outside them, these little ground squirrels still occasionally make homes in yards (so long as they do not have to deal with their great enemy, the house cat). These are completely enjoyable animals, and there's a lot more to say about the pleasure that comes from having them around than about any kinds of problems they may pose.

A few quiet moments in the woods, sitting and watching, reveals one, close by, then another, farther away, and another and sometimes even more going about their own business. It is clear that these animals are aware of one another, and a disturbance or threat that frightens one spreads rapidly to the others through the cascade of scolding barks used to signal alarm. All become alert and, if the disturbance is real, disappear into holes that are barely noticeable even after having watched the animals use them. Then they come out, cautiously, to resume the serious business that was interrupted.

Natural History

Classification and Range

Chipmunks are a member of the same family of animals as the larger tree squirrels (the *Sciuridae*). There is one species of eastern chipmunk *(Tamias striatus)* and more than twenty species of western chipmunks *(Eutamias* spp.*)* spread throughout the United States and Canada. The eastern chipmunk ranges throughout New England, the mid-Atlantic regions of the United States and corresponding areas to the north in Canada through about the middle of the continent. The western species take up where the eastern leaves off and virtually cover the rest of the continent.

Chipmunks are commonly distinguished by the broad stripes along the back. The eastern chipmunk is larger than most of the western species, reaching 10 inches (with tail) and weighing between 2–4 ounces.

Habitat

Chipmunks tend to favor deciduous forests with plenty of beech and oak trees. They may be most common around the edge of woods where they can also forage out into other habitat to add to their larder. Chipmunks readily adapt to suburban gardens with natural landscaping and often dig burrows around rock and woodpiles, retaining walls and fallen logs. They can easily climb trees but spend much of their time foraging along the ground. Chipmunks are active by day *(diurnal)*.

Diet

Chipmunks depend primarily on plants for food, concentrating on seeds and berries as well as acorns and other nuts. They also eat occasional insects, small amphibians and, in rare instances, birds. Like squirrels, their foraging is most intense in the fall as they gather food to store and use over the winter. Transporting food to larders is facilitated by the expandable *cheek pouches* into which quite a lot of material can be crammed—as anyone who watches these animals for long find outs. Chipmunks sleep through much

Chipmunk Tracks

of the winter but awake periodically to eat stored food and may even appear out and about during warm spells.

Reproduction

Mating begins as chipmunks emerge from their winter sleep in early spring (late February to early April) and again in early summer to produce two litters, each of four to five young. The young emerge from the burrow after about six weeks and set out on their own within the next two weeks. The western chipmunks only breed once a year unless a female loses her litter, in which case she may conceive again.

Burrows

Chipmunk burrows have been excavated by a number of investigators to reveal their internal structure. Two types of systems have been discovered. The first is relatively simple, with one or two tunnels leading to a single chamber that is probably only a temporary home used by young their first winter. The others are much more complex, with multiple openings and tunnels leading to nesting chambers, food storage areas and as much as a hundred feet of tunnel. Like many burrowing animals, chipmunks will use tree roots, rocks, sidewalks and any other firm object as support above their excavations. Stone walls are especially good for this and provide cover as well for coming and going to tunnel entrances. Sometimes tunnels appear close to reliable food sources, such as bird feeders, even when this leaves them rather exposed.

Public Health

Chipmunks are not considered to be a significant source for any infectious disease that can be transmitted to humans.

Problems and Their Solutions

Problems

Chipmunks do not usually cause property damage, although they sometimes are said to injure ornamental plants as they harvest fruits and nuts. It is easy to attribute squirrel damage to chipmunks and, unless an offender is caught in the act, often impossible to tell which species is involved when both are present. Like squirrels, chipmunks occasionally dig up and eat spring flowering bulbs, such as crocus. Some people get annoyed when chipmunks burrow in flower beds or under sidewalks and porches, but the burrows almost never are extensive enough to cause structural damage. Chipmunks found indoors are there accidentally and will leave as soon as the homeowner provides them with a means to do so.

Solutions

TOLERANCE

Most people enjoy watching these attractive animals, thinking the enjoyment outweighs any nuisance they may cause. We agree, and although we will go on to mention a couple of the common methods of excluding or repelling these animals from yards, we stress that only very rarely, if ever, is it necessary to employ these.

EXCLUSION

Chipmunks may be kept from burrowing around sidewalks, porches and retaining walls by using an L-shaped footer (Figure 11 on page 35). Flower bulbs may be protected from burrowing chipmunks if planted beneath a wire or plastic screen ground cover. This mesh should be large enough (1 x 1 inch) to allow plants to sprout but prevent digging.

REPELLENTS

There are no repellents registered for use on chipmunks, primarily because they have never been identified as causing significant enough damage to merit the elaborate series of tests necessary for approval. Commercial repellents labeled to repel squirrels will undoubtedly also repel chipmunks where both species are implicated in damage.

A Last Word

If you have chipmunks in your yard, watch and enjoy them.

Additional Source

Wishner, L. 1982. *Eastern Chipmunks.* Washington, D.C.: Smithsonian Institution Press. 144 pp.

11

Cougars

Found in the western United States and Canada, with a very small remnant population in the Florida Everglades.

Not usually found where people are; contacts and encounters are infrequent and uncommon.

There are more names for cougars listed in dictionaries than for any other animal in the world—in North America alone there are twenty-five Native American and forty English names for these animals.

THE COUGAR, OR MOUNTAIN LION, is the largest wildcat found in North America, except when once about every ten years a jaguar strays onto U.S. soil somewhere along our southwestern border with Mexico. Cougars were once distributed throughout almost all of North and South America but are now greatly diminished in number and presence. Their demise follows the usual pattern: persecution by humans and loss of habitat. Even with bounties and a concerted commitment to eradicate these animals as "varmints" they managed to persist long enough that our changing policies about predators were enough to buy a slight reprieve. Now that they are protected in many areas, there is hope they might finally be safe.

The spread of human development into cougar habitat has led to talk of a new threat, however. Increasing contacts between humans and cougars have been raised by some as a portent that attack, injury and even fatal encounters can be expected. In fact, such events are highly rare. There have been only thirteen fatal encounters by humans with cougars in the last century. To put this into perspective, about 300 people have been killed by bee stings and more than 1,000 have died in hunting-related accidents for *each* fatality from cougars. Many more people are attacked and injured each year by goats than by these big cats, yet little mention is ever made of the dangers to humans from goat attacks.

It is, of course, sensible and appropriate to seek ways to lower the risk of attack by cougars. It makes no sense at all, however, that this goal is taken by some to mean that the entire population, not just the offending animals, must be controlled. Harkening back to the turn of the century when predators were universally regarded as "bad" animals, the cougar is coming under renewed pressure. We know now that there are no "bad" species: each serves a purpose in nature's scheme of things. Now we stand ready to make a mistake as tragic as that of our forefathers in persecuting whole populations of these big cats for the harm done by a few individual cougars.

Natural History

Classification and Range

When Europeans first arrived in the New World, the cougar (*Felis concolor*) was probably the most broadly ranging mammal they encountered, being found from the tip of South America, north into southern Canada. Almost immediately upon settlement, the eastern population of these animals was pursued to near extinction. Today only a small remnant population remains in the Florida Everglades. Western populations managed a little better, although they were locally extirpated in many places.

Cougars are large and formidable predators. Males are on average almost 50 percent larger than females, averaging between 120 and 150 pounds compared to about 75 to 100 pounds for females. Including the tail, males can be more than 6 feet long, while females are usually about 5 feet long. The long tail itself is a key to identifying cougars because the only animal close in

appearance that might share the same habitat is the bobcat, who has but a stub to call its own tail.

Habitat

Cougars range throughout a wide variety of habitats, but really require fairly large undisturbed areas with vegetation suitable to supporting deer, their favorite prey. Places where humans have settled or forests that have been cut tend to be avoided by these animals. Their ability to move long distances means that cougars might appear in seemingly inappropriate habitat areas, even places densely settled by humans. Such appearances are almost always brief, with the animal moving along quickly in its search for a suitable permanent home.

Diet

Cougars are exclusively meat-eaters or *carnivores*. Although they will eat a wide variety of small- to medium-sized mammals, such as porcupine, raccoon and opossum, they strongly prefer deer and are generally recognized as dietary specialists on these animals. Deer and cougars have probably co-evolved over a long period of time, during which cougars have become more adept at preying on deer and deer have become adept at avoiding being made a meal.

One story is told of a cougar raised from birth in captivity that was quite tame and used by its owner to cap natural history talks by making a grand entrance on a leash just as the talk was winding to a conclusion. One of these, given at a museum, was never completed because the cougar, waiting outside the lecture hall, was led past a display that included a stuffed white-tailed deer. Instinctively, without any sound or smell to guide it, and without ever having seen a deer, the cougar leapt, shattering the glass to the display and profoundly startling its attendant, not to mention itself.

Reproduction

Cougars breed year-round, although there may be certain times, such as the spring, when breeding is more likely than others. Many of the long-range movements made by male cougars occur during searches for sexually receptive females. No long-term male-female bonds appear to occur, however, and the sexes avoid one another after mating has taken place. Gestation takes about three months, with from one to six (averaging two to three) kittens born in a litter. The sites chosen for raising kittens are often quite open and not exactly what seem to humans as suitable to this purpose; they apparently do for the cougar, however. The kittens will stay with their mother until the spring following their birth, and she will usually breed only every other year because of this extended maternal care. Orphaned kittens as young as six months have been known to be able to fend for themselves.

Public Health Concerns

Cougars do not carry any communicable diseases that are regarded as threats to the public health. Although they can get rabies, there is no indication that any attacks on humans or other animals have been caused by this disease.

Problems and Their Solutions

Problems

The most serious damage these animals do is their occasional predation on livestock and pets. Cougars will kill even fairly large animals, including cattle, although like most predators, they prefer young or smaller prey. Historically, cougar depredations on livestock have been mostly restricted to the Southwest. Estimates of the impact are debated, with less than 1 percent of all losses generally regarded as an accurate average. Individual livestock ranchers may be hard hit when a cougar repeatedly preys on their herd, but as always in such cases of depredation, it is an individual animal that is a problem, not the larger population. Cougar attacks on humans are increasingly regarded as potential problems in some parts of the country, even though they are very rare.

Solutions

TOLERANCE

Cougars are shy of human contact and are rarely seen. Like most large predators they may appear calm and confident when encounters with humans do occur, and this attitude can be disarming to people who expect all wild animals to be fearful of encounters with humans. An understanding of these animals and their habits, along with an appreciation of the fact that they may be close neighbors, is the first step toward living compatibly with them. Simply seeing a cougar sign is *not* a justification for alarm.

MINIMIZING CONTACT

Some simple steps can be taken to minimize the possibility of contact by people who live in areas where there are also cougars. One of the first is merely to be more attentive and alert. Be aware that you may encounter a cougar some day and remember the best way to react should that happen.

An important precaution is *not* to run if a cougar is encountered—this may simulate prey behavior and provoke an attack. Remain standing and try to appear larger, by raising your arms or opening your jacket. An umbrella rapidly opened and closed while facing the animal can be highly intimidating. Otherwise, throwing rocks or sticks and yelling are advised. Do *not* approach the cougar and expect it to be intimidated. In the unlikely event of an attack, it is recommended that you fight back in any way that you can. People have successfully intimidated attacking cougars by hitting them with sticks, their hands, baseball caps and even garden tools. Of course, hiking or jogging with a partner is a practical step when using backcountry trails. With children it is always best to keep them especially close at hand. The same goes for companion animals. It is prudent to keep your dog on a leash, and, in many parks and backcountry areas, it is the rule.

HABITAT MANAGEMENT

The possibility of visits by cougars to residential areas can probably be reduced with a few simple procedures. First, it is recommenced that wildlife (raccoons, deer and other mammals) not be fed. This activity, which we also discourage for other reasons stated earlier in this book, can lead to visits by cougars seeking their normal prey. Dense and low-lying vegetation or thickets can be removed or pruned to allow good visibility and discourage a cougar from trying to use them as cover. Good lighting around the house can be both a deterrent as well as reassurance that any animal (especially skunks) would be seen before one blundered into them. Pets should be kept inside or in a secure outdoor kennel, and livestock should be housed in secure outdoor buildings. These simple steps can go a long way toward lowering the possibility of visits from cougars.

REPELLENTS

Although there are no registered repellents for use on cougars, the pepper (capsaicin) sprays sold to deter attacks by dogs and humans should be effective in the extreme unlikelihood of a close encounter with one of these cats. No products are known to repel these animals from yards or areas around houses, although the many brands of repellents used to keep domestic cats away from flower beds or gardens may also do the same job with cougars.

A Last Word

Like many species of wild animals that were persecuted and driven nearly to extinction, the cougar is making a comeback. A lot of the credit for this has to be given to the animal itself because it was only by its hardiness and adaptability that it managed to survive the time when people were entirely bent on exterminating it. The majority of us no longer want to do that and are willing to question the few that still feel so inclined. The concept that cougar populations have to be hunted to keep their numbers low enough so that they do not conflict with humans is a remnant of the philosophy that all cougars are bad. Both arguments are groundless—one an earlier misconception that we have put behind us, the other a current one that still awaits retirement.

Additional Source

Hansen, K. 1992. *Cougar*. Flagstaff, Ariz.: Northland Publishing. 129 pp.

12

Coyotes

Coyotes are found throughout virtually all of North America and are increasing their presence in urban areas.

When seen, which is rarely, it will be passing through the yard or inspecting the garden.

Since the 1960s, coyotes have moved back to almost all the eastern states—even New Jersey, the most urbanized state of them all.

THE COYOTE IS THE most persecuted animal in North America. Coyotes have been hunted, trapped, poisoned, dug out of dens, shot from the air, gassed, burned and killed using trained dogs. And these are only a few of the less barbaric methods of destroying them. This all has been part of an ongoing struggle between those who raise livestock for human consumption and coyote the predator, whose nature it is to hunt.

By killing unwary coyotes we humans have provided this species with only the best genetic material to deal with the technology we aim at them. New strategies, newer tools, more extensive programs and more and more resources are aimed at the coyote to less and less avail, and the few voices that suggest looking at an ecologically based solution that acknowledges coyotes as an inevitable part of the natural scene are ignored.

In the face of the most determined assaults, the coyote has come back to places from where it had been extirpated, expanded its range into places it has not been known before and even has begun to explore the possibility of settling down with humans in their urban and suburban developments.

Natural History

Classification and Range

The coyote *(Canis latrans)* is a member of the same family to which foxes, dogs and wolves belong. The word *coyote* is derived from the Aztec *coyotl*, which loosely means "trickster." This animal's sharpened instincts, adaptability, intelligence and hardiness were well known to all of the original Americans, in a way that later colonizers seem to have been unable to fathom, respected. Nothing better illustrates the adaptability of the coyote than the fact that it is one of only a few species that are distributed throughout all of North America. Only where their larger cousins, the gray *(C. lupus)* and red *(C. rufus)* wolves, have established themselves are coyotes likely to be absent.

Habitat

Coyotes have adapted to virtually all *biomes* (areas habitable to wildlife) in North America. They may prefer grasslands, wooded hill country or wooded drainages, in part because these are areas where prey are common, but they are also found in scrub, deserts, Alpine heights and the subarctic tundra. Fox and coyote territories may overlap, but as direct competitors the presence of one species usually signals a lack of the other. Coyotes are territorial, with the males marking their boundaries, as many canids do, with urine signposts. The size of the territory is directly related to the quality of the habitat, and often it can take several square miles to support a coyote family.

Diet

Coyotes are opportunistic feeders who make use of an astonishing variety of plant and animal foods. In rural settings their diet may consist mainly of rabbits (or hares) and rodents, such as voles, with occasional vegetable foods such as berries and acorns and some insects to round out the list. In urban settings pet food, pets themselves (primarily cats), human food wastes and garden vegetables become alternative food sources. Coyotes are capable of inflicting substantial damage on livestock, primarily during the birthing season, and this is the characteristic of the species that most brings them into conflict with people.

Reproduction

Coyotes probably mate for life, although not as much is known about the phenomenon of *pair bonding* between male and female as we would like. Throughout most of their range, coyotes breed during February or March and give birth in April or May. The den may be an enlarged fox burrow, a rock ledge cave or a shallow pit under a wind-blown tree. Litter size varies, depending, in part, upon environmental conditions as well as coyote population density. Gestation averages sixty-three days, with an average litter size of six pups in older females. One- and two-year-old females tend to have smaller first litters, averaging three pups.

The female nurses the pups for up to two months, but starts offering regurgitated meals as early as three weeks. This form of feeding is widespread among canids and represents an economical way of weaning young from milk to semisolid meals. It is also a convenient way to transport food for animals that do not have pockets. The pups mature quickly and are fully independent at about nine months. The male coyote provides protection and food for the mother and offspring until the offspring are able to hunt for themselves.

Public Health

Coyotes, like all warm-blooded animals, may contract rabies. Their close kinship makes coyotes susceptible where there are populations of unvaccinated domestic dogs and is the principal reason that an outbreak, or epizootic, of rabies has recently occurred in parts of the Southwest.

Problems and Their Solutions

Problems

In the West, the long bitter war fought against the coyote as a depredator of livestock is its own issue. Books have been written about it, and little of what it has meant should be discussed here. It is important to note how much of the bitterness and misunderstanding of these animals transfers from range to suburb. In cities and towns where there are suitable habitats, coyotes will kill free-roaming pets and occasionally do some damage to home gardens. Exactly how much conflict there will be remains to be seen. First contacts are only now being made as the coyote, adapting as it goes, makes its way into this new environment.

Solutions

TOLERANCE

Often, people live with coyotes nearby and never see them. Occasional night choruses are the only evidence that they are there. Unless they cause a specific problem there is no reason to worry about coyotes. Even in the most intense battlegrounds on western rangeland, the perception of these animals and the formerly imperative "need" to control their populations are changing. Many ranchers now only attempt to capture or kill animals when specific damage has

occurred. Then the offending individual or pair is removed and other coyotes left unmolested. This strategy recognizes that it is better to leave coyotes that do not kill livestock on their territories alone so that they will keep other coyotes, who might be livestock killers, away. The same strategy is also true for suburbia.

DOMESTIC PETS

Individual coyotes can be serious predators on cats and small dogs. Coyotes are primarily nocturnal, and owners can minimize risk by not letting their pets out at night. It is most important not to attract coyotes by leaving any pet food, water or food storage areas available to them. Good housekeeping and trash sanitation will also contribute to discouraging coyote activity near residences. In areas where there is little natural tree cover, those who must leave cats outdoors can help protect them by installing "cat posts." These can be any type of long climbable wooden post (4 x 4 or corner posts) that stand out of the ground at least 6 to 8 feet. This post gives the outdoor cat an escape from pursuing coyotes.

HABITAT MANAGEMENT

Coyotes can only eat refuse that is improperly stored or disposed of. High-quality garbage cans with tight-fitting lids will solve most problems. If coyotes are able to get at them, the cans should not be put street-side until the morning of scheduled pickup. When especially attractive food wastes like chicken, fish or leftover pet food are bagged, a small amount of ammonia can be added to the bag. If it will be several days before garbage pickup, either temporarily freeze these wastes or haul them immediately to a dumpster or other suitable storage container. As we have said elsewhere and will repeatedly stress, the feeding of coyotes or other wild animals writes a prescription for conflict.

BACKYARD EXCLUSION

Poultry or hobby livestock can be well protected from coyotes with fencing (both structural and electric) and by ensuring that the animals are properly confined in well-built cages or pens each evening.

REPELLENTS

There are no repellents registered for use on coyotes. The aversive agents used for dogs and cats, however, should work to discourage these animals where both are a problem (see Chapter 3).

A Last Word

Our conflicts with coyotes have opened a window on ourselves as much as on these clever canids. Brute force and bitter feelings have been something of an order of the day for so long as to become culturally institutionalized in parts of the country. Clearly, no good has come of the massive programs to suppress this species—not for humans, their economic interests, for the environment and certainly not for coyotes. The coyote rebounds against our attacks and returns despite the most intensive efforts to eradicate it. That ability only heightens the feelings of antipathy some have toward them. A perpetual cycle of violence is created in the absence of any true understanding of the possibile harmony of people and coyotes on the land. Like all cycles, this one will be broken only by an applied force. Fortunately, reason is a force, and we still have time to apply it before urban and suburban coyote problems develop a legend of their own.

Additional Sources

Kinkead, E. 1978. "Coyote: The Species Indestructible." In *Wildness Is All around Us.* New York: E. P. Dutton. 47–88.

Leydet, F. 1977. *The Coyote: Defiant Songdog of the West.* San Francisco: Chronicle Books. 222 pp.

13

Crows

Widely distributed, year-round residents throughout the United States; also widely distributed throughout most of Canada, but tend to only summer there.

Seen in yards, along the streets, especially on trash collection day and often roost in large numbers in urban woodlots.

Make at least twenty-three distinct vocalizations in communicating with other crows.

CROWS ORIGINALLY WERE WHITE, but the Greek goddess Athene turned them black after one of their kind brought her bad news concerning her family. She also forbade them to ever land at the Acropolis, but we don't know whether or not that sanction is still in effect. There are certainly no such sanctions in any city in North America, where these birds have found safe and comfortable havens. There is fairly good evidence to show this trend is quite recent—traditional roosting areas in the country have been abandoned for those in towns and cities. Many crows still commute, however, to forage in outlying agricultural areas. Human commuters can see them across the sky, streaming purposefully in one direction at dawn and the opposite at dusk. Tens of thousands of these birds can occupy urban woodlots, raising human anger over the noise and commotion they cause, as well as raising concern for the potential transmission of disease through the accumulation of their droppings. Too often overlooked is the marvel of adaptation that crows represent: highly intelligent, perceptive, socially skilled and ecologically adaptable representatives of the order to which they belong. There is much more to these birds than meets the eye, and, sadly, far less human attention directed at them than there should be in attempts to understand what their life story is.

Natural History

Classification and Range

The American crow *(Corvus brachyrhynchos)* is one member of a fairly large group of birds that also includes many varieties of jays, magpies and birds like the common raven *(Corvus corax)*, which is more of a denizen of remote and mountainous areas than its cousin the crow. The American crow is found across most of the rest of the United States all year long and Canada in the summer. Its close relative, the fish crow *(Corvus ossifagus)* is found along the eastern seaboard, while the northwestern crow *(Corvus caurinus)* is found on the other side of the continent in Washington and Alaska. Both of these may be more specialized in their habitat preferences and selection than the American crow. One species of crow, *Corvus imparatus*, has just begun to make its way north into the United States from Mexico, and is commonly seen only at the municipal dump in Brownsville, Texas.

Habitat

The American crow is tolerant of many different habitats and has a special affinity for agricultural or urban settings that often brings it into conflict with humans. Still, these birds use almost any combination of woodland, farmland, orchard or suburban neighborhood, as long as enough shelter and suitable trees for nesting are available.

Reproduction

Crows are probably monogamous and mate for life; we just don't know for sure. We do know that they start nest-building in early spring and can often be seen carrying building materials of bark, branches and twigs at that time. Nests can be anywhere in areas with blocks of trees and, although it is rare, even occur sometimes on the ground. Usually four to six eggs are laid and incubated over a period of about eighteen days. The young are tended in the nest until they are ready to fledge at about a month of age. What happens beyond that is somewhat speculative, but the close association of crows in groups suggests that related birds flock with one another into the winter, when winter roosting groups form.

Public Health

The most important public health issue involving crows comes with the accumulation of fecal droppings at roosts and the potential for *histoplasmosis* to occur there. The issues and precautions associated with this disease are discussed in Chapter 2.

Problems and Their Solutions

Problems

Crows can cause damage to agricultural or garden crops that ranges from pulling up seedlings to harvesting fruit and attacking grain crops such as corn. Occasional bullying of other birds occurs at feeders, although this is not a serious concern. Crows are predators on other birds and take a toll of nestlings, which may, in combination with the many other factors of mortality or nesting failure that afflicts songbirds, have a cumulative negative effect. Crow damage to trash is widespread and perhaps the classic way in which they come into conflict with homeowners, although it is often confused with damage caused by other species.

Solutions

TOLERANCE

As anyone who has raised an orphaned crow or studied this bird to any extent can vouch for, crows have a high degree of what we would call intelligence—which may mean nothing more than that they are sociable and solve problems in ways a human being would. Most of the times we encounter them in yards and around neighborhoods are times when they are not really causing problems. Then, they should be left alone (and appreciated).

EXCLUSION

Keeping crows out of trash is easy, as long as intact and relatively secure trash receptacles with tight-fitting lids are used consistently. Trash bags placed alongside the curb or overfilled bins will invariably attract crows, who easily open the bags to retrieve what they want. This damage is done by day; scattered trash that has been left out overnight is the work of others—dogs or, perhaps, raccoons. Usually, daytime offenses can be observed, and the homeowner will know for sure whether it's crows or not. If so, securing the trash is the key to solving the problem, and the simple devices shown in Figure 21 are more than adequate. Usually, simply putting lids on is enough.

SCARE DEVICES

Visual and auditory scare devices can be quite effective against crows and can either be homemade, such as the pie tins hung out in the garden, or commercial products such as scare tape or balloons (see Chapter 3). Pyrotechnics, auditory alarms and scarecrows or effigies can also work, but must be used consistently to be effective, and often are restricted in urban areas because of noise ordinances.

Crow Roosts

Although many states do not accord them protected status, and the federal laws regarding migratory birds have been waived in regard to crows, there should be no efforts launched against them without tacit approval of federal and state authorities. This especially applies to roosts. Altering roosts or dispersing birds from them involves tactics that require experience and expertise to successfully implement. Some relatively noninvasive methods of altering roosting habitat so that large aggregations of crows do not occur around residential areas can be employed with success, providing that the timing is correct and that the measures used to disperse the crows are carefully planned and programmed. Better still is the dedication of woodlot space to roosting crows and the provision of adequate protection and security so that they do not conflict with people and people do not conflict with them.

Figure 21. *Simple tie-downs or weights on garbage cans can effectively exclude many kinds of animals, including crows and raccoons, from gaining access.*

A Last Word

Crows are currently enjoying a sort of golden era, where the pursuit and destruction they faced in the past has waned at the same time that they have learned how to use urban and suburban neighborhoods to their advantage. Hopefully, people will recognize and appreciate them for their intelligence and adaptability and enjoy their antics. However, as their populations expand it would be prudent to begin the research and long-term studies of urban crows that will help to head off problems *before* they become critical.

Additional Source

Angell, T. 1978. *Ravens, Crows, Magpies and Jays.* Seattle: University of Washington Press. 112 pp.

14

Deer

Two forms, the white- and black-tailed deer, range throughout most of North America.

People encounter deer in park and open-space areas, and around their homes, as these animals become increasingly adapted to suburban and urban environments.

The deer's hair is hollow, making it a superb insulator that protects the animal even when it is brutally cold outside.

DEER ARE ONE OF THE MOST easily recognized wild animals in North America, and in many places are the largest type of wildlife people encounter. Not long ago, deer were hunted so intensively they were almost completely extirpated from many parts of this country. Today, thanks to years of effort to restore populations, they are thriving. In fact, some argue that deer populations have expanded beyond acceptable limits, surpassing human tolerance, irreparably damaging natural plant communities and adversely affecting their own numbers as populations burgeon beyond the limit that the animals themselves need to remain healthy.

Even among the experts, however, there is considerable debate as to what "too many deer" means. While generations of researchers strove to understand how to improve deer habitats and increase the size of deer herds, little attention was focused on the larger issue of deer as members of ecological communities. No one knows yet whether the so-called deer overpopulation is a short- or long-term phenomenon. No one can say whether or not deer populations will regulate themselves before doing significant damage to the environment, nor under what circumstances regulation might or might not occur. Beyond such concerns it is a simple fact that many Americans are unfamiliar with deer and unaccustomed to seeing them, or damage done by them, around their homes. This lack of familiarity itself seems often to have led to intolerance.

Natural History

Classification and Range

The term "deer" can apply to several different kinds of animals in North America, including such well-known species as moose, elk and reindeer. The two smallest and most numerous North American deer belong to the genus *Odocoileus*. Mule and black-tailed deer *(O. hemionus)* are restricted mostly to the middle to western parts of the continent, while white-tailed deer *(O. virginianus)* are found almost continent-wide except for the northern tier of Canada and parts of the far West in the United States.

Deer are highly variable in size, ranging from the endangered Key deer of south Florida that rarely exceed 60 pounds, to a closely related subspecies farther north that reports males averaging more than 400 pounds.

Habitat

Mule deer appear more tolerant of semiarid grasslands than the white-tailed deer, but both species occupy a wide variety of habitats. Deer are traditionally thought of as a woodland species, but are actually ideally suited to exploiting "edge" habitat. Edges are created where a natural or human-made habitat break occurs, as in going from woods to croplands or pasture, or from woods to marshlands. One area (the woods) provides cover and shelter while the other (farmland or marsh) provides food resources. In more northerly latitudes deer may have "summer" and "winter" home range areas that can be

as much as 30 miles apart. Where winter snows are significant, deer "yards" may occur under evergreen cover where large numbers of animals congregate. Everywhere, deer are faithful to areas called *home ranges*. Home ranges are believed to be shared by related females that form matriarchies and exclude related males after they have reached sexual maturity. Deer can be active at any time of day or night, but are most commonly seen foraging or moving around sunset and sunrise. (This type of activity pattern is denoted by the term *crepuscular*.)

Diet

Deer are primarily herbivores, although they occasionally have been observed sampling such incongruous foods as dead fish. Their feeding habits and preferences can vary widely from one location to another, but each local population seems to have "preferred" foods that are chosen first, "marginal" foods that are eaten only after the preferred become rare and "starvation" foods that probably have no nutritional value, but are eaten because no other choices are available.

Deer eat an enormous variety of plants and eat different parts of plants in all seasons. The succulent leaves of growing plants are eaten in spring and summer, while fruits and seeds are consumed as they become available. The buds of woody plants comprise a mainstay of the diet in winter. Hard mast foods, such as hickory nuts and acorns, are an extremely important component of fall and early winter diets, when deer, like many wild animals, need to establish fat reserves. Deer can be quite selective about certain foods and are known to favor heavily fertilized ornamental and garden plants above others that have not been so well fertilized.

Reproduction

Breeding occurs from October to January, with the time of onset varying slightly across different geographic areas. This period is termed the "rut" and involves dramatic physiological as well as behavioral changes in male deer. The necks of males, for example, swell to more than twice their normal diameter during this time, in preparation for the quite serious contests of strength that usually determine mating rights. Nervous and almost constantly active, males during the rut are often oblivious to vehicles and frequently are so driven by events that they wander into residential areas and places where they would never be seen otherwise. Gestation is about 200 days, and from one to three fawns are born in the spring, the number conceived being in part dependent on the nutritional condition of the doe at the time of mating.

Public Health

Deer are important hosts of the ticks that carry Lyme disease, although their role in contributing to the spread and prevalence of this public health hazard is currently debated. The tick most commonly associated with Lyme disease lives on deer only as an adult and has alternate hosts for this life stage, and decreasing densities of deer do not affect the production of new ticks. Caribou and elk are known carriers of brucellosis, but their role in transmitting this disease to livestock or humans remains unclear.

Problems and Their Solutions

Problems

Deer damage is usually not difficult to determine, as these large herbivores are capable of rapid and widespread impacts, especially to small gardens or landscaped areas. Where deer damage might be confused with that inflicted by rabbits or woodchucks, look for

---

Orphan Deer

Every year wildlife departments and wildlife rehabilitators receive calls about "orphaned" fawns that people have stumbled across in the woods. Worse, they are often faced with the prospect of a concerned individual appearing at their door with the animal in hand! It is a perfectly natural occurrence in the spring to come across a deer fawn by itself in the woods. The fawn is actually not alone; its mother is nearby and certainly will be aware and attentive. The strategy deer have evolved to deal with their primary predators (which once were wolf and bear) is to leave their young hidden except when feeding them. The advice to anyone encountering a fawn in the woods is to leave it alone, with the assurance that a solicitous and anxious mother will be nearby and will be taking care of it once you move off.

Figure 22. *Deer and rabbit browse can be distinguished by the ragged appearance of twig ends browsed by deer and the neat, clipped appearance of those browsed by rabbits.*

Deer Browse

Rabbit Browse

a ragged, squared, torn appearance at the end of browsed twigs (see Figure 22). Deer do not have upper incisors and do not neatly clip-browse as do other species. Another fairly obvious sign that deer are at work occurs where browsing is obvious—3 to 5 feet from the ground (or even higher where snow accumulates). Woodlands in areas heavily populated with deer may exhibit a "browse line" in which the vegetation will have a neatly trimmed appearance up to the height they can reach. The forest floor is denuded of vegetation or completely dominated by plants that deer do not eat, such as hay-scented fern. An identical appearance occurs, we should note, where cattle and other domestic livestock have been pastured for any length of time. Deer sometimes damage small elm trees by stripping their bark for food, but this phenomenon is relatively rare. More frequently, damage to small trees occurs when males rub their antlers along trunks, stripping them of bark. These "buck rubs" occur most frequently in the fall, just prior to the start of rut.

Solutions

TOLERANCE
One of the best ways to address current problems, as well as to look ahead to future coexistence with deer, is to encourage understanding and a tolerance for these animals and the impacts they sometimes have on resources that humans seek to protect. This certainly is not to say that all of the damage that deer might cause has to be accepted, but only that it is inevitable that *some* will occur where deer and people share living space. Farmers and others whose livelihood depends on agriculture seem to have long understood this and have much to say about the ethics of tolerance and acceptance of nature's way to those of us who might fuss about occasional inconveniences.

DEER AND PLANTS
Deer damage can be considerably lessened and in some cases possibly eliminated all together by thoughtful landscape design that gives care to both the selection and placement of plants. Some plants (hollies and barberries are good examples) will be eaten by deer only when succulent growth is appearing, if then. Others (such as the popular annual plants, impatiens) are almost irresistible to deer.

A few state cooperative extension services and others have begun publishing lists of plants that are tolerant of or actually resistant to deer browsing. Those we are familiar with are listed below and should give some readers a place to seek information for their own areas. Beyond this, we encourage homeowners to contact local nursery and

Elk and Moose

Elk and moose are the heavy-weights of the ungulate division. Elk *(Cervus elaphus)* are found throughout much of the West. The moose *(Alces alces)* is more northerly in its distribution, but more evenly distributed throughout available habitat than the elk. Moose range from New England, north through all of Canada and into Alaska. In the West they range as far south as Idaho. The moose can stand up to 6 feet tall at the shoulders and weigh 1,000 pounds or more, while the elk, at less than half that weight, still remains a formidably large animal. The most serious conflicts with either of these animals are collisions with vehicles. As dangerous as deer-vehicle collisions are, the greater size of elk and moose make such encounters even more so.

on what is being eaten and *when* damage is occurring, the better. Sometimes the best source of information can be a next-door neighbor.

Here are some sources of information on plants susceptible and resistant to deer browsing:

Fargionne, M. J., P. D. Curtis, and M. E. Richmond. 1991. "Resistance of Woody Ornamental Plants to Deer Damage." Cornell Cooperative Extension Service Publication No. 147HGFS800.00.

Jensen, B. 1991. "Gardening around Deer." North Dakota Game and Fish Department brochure.

Another factor in deer damage assessment and planning for landscaping is the *current level* of damage. When damage is slight to moderate a wider variety of plants can be grown and a simpler and less involved set of strategies employed. Under heavy browsing conditions the options are more limited. Then, our recommendation is to either (1) enclose the areas or plants completely by using deer-proof fencing or (2) limit the plantings to those species that are the most resistant to deer browsing. To the extent that it is possible, the more natural the landscaping and the greater the number of native plant species that are used, the better. Naturalized plantings are less likely to attract special attention from deer, and native species are more likely to have evolved mechanisms to deter browsing or tolerate its impact.

landscaping companies for advice. One fact we know concerning deer is that their feeding habits and preferences vary enormously even within relatively small geographic areas. Plants that are not touched in one place may be severely damaged by deer in another. Accordingly, the more local the information

HABITAT MANAGEMENT

One key to predicting deer problems is simply knowing the animals are present and taking steps to deter them before they cause damage. The tracks left by deer are easily recognized and tell the homeowner that the yard or nearby areas are places used in the search for food or for travel. Tracks seen in or around the garden can be a distinct warning that any young plants set out in the spring are likely to be vulnerable. It is as plants are set out and not *after* damage begins that appropriate steps to protect them should be taken. Plant covers (see Figure 12, p. 36) and protective netting (see Figure 29, p. 88) on fruit trees are good ways to provide protection. Deer may be especially attracted to gardens in early spring when the plants there offer choicer and tastier morsels than the slower-growing native vegetation. Thus, damage may occur only until the native plant foods become available.

FENCING

Where deer are a serious problem the most effective and permanent way to protect resources such as crops or landscape plants is to install deer-proof fencing. No other method, whether it involves lethal or non-lethal means, is as effective over the long term as this. A variety of fence designs (see Figures 7 and 8, pp. 30 and 31) have been developed, ranging from high-tensile strand wiring that may be angled for better effectiveness to standard mesh-woven wire, chain-link designs or various types of electric wiring. The best type for any given area will depend on the situation, and local extension or wildlife specialists should be consulted for their recommendations before any expense is incurred. Where deer do have other available forage, quite simple fences can sometimes keep them out of yards and gardens. However, when they are stressed for food they may jump fences up to 10 feet in height.

PROTECTING TREES

Problems with buck rubs occur frequently where small trees (2 to 6 feet) are planted in yards that may be crossed or used frequently by deer. Wrapping (see Figure 13, p. 37) or corrugated plastic sleeves, as described under "Exclusion" in Chapter 3, can be used to prevent damage. Simpler protection (that would not, however, withstand damage from beavers or voles) can be achieved by using 2-inch wooden stakes (see Figure 14, p. 38), about 4 to 5 feet high, surrounding the tree to be protected. Many garden centers carry these types of stakes.

REPELLENTS

A variety of products (including some homemade remedies) can be used to repel deer. Some work directly by making the plants unpalatable to deer (taste and contact repellents), and others work by broadcasting an offensive smell or a disturbing sight or sound (area repellents). The key to using any repellent is to begin using it *immediately* upon observing the first signs of damage. With good reason, deer are extremely wary animals who will avoid places in which they feel threatened or insecure. If the gardener immediately launches a concerted effort to repel these animals when the first signs of their presence are found (usually tracks), then best success is likely to be had. Consult the section on "Chemical Repellents" in Chapter 3 for information on specific commercially available types of repellents. Home remedies, such as soap, hair and garlic, may be effective in repelling deer from gardens and small orchards.

SCARE DEVICES

Scarecrows and effigies may repel deer under appropriate circumstances, especially if they are moving. Lights set to go on by motion sensors may help protect gardens, or at least alert the homeowner to the presence of something outside that should be checked. Scare tape or balloons may also be effective in frightening deer. The key to using scaring devices is to couple them with other strategies and to vary them, moving scarecrows around or changing the place from which the frightening stimulus comes (when this can be done).

Educating Drivers

Students taking driver's education courses should be educated about the potential hazards posed by deer. In-service training, provided to groups such as law enforcement officers, should also be used to provide information about reducing the risk of deer-vehicle accidents. Not many people know that deer frequently travel in groups and that one animal seen crossing a road at night can often be followed by others, so that it is a definite signal to slow even if a deer is seen crossing at a distance.

DEER-VEHICLE ACCIDENTS

Deer are involved in a substantial number of accidents with vehicles every year, with some recent estimates ranging as high as a million deer deaths nationwide. Certainly, increasing human populations, congested roadways, driving habits and the abuse of alcohol by some who drive are contributory factors as well. Many tools can be employed to address this issue, including public education. Public announcements and radio spots during fall months can be used to alert drivers to increased deer activity, common with the seasonal onset of rut. Deer warning signs at least alert the attentive driver to look for these animals on stretches of road where they might not be expected.

Where particularly troublesome stretches of road occur (usually roadways that permit travel at high speeds through parks or wooded areas), high deer mortality and, presumably, high risk to drivers can occur. Often, little effort is made by authorities to identify and monitor such "hot spots," but they usually acquire local reputations. Both highway and wildlife administrations can work with such stretches of road to try to reduce accidents. Potential approaches include lowering speed limits, removing vegetation from road edges so that both driver and deer have better visibility, erecting woven wire fences to prevent or reroute deer crossings or using an "optical" fence as described below.

HIGHWAY REFLECTORS

The Strieter-Lite® highway reflector system (see "Highway Reflectors" in Appendix 2) consists of a specially manufactured plastic prism that is mounted along roadsides on steel fence posts and at prescribed distances that depend on road curvature and topography. The lights from oncoming vehicles at night reflect across the roadway into the area of woods or field where deer are (see Figure 23). The light steers deer away from the road when vehicles are passing. The system has been extensively tested and looks promising in applications where the reflectors have been maintained in good condition. Installation on public roads, of course, requires planning and approval through state and local Department of Transportation offices.

A Last Word

There are some knotty problems ahead of us in our relationship with deer that will

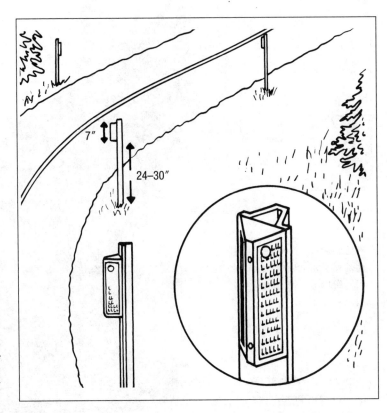

Figure 23. *A highway reflector, or "optical fence," system is available for use on stretches of roadway where deer-vehicle collisions are high. The specially designed prisms catch the headlights of approaching vehicles and reflect it across the road at deer preparing to cross.*

Deer Whistles

Many people use deer warning whistles that can be mounted on a car's hood or bumper, and claim to have alerted deer to oncoming traffic by ultrasonic signals. No information exists at the time of this writing to support that claim. It may be true, though, that people prone to use these whistles are likely to be more sensitized and alert to the possibility of deer on roadways and are more attentive for that reason.

have as much to do with the values and attitudes we hold about these animals as the demonstrable facts about their interactions with their environment. We must acknowledge that these animals will be a continuing part of our lives. Let's start by accepting and appreciating them for what they are before seeing them as a problem-causing crisis that has to be "solved."

Additional Sources

Curtis, P. D., and M. E. Richmond. "Reducing Deer Damage to Home Gardens and Landscaping Plantings." Cornell University, Department of Natural Resources. 22 pp.

Hall, L. K. (ed.). 1984. *White-Tailed Deer.* Washington, D.C.: Stackpole Books. 870 pp.

15

Foxes

Between the two species of foxes discussed here, almost all of North America is covered.

Occasionally make dens under decks, patios or outbuildings. Visit gardens and yards, sometimes to hunt, sometimes just passing through.

WHAT IS THE MOST STUDIED urban wildlife species in the world? If you guessed the red fox you are right. Thanks to work that is being done in Europe and Great Britain there are numerous research papers, ranging from population and behavioral studies to reviews of injury and disease, devoted exclusively to urban foxes. The research expands upon what anyone who has observed or read about foxes already knows: these are fascinating animals that combine many of the behavioral and ecological traits of *cats* with their obvious background as *dogs*—enough so that the red fox is often been called the "catlike canine."

To many people, the fox is the least expected of our urban animals, and it's common to hear people remark that they had no idea such animals lived in cities. In fact, they are well adapted to do so, being what most other successful urban mammals are: generalists who are able to use a wide range of habitats, exploit a wide range of natural and human-produced foods and alter their activity schedules, if necessary, to be primarily active at the times when humans are not. The reward for this is a longer life than their rural counterparts and a death that is more likely to come from disease or an accident than by predation, hunting or trapping.

Natural History

Classification and Range

There are five species of foxes found in North America but only two—the red *(Vulpes vulpes)* and gray *(Urocyon cinereoargentus)*—are town or city dwellers. Foxes are *canids* and close relatives of coyotes, wolves and domestic dogs. No fox, however, interbreeds with these other forms. Furthermore, there are considerable differences among fox species. For example, the red and gray foxes have characteristics so different and distinct from other species that they're placed in separate genera, which is the level of classification above species.

Gray foxes are known to be native to North America, but whether or not the red fox was ever native is still debated. It seems likely that they were, arriving by the same land bridge that the first humans did during the last Ice Age. Many certainly were brought here from Europe in the 1700s to carry on the hunting traditions started there.

Foxes are not large animals, although their relatively long legs and bodies elongated by bushy tails make them appear to be. The red fox is the bigger species, weighing 7 to 15 pounds and reaching about 3 feet in length with an extra foot- or foot-and-a-half-long tail. Gray foxes rarely exceed 11 or 12 pounds and often are much smaller. Because there is a great variety of color types among foxes, it is not always a sure bet that a red-colored fox is a "red fox" or a gray-colored fox a "gray." Where a close examination can be made, the white tip at the end of the tail is indicative of a red fox.

Habitat

Both red and gray foxes prefer diverse habitats that have fields, woods, shrubby cover, farmland or other variety. Gray foxes are more linked to woodlands than red, and are actually capable of climbing trees when in the mood (or required to do so). Both species readily adapt to urban and suburban parklands, golf courses, mixed suburban developments and other built-up areas.

Foxes are primarily nocturnal in urban areas, but this seems to be more of an accommodation to avoiding humans than it is a preference. (It doesn't always mean a fox is disturbed or sick if it's out and about by day.) They will be active by day as long as they feel secure and in or near enough to escape cover. This is when they pursue prey that are also active by day, such as squirrels.

The Bold Fox

Sometimes red foxes will exhibit a brazenness that is so overt as to be disarming. A hiker along a woodland trail may encounter a fox that does not retreat, but sits and watches the human approach. Likewise, a homeowner hanging laundry may watch a fox walk through the yard, going about its business, seemingly oblivious to the human nearby. Why this occurs is anyone's guess.

Diet

Foxes, like many urban adapted species, have a wide variety of plant and animal matter in their diet. Although far better adapted and more capable hunters than, say, raccoons, at some times of the year fruits will be more frequent elements of the diet. One of the reasons they are described as catlike is that foxes tend to hunt more by stealth than the pursuit typical of many other canids. A hunting red fox is all ears, literally, as it seeks the faint rustling sounds made by its prey, stalking it closely and launching a long, graceful, leaping pounce at the moment it feels it has the prey's location marked.

Reproduction

Kits, as the young are called, are born in the spring, usually in March or April. As many as eight or as few as three are born, with litters averaging four or five. The kits are weaned by nine weeks and begin to hunt with their parents. They may remain nearby the parents until late summer or early fall before dispersing to establish their own territories.

Dens

Dens are mostly used as an escape from severe winter weather, or when pups are being raised. Even when winter weather is uncomfortable to humans, foxes will use brush piles or fallen logs to rest under. Both species may dig their own dens, or they may occupy the abandoned dens of woodchuck, badger or other burrowing animal.

Public Health

Foxes are a vector species for rabies (see Chapter 2), which means that they are the primary carrier of one of the major strains of this disease that infects different animal species. In some parts of the country foxes carry the echinococcosis tapeworm that can cause a serious and sometimes fatal disease in humans.

Problems and Their Solutions

Problems

People may be surprised and sometimes frightened to discover that foxes live in their neighborhoods, but these fears are almost completely groundless. Foxes are not dangerous to humans in any sense, except when they are rabid (which is rare) or have been captured and are being handled. Even then, it takes a lot of handling for a fox to even defend itself by biting, and the natural tendency is for the animal to flee rather than

Fox Tracks

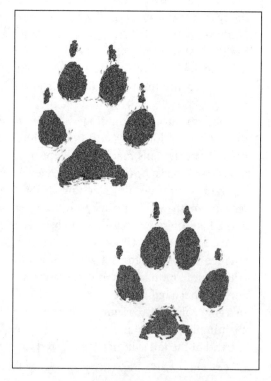

fight. Red foxes will occasionally prey on small house cats or kittens, and certainly will take small animals such as rabbits and guinea pigs when they are left outside unprotected. Both red and gray foxes will eat grapes, raspberries, windfall persimmons, apples and other fruit, but garden vegetables are usually not bothered. In all, foxes do such little damage and engage in so few conflicts with people that we hesitate to characterize them as problem animals at all.

Solutions

TOLERANCE
Sometimes foxes are blamed for damage they did not cause. The trash can that was knocked over by the neighborhood dogs or a visiting raccoon may attract a fox who is observed and then blamed for their nuisance. Foxes may cut through yards when moving from one hunting area to another, and the homeowner often becomes concerned over what they are doing. In fact, they need not be bothered at all and, if left alone, will probably do the homeowner a service by performing free rodent control on their way by.

EXCLUSION
Outdoor pets such as rabbits and poultry should be protected by housing them in secure hutches or pens that are built to withstand any effort by foxes, raccoons or dogs to break in. Because all these animals will dig under fences, it is important to make sure that an 8-inch or greater L-shaped footer on this outer perimeter is buried at least a foot deep. Electric fences can also be effective in excluding all of the species that might be attracted to poultry or small animals, but these are best when used in conjunction with other permanent perimeter fencing. The electric fence could be single-strand and placed in front of a perimeter fence to enhance the effect of repelling as well as excluding any inquisitive predator.

REPELLENTS
No repellents are registered expressly for use in repelling foxes, although the many products sold to repel domestic dogs from yards and gardens will undoubtedly have a similar effect on a passing fox.

SCARE DEVICES
Because they are active mostly by night and are very cautious about people when out and about, foxes are rarely seen by suburbanites. Noise-making devices, ranging from transistor radios to the motion-sensitive alarms that are on the market (see Chapter 3) can be quite effective in combining repelling and harassing strategies. The automatic sprinkler system (see Chapter 3), can be an effective deterrent for lawns or gardens. Even a loud voice or the banging of a pan or dish can frighten these very sensitive animals and keep them out of an area where they are not wanted. Any sound or sight (that is the least threatening) will cause their retreat.

HARASSMENT
Foxes that have made dens under porches and decks are one of the most common problems homeowners experience with these animals. As with all such situations, we recommend tolerance until young are old enough to follow the parents on nightly forays, then exclusion to keep them from reusing the den. In fact, the kits will spend time playing and loafing outside the den just before they are able to go out with their parents. This is one of the most enjoyable wildlife viewing experiences people can have.

However, some people want the family to move. In these cases, mild harassment

Do Foxes Eat Cats?

People are frequently concerned about their pets being outdoors when foxes are around. We do not recommend that cats be allowed to roam freely, and suggest that the best way to avoid encounters between foxes and cats is to keep the cat indoors. By and large, however, foxes seem to pay little heed to adult cats, recognizing that they are dealing with an animal that is almost their size (often) and certainly one that has a well-deserved reputation for self-defense. Kittens, however, could be easy prey for a fox, as might small adult cats; therefore, caution is suggested whenever the two might come into contact.

putting smelly sweat socks or old sneakers around the area where foxes come and go. Recently, some people have claimed success in getting fox families to move by using scare balloons (see Chapter 3) mounted about 2 to 3 feet off the ground, just outside the entrance to the den. In all of these strategies the idea is to make the parents uncomfortable and get them to move the litter—after that, make sure the move has occurred before trying to exclude them (see Chapter 3).

HABITAT MANAGEMENT

Food lures foxes into suburban yards. Compost piles should never receive meat scraps, and garbage should be placed outside only the morning of collection. If that is not possible the cans must be secured from access. This can be done by simply providing tight-fitting lids if only foxes are involved, or more secure fasteners if other, more persistent trash specialists such as the raccoon are involved. A cord threaded through the handle of the lid and hooked onto the sides of the can is a simple yet effective tactic. Dishes of pet food should not be left outside overnight. Foxes will be attracted to bird feeders and may even eat spilled sunflower seeds if hungry enough. Mostly, however, the sight of a fox around a feeder suggests that the spillage is being used by rodents, who have left their scent there and attracted the fox to the site.

may encourage a move. Start with placing objects or moving leaves, soil or mulch around to disturb the denning animals. Ammonia-soaked rags placed at the entrance of a burrow or around the place where animals come and go under the porch may encourage their leaving. Anything with a human scent will alarm the foxes as well, and some have recommended

A Last Word

There may already be two dozen good studies that have been conducted on urban foxes. But many more have been conducted on foxes in rural areas, and these are only a few studies when compared to those that have been devoted to animals such as deer, bears, and even quail. The reason for this is that game animals (those that are hunted and trapped) have always received more emphasis in our society than *nongame* animals. A slow change is occurring, as we have become increasingly aware of the importance of all species of animals and of the need, as conservationists have said repeatedly, to preserve all species. Still, with eight of every ten Americans living in cities and towns, one would think that more resources would focus on issues that affect *them*.

Additional Sources

Harris, S. 1994. *Urban Foxes.* London: Whittet Books. 128 pp.

MacDonald, D. 1987. *Running with the Fox.* New York: Facts on File. 224 pp.

16

House Mice

Mice are found throughout North America and are intimately associated with humans and their developments.

Mice prefer living in buildings—behind walls and appliances, in unopened drawers or where any tiny niche presents itself.

In England, mice have been found living 1,800 feet below ground in coal mines; many mouse colonies live and grow in warehouses and cold storage areas that never get warmer than 24° F.

FOR AN ANIMAL THAT usually weighs less than an ounce and eats about one-tenth its weight in food each day, the house mouse gives humans a good deal of grief. Preadapted to a diet consisting largely of seeds and grain, the agricultural revolution that swept through Europe and central Asia more than ten thousand years ago also swept mice right up to humanity's front door. So intimate became our association that today house mice (and their larger cousins, the Norway and roof rats) are described using the term "commensal," which literally means "sharing the table."

House mice followed the first Europeans to the New World and have since become established almost continent-wide. They are most common around human residences, farm sites, industrial areas and commercial complexes. In England, wild house mouse populations may be seasonal, going extinct in the winter and rebuilding in other months as the overflow from human buildings spreads out into the fields and surrounding woods. Perhaps the same occurs here, but generally these house mice do not do well in competition with the native species that have had longer to adapt to circumstances here.

Natural History

Classification and Range

The house mouse *(Mus musculus)* is just about what you'd expect a mouse to be—small (2 to 3 inches), gray-brown, with an almost naked tail as long or longer than its body. It is, of course, one of a variety of animals called "mice" and is often confused with native species such as white-footed and deer mice *(Peromyscus* spp.) or meadow voles *(Microtus* spp.). Native mice often cause problems that house mice get blamed for, although the techniques for ensuring that mice do not invade the house apply equally to all these animals.

Habitat

House mice prefer to live inside buildings, whether these be apartment complexes, single-family homes, granaries, barns or sheds. The entire area occupied by a mouse during its lifetime may be less than the size of an average room. Much of its life is spent in secure comfortable niches between walls and behind cabinets and appliances—the only sign of mouse occupancy being the evidence of gnawed foods and droppings on floors, shelves and countertops.

Diet

Mice are omnivores and eat a variety of foods, preferring seeds, grains and nuts. They require only about $1/10$ ounce of food each day and, unlike rats, can live without access to fresh water if the solid food they eat is somewhat moist.

Reproduction

House mice breed year-round and can raise as many as eight litters annually. Re-productive life begins for females at one and a half to two months of age. With an average of four to seven young per litter, the reproductive potential of these animals is considerable. Under the right conditions, mouse populations can grow almost explosively (the term for such events is *irruptive*). This potential is only partially counterbalanced by the tendency of mice to be short-lived; one year is about the longest any wild mouse could expect to survive.

Public Health

Mice, like their larger cousins the Norway and roof rats, can carry a wide variety of diseases transmissible to humans. Hantavirus is an important public health concern that is present in both wild and domestic mice. This disease has not emerged as a serious concern yet except in the arid southwestern part of the country. Salmonellosis can be transmitted by mice and is an important concern in food storage and preparation areas. The native white-footed mouse is an important host to the tick that causes Lyme disease.

Problems and Their Solutions

Problems

When mice are present in large numbers, they can and will consume considerable quantities of stored seed and grains. However, this type of damage will still be much less than that caused by the contamination of food with urine and feces. By gnawing wood, paper, cloth, books and insulation on wiring, mice may also cause considerable property damage. Direct observation will indicate damage, as gnawing leaves paired tooth marks about $1/8$ inch wide. Nests may be found in hidden places, such as little-used drawers or cabinets, and are made from loose assemblies of paper, cloth, twine and other material. Droppings are rod-shaped, about $^1/_3$ to $^1/_4$ inches long and one of the best indicators of mice.

Solutions

TOLERANCE

Sometimes people don't even know they have mice and live for years with a self-regulating population. Sometimes they'll know the mice are there, but be indifferent or tolerant of their presence. And sometimes the discovery of a mouse will immediately be regarded as a crisis in which the animals have to be disposed of immediately.

On occasion, native mice move into a building during the early fall or winter as a part of normal movement patterns. Usually a *Peromyscus* or other woodland mouse species, these animals can be humanely live-trapped and put back where they came from—the great outdoors. House mice would probably not do well in such evictions, but given the alternative, many homeowners are willing to try. With any mouse problem, it is important to recognize signs of mouse presence early, identify the source of food that attracts them, remove it and the mice and, after the mice are gone, keep others from gaining entry to the house.

LIVE TRAPPING

For those who wish to live trap and remove mice from the house, there are a number of commercially available devices that let this be done easily. Most grocery or hardware stores carry one or more brands of these.

Before going to any expense, however, the homeowner may want to rig an improvised live trap by using a bathroom wastebasket. The basket is baited with bread, sunflower seed, peanut butter or another proven mouse attractant and taken to a place where mice are known to be present. Because mice like to move along a wall or other barrier pressing against their side (a tendency labeled *thigmotropic*), traps set along walls are usually more successful than those set in the open. Preferably left along a travel route, the basket is tilted on its side, usually with a "ladder" of bricks or books that the mouse must climb to get to the rim. From there it has to jump or slide down the side of the basket (which it will do) and then ends up being unable to climb back up the slippery surface. Set before going to bed, the trap should be checked early the next morning. If a mouse is caught, it can safely be transported outside. Afterward a dilute (1:30) solution of bleach cleans the basket thoroughly.

LETHAL CONTROL

The killing of commensal rodents is commonly regarded as a necessary step in the management of problems. Usually this killing must be repeated again and again as the rodent population cycles back. How often this could be avoided through early recognition and response cannot be said; undoubtedly, it is more often than not. Unfortunately, lethal control usually occurs without following up with habitat management, sanitation or exclusion to provide long-term, economically sensible and environmentally reasonable management practices. The simple rule is that lethal control can never be justified without an effort to apply other controls to prevent the recurrence of problems.

EXCLUSION

Mice can enter buildings through openings no larger than the size of a dime and can easily climb interior walls, making exclusion sometimes very difficult. Nonetheless, this procedure is the *best* and *only* effective way to permanently deal with mouse problems.

The key to excluding mice from buildings is to conduct very thorough examinations of possible points of entry around foundations: where utility pipes and wires pass into the house, where siding has deteriorated and holes occur, cracks in foundations or any other places where an entryway might be suspected. Powder (either baby powder or talc) that is sprinkled along the inside perimeters of walls and thresholds will show tracks where mice are active and can be instrumental in helping decide where exclusion efforts are needed. The process of excluding mice nicely complements the examination and sealing of a house that would be done for good summer or winter insulation. The two can simply be done hand in hand.

Many different tools can be used to exclude mice from buildings. Wire mesh or quick-drying cement can plug cracks around drainpipes and small openings where mice may gain access. Galvanized window screening can be balled and stuffed into larger openings that are then finished with caulking or cement. The expanding-foam insulation sold in many hardware stores is excellent for filling small- to medium-sized openings and has the advantage of being available in commercial kits for larger jobs (see Appendix 2 under "Caulking and Foam Sealants").

Habitat Modification

The removal of food sources through proper sanitary techniques is essential. Because mice eat so little, attention should be paid to both obvious and not-so-obvious sources of food. A small amount of spillage from birdseed stored in a garage or shed can be more than enough to sustain a mouse. Dry pet food left in the garage overnight or next to an appliance behind which there is access from the wall is a bonanza. Appliances also offer security from which foraging trips into the kitchen can be made to pick up the tiny amounts of spilled food that makes a meal.

Household food items that are accessible to mice should be stored in metal or plastic containers. Outside protective cover can be eliminated by removing weeds and trimming a vegetation-free perimeter for at least 18 inches out from the foundation of the house or building to be protected. This procedure allows better recognition of entry points as well. Pets should be fed indoors and uneaten food picked up where mice are known to be a problem.

Ultrasonic Devices

There are such devices commercially marketed as described in Chapter 3. There are no credible scientific studies to validate the effectiveness of any such device.

A Last Word

Our conflict with mice may be our most ancient engagement with any animal. Once humanity chose a settled agrarian lifestyle, mice moved in to flourish off our goods. If it were only a matter of their eating their share of our foodstuffs, then we could probably coexist with many millions of them and not feel any effect. But by contaminating so much more than they eat, and by serving as a source or vector for diseases that endanger humans, mice are clearly at odds with humanity. The key to managing our conflicts with them, of course, comes in better habitat management: of ours, to eliminate attraction, and of theirs, to make it less suitable.

Additional Source

National Park Service. 1993. *IPM Training Manual: Commensal Rodents.* Washington, D.C.: Department of the Interior. 72 pp.

17

House Sparrows

House sparrows are everywhere, except in parts of Antarctica and the far North.

House sparrows live near houses, especially older buildings with crevices in which they can build nests.

The house sparrow is actually not a sparrow at all, but a type of weaver bird or finch. The first house sparrows were imported into the United States by a dentist and a sea captain to help control insects.

HOUSE SPARROWS ARE not native to the New World; they are one of the increasing numbers of non-native, or introduced, species that occur as the world becomes more connected by humans. Introduced species, whether they be plants or animals, can be highly controversial if they successfully colonize an area. Once getting a good start, they undergo rapid population growth and expansion in places where they have no effective predators, diseases or environmental restraints to hold them in check. Later, they may integrate themselves into natural communities, but by then they often have had a negative impact by displacing native species.

The house sparrow is a prime example of an aggressive introduced species, with expansionist tendencies that may take a backseat only to those of our own kind. First imported in about 1850 to the East Coast, house sparrows quickly filled an "urban" niche that native birds were not fully exploiting. Brought in to deal with insect pests that were destroying the urban street trees of that time, they apparently did that job well before reverting to their preferred niche of its kind—that of a seed-eater. From that point on there have been enormous conflicts between people and house sparrows: in agriculture, gardening, among lovers of wildlife and in cities and towns where some people regard them as nuisances.

Natural History

Classification and Range

The house sparrow (*Passer domesticus*) is one of the most widespread vertebrate species on this planet. It is found on all continents except Antarctica and may occupy as much as a quarter of the 50 million square miles of the earth that is habitable by land-based animals. It is not found in Japan, nor Alaska (yet), but completely wild populations live in the Australian Outback, far from any humans. In North America it is found as far north as the Hudson Bay, where it tolerates long and cold winter seasons. In Asia, house sparrows have become migratory in at least two places, while everywhere else they seem content to dwell as year-round residents.

Diet

House sparrows are *omnivorous*, meaning they eat both plant and animal (insect) material. Adults tend toward being *graminivorous*, however, meaning having a dietary preference for seeds. The young, however, are mostly fed insects, perhaps because these are easier to catch and transport in bulk to the nest. Most of the insects eaten are injurious, and it is probably true that sparrows not only served their original purpose in saving the urban trees of New York from insect infestations, but continue to serve a beneficial purpose today in removing many insect pests from urban areas.

The enormous quantities of grain used to feed horses in the 1800s led to optimal conditions for these birds, and their populations literally exploded. As gasoline-powered vehicles replaced horses, the once-abundant food supplies dwindled to insignificance, and the sparrow population declined dramatically. Of course, "decline" has to be taken as a relative term, because these birds are so numerous that they continue to be regarded as serious problems in cities and towns. Early morning commuters rarely notice the small brown birds that dart from the road just in front of them. The house sparrows are up early also, gleaning the moths and other insects struck by cars the night before.

Reproduction

Depending on geography, climate and other factors we do not yet understand fully, house sparrow breeding begins any time from February onward, with a courtship so noisy and boisterous that they are oblivious to anything else. As many as nine eggs are laid in one clutch, but between four and six is the most common number. Incubation is sometimes shared, but the female usually bears most of this duty, with young born about twelve to fourteen days after the eggs are laid. The young will stay in the nest and are fed by both parents for about as long as they took to hatch, and they are fed as fledglings for several days after that. Then they are on their own, as the parents get a brief rest, regroup and prepare for the next brood. Two or three, and sometimes four, broods are raised each year, usually between spring and late summer, but occasionally later or earlier than that.

Public Health

House sparrows generally have not been implicated in the transmission of any serious disease problems to humans. Potentially, the accumulation of droppings at sparrow roosts or nesting sites could contribute to the rise of histoplasmosis. House sparrows can carry salmonellosis and potentially transmit it to humans or other animals.

Nests

House sparrows are both cavity and crevice nesters and occasionally build their odd side-entrance nests in evergreen trees. They fiercely compete with native species for access to nesting sites and are known to destroy eggs laid by other birds (and sometimes even harass and beat adults to death). Contrivances such as window-mounted air conditioners provide ideal crevices for nesting, and young are frequently raised amid the nest material stuffed alongside of these devices, despite the noise and vibration there.

Problems and Their Solutions

Problems

The economic damage house sparrows do to grain crops has generated considerable negative feelings from humans. As many as seventy species of native birds have been documented as subjects of bullying by house sparrows, and many ornithologists attribute declines in some of our more popular species, such as the bluebird, as coming from competition with sparrows. House sparrows nesting near windows can create unacceptable noise for many people, especially because it is likely to begin at first light. Crowding and bullying by sparrows at winter bird feeders denies many bird enthusiasts the opportunity to enjoy other species.

Solutions

TOLERANCE

Much of the minor inconvenience and annoyance of the house sparrow at feeders and around homes can be eliminated very easily through a little conscientious attention to the biology and behavior of these birds. By treating sparrows as naturalized citizens,

which they certainly seem to have become, half the battle in considering what to do with them will already have been waged. Once accepted as a permanent presence, we can stop waging war against the birds themselves and start fighting the battles to modify the environmental conditions *we* create that lead to their becoming problems.

EXCLUSION

Problems from nesting sparrows on buildings can and should always be solved by excluding the birds from access to any crevice or hole they might try to take advantage of. The primary tools in this are netting and hardware cloth (see Chapter 3). Any of the commercially available netting material that has an acceptable UV rating (meaning that it will not deteriorate under sunlight) and is strong enough to repel the sometimes persistent attempts sparrows will make to breach it will provide the most reasonable cost-effective means of keeping them out.

Where house sparrows are taking over birdhouses and expelling preferred species (wrens, swallows and bluebirds are good examples), an excluder or baffler may work (see Chapter 3). Timing is important because house sparrows start nesting before most other species, and if birdhouses are taken down in the fall and not put back up until late the next spring, some of the conflict that arises with these birds can be avoided.

SCARE DEVICES

Auditory and visual scare devices that might be effective on other birds typically have less effect, if any, on house sparrows. Scare tape and balloons may be effective if the homeowner wishes to keep sparrows away from specific areas, and apartment dwellers may use them on patios along with bird wires to keep these and other problem birds away.

REPELLENTS

The polybutene repellents registered for use on house sparrows and other birds may be effective but have serious drawbacks that argue against their use as described in "Chemical Repellents" in Chapter 3. Ro-Pel® is registered to protect seeds and bulbs from birds in general, and might be used where house sparrows are a problem during broadscale seeding efforts such as new lawns.

HABITAT MANAGEMENT

Over the long run, one of the principal means of "controlling" house sparrows is habitat management. Specific efforts to exclude birds from nesting sites will work, but only if sparrow activity is monitored and nesting prevented at its earliest stages. By excluding birds from the few available nesting locations on the typical house, their activities may be seriously curtailed. Feeding is also a way to manage house sparrows because so many of them are sustained by the types of seeds found in the mixed bird foods people put out in backyard feeders. By substituting only sunflower or niger thistle, which will attract many desirable birds, house sparrows, who do not favor these seeds, may be practically eliminated. Many wild bird specialty stores make up mixtures of seeds that are less attractive to house sparrows, or sell feeders that deter them but encourage other, desirable species.

A Last Word

Humanity is in the midst of an experiment with introduced animal species that began in some cases over a century ago and will continue to run long into the future. Unlike a well-planned laboratory procedure, the documentation and recording on this one has been a little sloppy. A lot of minor perturbations have effected it also, such as eradication programs that are started with much fanfare, achieve short-lived "success" and are then forgotten—until brilliantly reinvented at a later time as the "new" solution to a wildlife problem. Regardless of its fits and starts, the experiment will still run its course. Ultimately, it may tell us whether species that are introduced into ecosystems can actually prevail over those systems or not. Our money is on the ecosystem, but only time will tell.

Additional Source

Kinkead, E. 1978. "A Very Familiar Wilding." In *Wildness Is All around Us*. New York: E. P. Dutton. 89–178.

18

Moles

Primarily found in the eastern and western parts of the continent; only one species; the star-nosed ranges very far into Canada.

Lawns, gardens and occasionally crop fields are the domain of the mole.

Putting chewing gum into mole tunnels to eliminate these animals is a good way to bury used gum where it won't be stepped on (and that's about it).

CONFLICTS BETWEEN PEOPLE AND MOLES would almost never take place if it weren't for our country's love affair with the lawn. For reasons buried deep in our psyches, Americans have long demanded our landscapes be dominated by open expanses of fastidiously tended greenery, trimmed to a level that requires phenomenal amounts of water, fertilizer and pesticides to maintain. Literally billions of dollars are spent every year to sustain lawns. Only recently have the embarrassing environmental effects of this obsession come to be recognized, including pesticide, herbicide and fertilizer runoff, toxic effects on birds and, of course, the loss of habitat for many species when new lawns are created.

One animal that does tolerate and may even benefit from the lawns people create is the mole. Moles cause a visual impact to lawns by tunneling, pushing up mounds of earth and (occasionally and then only temporarily) undermining the root systems of growing plants. Environmentally, they provide benefits by turning soil, mixing soil nutrients and improving soil aeration.

The mechanical damage they do, however, will simply not be tolerated by many homeowners, and a cottage industry has sprung up to advocate a variety of home-made "remedies" to solve mole problems. The result has been the invention of wildly imaginative devices to kill offending moles in their tunnels, somewhat reminiscent of medieval weaponry. The world has yet to beat a path to the door of the inventors of these for the simple fact that moles do not actually cause all that many problems for humans. In fact, a close examination of the problems that exist between people and moles suggests that we may have been making mountains out of them all along.

Natural History

Classification and Range

Moles are not rodents although often mistaken as such. Both are small, usually gray or brown mammals, but there the similarities end. Moles have eyes often hidden in fur, naked snouts, no external ears and characteristic paddle-shaped large forelegs that clearly distinguish them from mice. They belong to their own family *(Talapidae)* and are insectivores, meaning they have a dietary preference for worms, grubs and other insects that can be found beneath the surface of the ground.   Seven species occur in North America, with eastern *(Scalopus aquaticus)* and star-nosed *(Condylura cristata)* moles the most widely distributed. Moles do not occur throughout most of the Great Plains, Great Basin and Rocky Mountain areas of the West.

Habitat

Moles spend most of their lives underground—a trait we designate by the term *fossorial*—and rarely make an appearance on the surface. They prefer moist loose soils of the sort favored by the grubs and earthworms that are their main source of food.

Diet

The diet of moles consists almost exclusively of earthworms and the grubs that are the larval forms of many insects, such as beetles. Where plant damage and mole tunnels are associated, it may be because of rodents (mice and voles) using the tunnels, rather than from the mole itself. The townsend mole *(S. townsendii)* of the far northwestern United States is the one species likely to eat plant material and sometimes even attack root crops and tubers.

Reproduction

Breeding occurs in late winter and early spring; litter size usually ranges from three to seven. The young are born in a deeper burrow than those normally seen on the surface and become active within the burrow runs at about four weeks of age. Moles are very territorial and will not tolerate other adults in their territory, except during the brief mating season.

Public Health

Moles are not considered to be a significant source for any infectious disease that can be transmitted to humans.

Problems and Their Solutions

Problems

Moles are often blamed for damage caused by other species. On golf courses and lawns the evidence of mole presence is frequently seen in their excavations, either in small mounds of earth (molehills) resulting from deep tunneling or shallow surface tunnels or runs that collapse underfoot and may result in dead patches in lawns. Damage to lawns can occur when the raised turf over the surface tunnels is hit with mower blades (but only when the lawn is being clipped very short).

Solutions

TOLERANCE

Because moles feed on insects and earthworms below ground, it fits to reason that part of their diet should consist of grubs, which can be harmful to lawns. How much they help the homeowner in regard to grub control is not known. When moles are abundant and perceived to be a problem, harmful insects are likely to be abundant as well, and the removal of moles may expose the homeowner to an insect problem. In response to insect abundance, mole activity in a given area is also likely to be episodic or seasonal and often stops before any control action can be undertaken. Accordingly, we do not advise any direct efforts to control moles or their habitat as necessary except in extreme cases. Then, the techniques of habitat management and exclusion should be used.

HABITAT MANAGEMENT

Where a problem exists with mole tunnels that is the result of mechanical damage caused by a lawnmower hitting raised mounds of earth, this can be avoided by flattening the mole runs by foot or with a lawn roller before mowing. Overwatering lawns can keep earthworms and other mole prey near the surface and result in increased surface tunneling. Encouraging native plant species to establish themselves in the lawn and keeping lawn size to a minimum whenever possible are also good approaches to

dealing with mole problems. "Natural" lawns that rely on native grass or forb plants and do not emphasize the Bermuda and rye grasses that require fertilizer, frequent watering and herbicide and pesticide applications to be maintained in good health would aid tremendously, not only in minimizing conflicts with moles and other wildlife, but as generally sound environmental constructs. For some, the tunneling activity of moles is welcome because it turns the soil, increases biological activity and may, in the long run, improve the quality of a site.

EXCLUSION

Barriers can be erected around flower or garden plots by burying hardware cloth ($^1/_4$ inch mesh) in the recommended L-shaped footer configuration (see Chapter 3). Concrete edges buried 8 to 12 inches underground or similar barriers used in addition to keeping weeds from spreading into flower beds may repel tunneling moles. These approaches are labor-intensive and costly, however, and would be recommended only for exceptional situations or if the homeowner has reasons other than moles to be using them.

REPELLENTS

Castor bean or castor-oil plant *(Ricinus communis)* and a species of spurge *(Euphorbia lathris)* are often recommended mole repellents, but need research to document when and to what extent they might be effective. A recently registered repellent sold under the brand name Mole-Med® (see "Chemical Repellents" in Chapter 3) uses an extract of the castor bean plant as a spray to repel moles from lawns. Careless people put all sorts of things down mole tunnels to discourage them, ranging from Napthalene to gasoline. This may discourage the mole from using that tunnel, but not address the problem. We do not recommend any of these sorts of solutions to problems with moles.

SCARING DEVICES

Some success has been reported by using garden pinwheels that transmit vibrations into the ground and supposedly frighten moles away from an area. Commercial battery-operated devices of this sort are available and claim effectiveness over areas of as much as 3,000 square feet. As with all such products and claims, the buyer is encouraged to be skeptical and to seek money-back guarantees if the product proves ineffective.

A Last Word

As goes our national love affair with the lawn, so goes our attitude toward moles. It certainly does not seem that we will abandon our cultural preference for lawns anytime soon. If anything, there will be more acreage for this peculiar habitat and more resources devoted to its maintenance. No other ornamental landscape element on this planet receives such attention. Undoubtedly, some people will feel it necessary to battle moles over the appearance of the landscape until our attitude toward the lawn has changed.

Additional Source

Yates, T. L., and R. J. Pedersen. 1982. "Moles." In J. A. Chapman and G. A. Feldhamer (eds.), *Wild Mammals of North America*. Baltimore: The Johns Hopkins University Press. 37–51.

19

Muskrats

Found throughout Canada and most of the United States; absent from drier parts of south-central and southwestern United States.

Occasional problems when burrowing into earthen dams.

Closely related to the meadow vole, the muskrat is adapted to an aquatic environment, while its smaller cousin is wholly terrestrial.

MUSKRATS ARE INOFFENSIVE water-loving animals that have readily taken to the many artificial ponds and other impoundments created by humans. Often mistaken for their larger cousin, the beaver, they have quite different habits and lifestyles. Muskrats are not the engineers that beavers are, contenting themselves with cruder houses and bank dens and declining to build dams at all. Muskrats are important contributors to the healthy functioning of many aquatic ecosystems, most especially freshwater marshes. Most of these lands were long ago drained and refilled, first because it was believed marshes bred pestilence and later because the land was coveted for development. Now that we are beginning to recognize the many important functions marshes perform, such as holding and filtering polluted water, taking runoff to prevent flooding and helping to preserve plant and animal species diversity, we regret the loss of so many of them. Muskrats are a keystone species in these threatened ecosystems and can help in the enormous task of their restoration—if we allow them to.

Natural History

Classification and Range

The muskrat (*Ondatra zibethecus*) is a rodent and the largest member of the group called the "microtines," to which meadow voles also belong. Muskrats are widely distributed throughout North America. They are absent, however, from Florida, where a relative known as the round-tailed muskrat (*Neofiber alleni*) can be found. This rabbit-sized animal is well adapted to an aquatic life, with partially webbed hind feet that function as paddles, a waterproof undercoat and a long naked tail that is flattened from side to side. The average weight of an adult muskrat is 2 to 3 pounds, with a total length between 16 and 26 inches. The normal coat color is dark brown, but individuals can range from black to almost white.

Habitat

Muskrats may be found in almost any body of water throughout their range, including drainage ditches, streams, ponds, lakes and both freshwater and brackish marshes. Muskrats are active all year. They restrict their movements, except during dispersal, to home ranges that may extend no more than 100 feet from their main dwellings. Young animals will disperse from their natal areas, but often not until the spring following their birth. Still, both autumn and spring are times when movements occur, and the animals without established territories (called "runners") often move considerable distances. Like beavers, muskrats can slow their heart rate and utilize stored oxygen efficiently enough to remain under water for as long as fifteen minutes. Muskrats are creatures of habit and repeatedly follow the same paths from their lodges, leaving visible channels in mud and marsh vegetation.

Lodges and Shelters

Muskrats build a variety of structures, the most common being a "house" or lodge of piled vegetation and mud that rises out of the water. While this resembles the living quarters built by beavers, the muskrat lodge is usually made from soft vegetation, such as cattails, rather than the tree limbs and other woody vegetation used by beavers. Muskrat lodges can be from 3 to almost 9 feet across and are usually built in water that is 2 to 4 feet deep. The lodge can have several underwater entrances that lead to one or more internal nest chambers. Muskrats also build feeding huts and even more temporary feeding platforms where they can consume collected plants without having to go all the way back to the lodge.

In frozen or snow-covered marshes muskrats often build what are called "pushups" by cutting a hole through the ice and pushing vegetation through it to construct a cavity that rests on top of the ice. These can be used to rest or eat on during severe weather. Bank dens are also built by muskrats. These range from superficial shallow tunneling just below the surface of the water to long (45 to 50 feet) complex systems that have nest chambers, air ducts and multiple entrances (as many as nine have been found), some of which may be plugged with vegetation and difficult to find.

Diet

Muskrats are primarily plant-eaters and prefer to feed on soft aquatic plants such as cattails, bulrushes, arrowhead, reeds and algae. Plant roots and tubers are staples of their winter diets. They may occasionally eat small aquatic animals such as clams and crayfish. By closing a special flap of skin in their mouth muskrats can cut and carry feeding material under water.

Reproduction

Muskrat breeding varies from one area of the country to another, with a tendency to larger litters and restricted breeding periods in the North and smaller litters and unrestricted breeding in the South. Usually, breeding in the northern half of their range occurs from April to August, while in the Deep South it is likely to be curtailed only during the hottest summer months. Gestation is about twenty-five to thirty days, and litters normally vary from three to eight. Young muskrats grow rapidly and may be able to swim by the end of the second week after birth. The mother will swim with young attached to her nipples or belly skin and may even dive underwater with them. The young usually reach the age of independence at about four weeks, when the mother is ready to give birth again. Unlike many other mammals these young do not get chased off or voluntarily leave the natal (birth) den, and the mother may simply excavate a new chamber in the lodge to bear her next litter. Sexual maturity is usually not reached until muskrats are one year old, and three to four years is probably the average life expectancy. In prime habitat, twenty-five muskrats can live in an acre of marsh, but fifteen animals is more typical of the capacity of such an area.

Public Health

Muskrats may become infected with tularemia, which may be transmitted to people through blood-to-blood contact or by eating inadequately cooked muskrat meat (see Chapter 2).

Problems and Their Solutions

Problems

Local populations of muskrats occasionally increase to such densities that the habitat becomes overcrowded and animals denude aquatic vegetation. Such events, called "eat-outs," are most likely to occur in coastal saltwater marshes. Eat-outs put pressure on the population, resulting in hunger and predation, and are normally followed by sharp declines in muskrat numbers. To that end, their populations appear to be self-controlling. Muskrat burrows are often cited as threats to the structural integrity of ponds. Muskrats occasionally feed on agricultural crops growing near water, but their limited home ranges usually restrict the amount of damage they can do.

Solutions

TOLERANCE
Muskrats rarely cause problems for people and add greatly to the biological activity of marsh communities. Where they become so numerous that they threaten to "eat-out" aquatic vegetation, this does tell us something is wrong—but not with the muskrat.

MANAGING IMPOUNDMENTS
Because muskrats prefer steep slopes with dense cover in which to start burrowing, a gently rising incline (about 3 feet of slope for each foot of depth in water) and limitation of dense woody cover along the banks may deter burrowing. Where breaches occur, it is often because fluctuating water levels flood the initial burrow and encourage the muskrat to burrow farther into the dam core. Eventually, a burrow system may completely pierce a dam in this manner. Restricting fluctuations in water levels to no more than 6 to 8 inches will help to control burrowing. When the dam itself has a free-board (the height of the dam above the normal water level) of not less than 3 feet, the structure will be generally resistant to any problem arising from muskrat burrowing.

In addition to proper construction, dams that are imperiled by borrowing can be protected by the placement of a continuous layer of riprap (4- to 6-inch coarse stones or gravel) that extends from 2 feet below the normal water level to 2 feet above. A barrier can also be fashioned from welded wire, galvanized hardware cloth or plastic netting buried along the same area, with plastic being the least costly and most durable of these materials. The barrier should be placed flat against the bank and anchored every few feet along the perimeter.

In extreme cases, a trench can be dug in the middle of the pond berm and filled with concrete. The trench should be dug to a depth of 3 feet below the water level. The resulting concrete core will block muskrats from digging through the dam. While this method of control is labor-intensive and costly, the trouble and expense may be justified if flooding poses a substantial risk to buildings or crops.

A Last Word

People often ask what good animals are as if the services they provided to humans were the measure of their worth. Even animal advocates lapse into this faulty way of thinking. Bats are important, many say, because they perform mosquito control; snakes are valued because they eat rodents. Here's the benefit muskrats provide: They will help us regain the wetlands we have wantonly destroyed and bring us back from the brink of the near ecological disaster we face by having done this. And for this they will not even charge.

Additional Source

Perry, H. R. 1982. "Muskrats." In J. A. Chapman and G. A. Feldhamer (eds.), *Wild Mammals of North America.* Baltimore: The Johns Hopkins University Press. 282–325.

20

Opossums

THE OPOSSUM IS THE ONLY MARSUPIAL found north of Mexico. The marsupials are distinguished by their unique mode of reproduction in which the young are born in an almost embryonic form and make their way into a pouch, or *marsupium*, where they are nourished for what in other mammals would be most of the gestational period. As with some of the other mammalian generalists common in urban and suburban areas, the opossum may have benefited from European colonization and extended its range because of advantageous alterations humans have made to the landscape. It is also fairly clear that a natural northward expansion of these animals was occurring at the time that Europeans arrived because there was so much comment among the native peoples that the first colonists spoke about the novelty and strangeness of these animals.

Opossums figure prominently in the folklore and regional culture of many parts of the country. During the presidential campaign of 1912, Americans even flirted with the possibility of a "possum" party, led by the redoubtable "Billy Possum" (William Howard Taft).

Natural History

Classification and Range

The opossum (properly, the Virginia Opossum—*Didelphis virginiana*) is a medium-sized mammal about the size of a house cat, with long guard hairs that give the fur a very coarse appearance. It also has naked ears and a long almost hairless tail. Its coat color varies from light, almost white, to almost black, but most usually appears an off gray. It has a *prehensile* tail—a tail that is capable of grasping and holding objects. While it might support the opossum's full weight briefly, the animal usually holds on with at least one foot as well as the tail when dangling from a limb. Perhaps because of the naked tail, opossums are often mistaken for rats. A large adult male opossum (the males on average are larger than females) may weight 12 or 13 pounds.

Opossums grow throughout their life, but these lives are usually short ones. The average opossum female probably only lives through one breeding season, during which she raises two litters. A four-year-old wild opossum is exceptional. When confronted, opossums sometimes open their mouths to display their teeth and may even hiss. Although this appears to signal a formidable opponent, these animals are actually shy and inoffensive. Rather than fight, when hard pressed they will sometimes slip into the death-feigning catatonia that we have come to term "playing possum." This state of apparent death can last a minute or two or upwards of two hours before the "dead" opossum revives, looks around and moves off (if the danger it previously confronted has disappeared). What is happening at a physiological level to the opossum when feigning death is not yet well known. The cautionary tale, however, in dealing with playing-dead opossums is to never touch an animal without gloves or better protection.

The opossum is found throughout the East and midwestern parts of the United States, is absent from much of the West and is found again in the far West where humans have imported it into California, Oregon and Washington. Opossums occur on a very limited basis in parts of eastern and western Canada, but the length and severity of the winters appear to limit their presence. Temperatures that average less than 20°F for any extended period of time severely tax these animals, who do not hibernate and either must live off stored fat or count on frequent periods of mild weather when they can become active and search for food. Veterans of hard winters can usually be recognized by the absence of parts of ears and tails lost to frostbite.

Habitat

Opossums are found across a variety of habitats but prefer deciduous woodlands. The opossum lifestyle has been aptly characterized as that of a terrestrial gleaner. This refers to their habit of ceaselessly moving along the ground in search of food, without following prescribed trails or travel routes to places of known food reserves. In

Opossum Tracks

fact, adult male opossums may wander continuously, while females spend their lives in more defined areas, but still move around almost randomly. While they may be more sedentary during the winter and when reliable food sources are available, most opossums seen in yards and neighborhoods are likely to move on without human encouragement or intervention if given enough time. Opossums are most active at night and will begin movements after sleeping by day in a ground den, brush pile or, less commonly, a tree cavity.

Diet

Opossums are omnivorous and consume an amazing variety of plant and animal foods. They are not above scavenging carrion and raiding garbage that has matured beyond the point where other animals would turn it down. Invertebrates, including many types of insects, slugs, snails and earthworms, can comprise a large part of the diet. Raids by opossums on poultry houses and gardens are rarer than popular folklore insists.

Reproduction

Birth is given to young that are little more developed than embryos. Amazingly, these tiny newborns will crawl instinctively upward into the mother's pouch, where they attach themselves to a teat (there are usually thirteen available) and fix themselves firmly to nurse for about fifty days before beginning to wean. Females may breed twice a year and, with litters of as many as a dozen young, they accommodate for the high mortality most opossum populations face. The young become independent of the mother at about three months of age, and a mother opossum with young clinging to her back and side is a popular image of these animals. It is said of opossum young that they do not engage in play. If true, this is a remarkable exception to a behavior that is quite widespread among mammals.

Dens and Nest-Building

Opossums are capable climbers and may take shelter by day in tree dens, old squirrel nests or nests they have built themselves above ground. Nest material is accumulated between the legs, and the tail is used to support it for transport. Ground dens are probably preferred over those in trees, at least in winter, and old woodchuck burrows may be the most ideal from the opossum's point of view. Nest material is also transported into these and the openings are plugged, sometimes quite tightly, with leaves and other material. The preference opossums have for using dens on the ground can lead them to take up residence under decks and in crawl spaces, where they are often considered unwanted guests.

Public Health

Opossums are susceptible to a variety of diseases of significance to humans, but their role in the transmission of any is uncertain. Rabies occurs in opossums, as it does in all warm-blooded animals, but it is very rare. Opossums can serve as hosts for the ticks that transmit Rocky Mountain spotted fever.

Problems and Their Solutions

Problems

Opossums hardly ever raid garbage cans or damage fruit and vegetable crops. In some places they acquire unsavory reputations by killing an occasional bird in a poultry yard, but in sum, all of the possible and even imagined depredations of these animals have to be recognized as slight. Opossums are undoubtedly more beneficial as scavengers and consumers of undesirable invertebrates than harmful for any damage they cause. It is likely that far more complaints about opossums are generated out of mere concern for the presence of these animals rather than for any problems they create.

Solutions

TOLERANCE

The primary message to homeowners who have seen an opossum in their yard and are wondering what, if anything, they should do is not to worry—the animal will likely be moving on in very short order and will not be a threat or a concern.

EXCLUSION

Where an opossum is known to be denning under a porch or patio, the eviction strategy is much the same as for skunks. If anything, it may be slightly easier because the opossum carries her young with her, and the probability that helpless young would be left behind is of far less concern than with other species. Exclusion using one-way doors is effective (see Figure 10, p. 33) and so is simply waiting until the animal has begun its nightly foray (two hours after dark is generally a safe time) and loosely closing the opening with netting, straw or other fibrous material that an animal trapped inside can push away, but which one outside will be less likely to disturb to get back in. The most effective method of discouraging visits by an opossum is to secure trash containers with tight-fitting lids and pick up food at night if pets have been fed outdoors.

Opossums will occasionally find their way into houses through pet doors. The general rules for encouraging an animal to move out of the house, as described for raccoons, apply to opossums, but they can also be directly guided out with as little as a broom to gently nudge them along to an open door. Opossums are very slow moving and easy to evict when they have wandered into buildings where they are not wanted.

A Last Word

There are many myths and misconceptions surrounding opossums. Perhaps the most widespread is that they are more primitive than other animals—so much so as to lead some to describe them as "living fossils." In an evolutionary sense, they do retain an ancient mode of reproduction when compared to the pattern of most contemporary mammals. Unfortunately, the implication of primitiveness usually goes beyond that to reflect their conservative behavioral traits and to the so-called "lower" intelligence they exhibit. This perception of low intelligence may come from the fact that opossums do not do well in problem-solving settings or tests designed by humans to measure intelligence. Regardless, however, the bottom line on opossums is that they have survived far longer than most other contemporary mammals and clearly have passed nature's test of time well enough to be declared a resounding evolutionary success.

Additional Sources

Gardner, A. L. 1982. "Virginia Opossum." In J. A Chapman and G. A. Feldhamer (eds.), *Wild Mammals of North America*. Baltimore: The Johns Hopkins University Press. 3–36.

Sidensticker, J., M. A. O'Connell, and A. J. T. Johnsingh. 1987. "Virginia Opossum." In M. Novak, J. A. Baker, M. E. Obbard, and B. Malloch (eds.), *Wild Furbearer Management and Conservation in North America*. Ontario: Ministry of Natural Resources. 246–63.

21

Pigeons

PIGEONS ARE THE QUINTESSENTIAL URBAN BIRD; they are the mold from which all of our perceptions and feelings about birds in cities are formed. And those feelings often are not kind. Variously referred to as nuisances, pests and even "feathered rats," pigeons are doing nothing more than utilizing an environment provided to them for which by chance they are preadapted. Originally, these birds, often called *rock doves*, inhabited cliffs and rock ledges in Europe and Asia, nesting in these inaccessible places and foraging on the ground below. Some still live this way. Imported to this continent as food animals and to serve as carriers of messages, some pigeons escaped captivity to find shelter in the artificial cliffs of the cities. Pigeons are simply another fine example of an animal doing what it is supposed to do: survive in a world whose odds are set against survival. That they live in a human-created habitat doesn't seem to bother them. We accuse them of making nuisances of themselves, but increasingly provide more and more habitat opportunity for them. If problems with pigeons exist, they are of our own making—not theirs. If we truly want to deal with any inconvenience these birds might cause, we must modify the habitat that *we* have made so suitable for them.

Natural History

Classification and Range

The common pigeon *(Columba liva)* of city and suburb is an introduced or *alien* species brought over by early settlers (as were other domestic pets). Pigeons have long been kept and raised in captivity, and an astonishing variety of forms attest to long human experimentation with genetic variants. This introduced species has close relatives in a few very locally distributed species of larger birds like itself that reach a foot or more long, and many other smaller members of the family to which it belongs that are commonly referred to as doves. The classic appearance of the urban pigeon is of a plump-bodied bird with a small head, black bars on its inner wings, a white rump and a dark band at the end of its tail.

Habitat

Pigeons occur throughout the United States, Mexico and most of southern Canada. They have not yet established a foothold in northern Canada and Alaska. Although primarily a bird of urban settings, large populations of pigeons are found in small towns as well. Under some conditions, such as around grainaries, large flocks of pigeons may occur in rural areas as well. Pigeons are gregarious and tend to be found in small flocks of around twenty to thirty birds, although far larger *aggregations*, which are made up of numbers of flocks, also occur.

Diet

Pigeons appear to be dietary generalists because they do sample all of the many foods offered them by people in city parks, but they specialize in seeds and grains. They are regarded as inveterate panhandlers by humans, but where they have been studied (and that is not all that many places), the bulk of the diet is found to come not from foods (bread, leftovers or birdseed) directly provided by people but from waste grain or seeds from city flora.

Reproduction

Pigeons breed throughout the year, even during winter, and can raise four or five broods annually. The female usually lays two eggs (less often one or three and, rarely, four), sheltering them on a crude and loosely constructed nest structure without a lining. The nest of branch and root pieces and occasionally leaves is built on a ledge, such as a building windowsill or a bridge girder. Incubation takes about sixteen to nineteen days, and the young are fed crop milk for about the first two weeks. (Crop milk is a specially produced secretion that both parents produce from the lining of the crop, a saclike food storage chamber that projects outward from the bottom of the esophagus.) Crop milk is a highly nutritious

Pigeon Tracks

and efficient way of feeding young. Apparently, this way of feeding young has been acquired independently in such diverse bird groups as flamingos, pigeons and penguins.

Public Health

Pigeons play a role in the environmental concern of histoplasmosis, and are known carriers of cryptococcoses and salmonella. However, there is little evidence linking pigeons directly to infections in humans.

Problems and Their Solutions

Problems

To some, pigeons are a visual and aesthetic problem. To others, they are only a problem when present in great numbers or when roosting on buildings or under bridges. Their droppings can disfigure buildings, and if left to accumulate, can cause serious disfigurement due, probably, to their acidic nature. But usually, pigeons do little if any actual structural damage to buildings.

Solutions

TOLERANCE
To those for whom pigeons are an irritant or eyesore, remember that they are one of the few animals that will tolerate the environmental conditions humans impose on the inner city. We think of deserts as barren places, but they team with life in comparison to the industrial core of some of our cities. The pigeons that are there can be considered a vanguard of other species that might come when the condition improves.

HABITAT MANAGEMENT
One of the essential keys to controlling excess numbers of pigeons around urban neighborhoods and parks is to limit the amount of feeding done by humans. Frequently, large numbers of these birds are supported by well-intentioned individuals who regularly supplement them with bread, table scraps or birdseed. Generally, feeding is incremental. From a modest beginning the individual feeder encourages more and more birds to appear or stay in the area, thus requiring more feeding and further enhancing bird numbers. Eventually, the situation gets out of control, to the detriment of all concerned.

The golden rule to pigeon feeding is moderation. Feed only as much as birds will consume in five to ten minutes and do not feed with the clockwork regularity that conditions the birds to appear at the same place, same time, every day. When excess feeding situations have occurred, a gradual reduction over a period of several weeks to a reasonable baseline amount is recommended. Feeding schedules and amounts can be adjusted for weather or any unusual circumstances, provided that the feeder is aware of and responsive to the adverse effects of this activity as much as their positive ones.

EXCLUSION
Pigeons prefer to perch on flat surfaces and certainly need these to nest. Nests are usually built under shelter and as much in a cubby as the parents can find. Wood or metal sheathing can be installed on a ledge at an angle that denies pigeons the opportunity to use that surface. An angle of at least 45° is needed, and 60° is required to ensure that even the most determined attempt to land will be rebuffed. Bird wires (see Chapter 3) will exclude pigeons from ledges, railings, awnings and rooftops. Any of the types—single-strand, coils or porcupine wire—will be effective, but where problems are severe or pigeons numerous and persistent, the porcupine wire has been used most

frequently. Electricity was once commonly used to enhance the effectiveness of wire barriers, but is now considered largely an unnecessary refinement.

Netting (see Chapter 3) is the tool of choice for many conflicts with pigeons as well as other urban birds when large areas have to be treated. Netting can be used to exclude birds from virtually any type of structure, from a detached house to an office building. To evict birds from window ledges, the netting is anchored to the roof, draped across the front of the structure and then tightly secured to the base and sides of the building. Netting can be used under bridges or inside buildings where pigeons perch on beams, girders, struts and supports. The netting can be suspended below the perches to create a false ceiling that excludes the birds. Large-scale applications of netting almost always require the experience and tool kit of professionals, of which a growing number provide excellent long-term solutions to urban bird problems (consult private companies listed in Appendix 1).

Door curtains (see Chapter 3) can also be used to prevent bird access into buildings, such as warehouses, that must be somewhat open to access and daily traffic. The netting is installed in overlapping strips so as to form a protective curtain that parts to allow the passage of personnel and vehicles and then falls back into place to seal out pigeons.

SCARE DEVICES

Effigies and homemade or commercial scarecrows (see Chapter 3) are often used to attempt to frighten pigeons away from an area, especially where no strong attraction such as a food source occurs. These may or may not work. The types that move or are even motorized stand a better chance of achieving some result, but pigeons often accommodate quickly to any type of scarecrow used against them.

REPELLENTS

Polybutene repellents are registered for use on pigeons and may be effective, but involve so much danger to smaller birds and create so many other problems that we do not recommend their use. The chemical product Avitrol® is also registered for use on pigeons and classified as a frightening agent. It has, however, lethal consequences for at least some birds (see Chapter 3), and we do not recommend its use.

A Last Word

The cities we have so proudly built contain many artificial cliffs and ledges that attract pigeons, while residents provide many offerings of the various kinds of foods that sustain them. Ecologists looking at urban habitats describe them as cliff-detritus zones—areas in which our skyscrapers function much as mountain ranges do to set wind circulation patterns and microclimates about themselves and to capture windblown seeds and other organic detritus. No one has yet studied this habitat in any detail, but certainly when aspiring ecologists do, they will no doubt find a surprisingly high biological diversity, with many species of microorganisms, insects, plants and animals adapting rapidly to this special niche provided by humans. At somewhere near the top, and likely to represent the greatest total biomass of all, will be the pigeon.

Additional Source

Johnston, R. F., and M. Janiga. 1995. *Feral Pigeons*. Oxford: Oxford University Press. 320 pp.

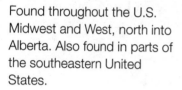

22

Pocket Gophers

Found throughout the U.S. Midwest and West, north into Alberta. Also found in parts of the southeastern United States.

Mostly a problem in agriculture; restricted to yards and gardens in residential areas.

By itself, one pocket gopher may bring from 2 to 4 *tons* of soil to the surface in a year's time.

LIKE MANY OTHER SMALL RODENTS, under appropriate circumstances pocket gophers can undergo dramatic population increases or *irruptions*. The appropriate conditions are often provided by humans preparing agricultural land. By removing a natural community of plants to prepare land for a single crop, or *monoculture*, we create superabundant food resources that are bonanzas to animals like pocket gophers. The population increases that logically follow can generate substantial economic loss—as much as 25 percent of a crop. Loss such as this is certain to evoke significant responses, leading to major efforts to destroy the "pest" in accordance with the damage it does. If this works at all, it is briefly and almost always followed by adaptation of the problem species to the technology directed at it. Even those who have spent much of their lives in this effort are recognizing the inevitable circular path this course follows. Breaking out of that circle begins with a better understanding of the place these animals hold when they are a part of the natural ecosystems in which they have evolved. This leads to understanding their role in the new ecosystems imposed by humans. Not all ecosystems are natural (deserts or woods or tundra). Some are *agricultural,* and those that are mostly the object of this book are *urban* or *human-dominated.* They still function as ecosystems even where human hands have dramatically altered them.

The control of problems with wild animals in any of these systems must ultimately focus on natural processes that will work not to destroy species but to bring them into balance with other parts of the system.

Natural History

Classification and Range

Pocket gophers are rodents belonging to a family *(Geomyidae)* that is only found in the New World. There are three genera of pocket gophers *(Thomomys, Goemys* and *Pappogeomys)* in the United States and thirteen species. Pocket gophers are found throughout most of the Midwest and West, as well as in the southernmost parts of Alabama and Georgia into Florida. They also range north into parts of Canada through Alberta. Like many other rodent groupings, the family relationships are highly complicated, and a good deal of diversification and specialized adaptation to specific microhabitats has occurred to make the group's taxonomy either a joy or a curse, depending on how you feel about taxonomizing.

To the homeowner with pocket gopher problems the taxonomy of the group is probably not a high concern. To anyone who wonders about the variety of life and its adaptations and diversification, groups such as this can be highly significant.

Habitat

Although they are burrowing *(fossorial)* animals, pocket gophers occupy a surprising range of habitats, including some that are fairly rocky. Exactly what types of soils support them in their greatest abundance remains to be determined, but lighter and more friable types are clearly preferred. In fact, the diversification these animals have undergone is thought by some to have happened by their adaptation to different types of soils.

Diet

Pocket gophers are herbivores—they live almost entirely on plants. Much of their feeding occurs in tunnels, where they consume the roots of the plants they encounter. They will also feed on the surface, in brief bouts of activity right outside a tunnel exit. The roots of dandelion are an important food for pocket gophers, and the entire plant may be consumed when it can be pulled into the tunnel. Grasses and *forbs* (plants that die back in winter) make up the bulk of the diet, but many agricultural crops are readily consumed—especially alfalfa.

Reproduction

In the northern part of their range, pocket gophers usually have one litter each year but may give birth twice in the South. The average litter ranges from three to five young,

Pocket Gopher Tracks

but as few as one or as many as ten have been found.

Burrows

Burrows are sometimes quite close to the ground and sometimes are as much as 2 feet down. The industry and energy that goes into burrowing and the amount of earth that is cast off is hard to imagine. Using its teeth and its claws to tunnel (different species vary in the amount to which they use one or the other technique), the pocket gopher loosens soil, then somersaults in the tunnel to turn around so that it can push the excavated material to the surface. The amount of material a local population of pocket gophers can bring to the surface has to be measured in tons, indicating a significant influence on the soil ecology of regional areas when these animals are present.

Public Health

Pocket gophers are not implicated in the transmission of any serious zoonotic disease to humans.

Problems and Their Solutions

Problems

Extensive burrowing, numerous mounds of excavated earth and plugging of burrow entrances with earth or grass are indicators of their presence and a source of concern to anyone trying to maintain a lawn with these animals in it.

Solutions

TOLERANCE
Most people would not think to tolerate pocket gopher problems because of the logical concern that leaving them alone would lead to even more damage. For those trying to raise crops this may be true, although it does not mean that a better understanding of these animals and their ecology is not germane to dealing with the problems they cause. In fact, it is highly relevant and likely to be the best way to approach dealing with them. For the homeowner and small-time gardener, pocket gophers may be an occasional nuisance and problem on lawns, ornamental or garden beds, but not a long-term problem or threat. Where the animals are not so numerous as to be causing heavy damage, the homeowner should consider them as neutral.

EXCLUSION
Fencing or other exclusion techniques can be expected to have only a limited applicability in controlling pocket gopher damage. Individual trees or plant beds that are of special value can be surrounded with hardware cloth or a plastic mesh that is no more than $1/2$ inch. This must be buried at least a foot deep, and the effort required to do this, as well as the possibility of disturbing plant roots by digging, does not make this a particularly attractive solution.

HABITAT MANAGEMENT
Where they are problems in agricultural settings, success in limiting the amount of damage pocket gophers do has come through a variety of habitat management practices, ranging from the planting of alternate crops to crop rotation and flood irrigation. All of these lower the suitability of the habitat for pocket gopher occupancy. Some success may be achieved in residential areas by heavily watering lawns periodically to create an unsuitable soil structure for burrow maintenance. As with any rodent problem, the tolerance and encouragement of natural predators leads ultimately to some of the best solutions. Artificial perches for raptors

and tolerance of fox and even coyote presence can go a long way toward creating a predator-prey balance.

REPELLENTS

There are no repellents currently registered for use on pocket gophers, and home remedies that might work on other species are less likely to be usable for them because of the difficulty of reaching animals underground.

A Last Word

The positive and beneficial environmental roles of pocket gophers have been little acknowledged in the past and, even when they have, not taken to heart. The enormous amount of soil they move alone suggests they serve an important function in directly influencing the soil and plant communities. Rather than destroy, we should understand.

Additional Source

Chasse, J. D., W. E. Howard, and J. T. Roseberry. 1982. "Pocket Gophers." In J. A. Chapman and G. A. Feldhamer (eds.), *Wild Mammals of North America.* Baltimore: The Johns Hopkins University Press. 239–55.

23

Porcupines

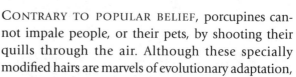

Found throughout most of Canada and the western United States. Limited presence in the eastern United States.

Only an occasional visitor to residential areas; more likely to be encountered on hikes.

The quills are present from birth and functional once dry—all thirty thousand of them.

CONTRARY TO POPULAR BELIEF, porcupines cannot impale people, or their pets, by shooting their quills through the air. Although these specially modified hairs are marvels of evolutionary adaptation, they can only do so much to help this slow-moving and (to be honest) clumsy rodent protect itself. So, you must actually be in contact, however slight, before the quills can become dislodged and attach themselves to you. If you leave the porcupine alone, then it will go its way and certainly not interfere with you going yours.

Natural History

Classification and Range

The porcupine *(Erethizon dorsatum)* is a large-bodied slow-moving rodent that would be ill equipped to avoid any sort of predator were it not for the unique defensive system nature has provided it with. Porcupines range throughout most of Canada and the western United States, and can be found in the East throughout the New England states, New York and Pennsylvania, and even into parts of northern Maryland.

The adults vary little between the sexes. A full-grown porcupine is about 2 to 2 $\frac{1}{2}$ feet long and weighs up to 30 pounds. The quills are the hallmark of these animals. A sheath of muscle controls quill movement so that they can be raised in a sign of warning when the porcupine is threatened. As many a dog owner living in porcupine country has discovered, ignoring this warning can lead to big problems for the overly inquisitive or aggressive pet. The end of the quill is made up of overlapping shinglelike sections called *barbules* that, once imbedded, cannot easily be pulled out. Serious injury, even fatalities, can occur to both wild and domestic animals that have come into contact with a porcupine. In fact, one human fatality has even been documented, this coming to an individual who ingested a quill in a porcupine meat sandwich.

Habitat

Porcupines are most commonly associated with coniferous or evergreen forests. They also range into deciduous forests, and in parts of the West are felt to cause serious damage, at times, to stands of cottonwood trees.

Diet

Porcupines are herbivores (plant-eaters). They specialize during the winter on utilizing the woody parts of plants, especially the inner bark (the *cambium*) of trees that also is so favored by beavers. The *bark stripping* that occurs when a porcupine has worked on a tree is fairly obvious and distinctive, being only occasionally confused with similar damage caused by squirrels. Virtually all species of trees found within the porcupine's range are eaten. Porcupines may have preferences for hemlock, Douglas fir and ponderosa pine among evergreens, and

maples, oaks, beech and birch among deciduous or hardwood trees. In summer, porcupines will eat herbaceous plants, but the significance of these food items is probably always less than the food derived from the woody plants.

Reproduction

Breeding occurs in the autumn and is followed by about a 210-day gestation period. This is unusually long for a rodent—almost five times longer than the gestation period for the squirrel and about equal in length to that of the white-tailed deer. Much humorous speculation is traditionally associated with the act of mating in these animals, but from what we know, it is not different from most other mammals. It does appear that porcupines have quite meticulous behavior during the brief period of sexual

Porcupine Tracks

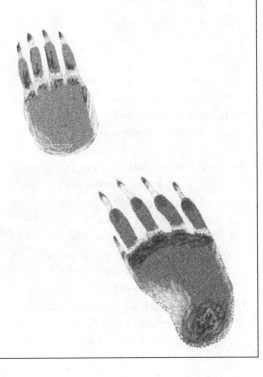

activity, but they also are sometimes quite aggressive and combative with one another, all done *without* the use of the most formidable weapon in their arsenal, the quills.

Public Health

Porcupines do not carry any communicable diseases that are of concern to humans. The main safety issue associated with these animals is the possibility of being quilled. The reflexive twitching of muscles tends to pull quills in deeper, and a quick response is recommended to minimize this. Pets that have had a run-in with a porcupine should be treated by a veterinarian, both to ensure that quills are removed correctly, with as little discomfort to the pet as possible, and for evaluation and treatment with antibiotics if deemed necessary. Humans who have imbedded quills should consult a physician to determine a course of treatment.

Problems and Their Solutions

Problems

Porcupines occasionally damage structures and implements that are used in outdoor work or recreation, and are sometimes responsible for damage to trees. People who spend time outdoors in porcupine country know that these animals are attracted to tools and implements that have salt on them (as from sweating). Even aluminum oars are occasionally found to have been gnawed to get at this mineral. The wooden parts of structures that are attacked usually are bonded plywood that contains a layer of glue that attracts the porcupine. Car tires and hoses may also attract attention because of their mineral content. Tree damage, including bark stripping, is occasionally an impor-

tant issue in commercial forest stands, but this is rare. Damage to individual trees in settled areas doesn't happen very often and is easily addressed by the methods described below.

Solutions

TOLERANCE
To emphasize a point made earlier, we note again the appealing and almost entirely benevolent disposition that makes porcupines thoroughly enjoyable animals to be around. The mistaken impression of the porcupine is that it is a dangerous or harmful creature that will ultimately cause people and their pets harm. The truth is that unless there is provocation, no harm is likely to ever come from these animals.

EXCLUSION
Where individual trees need to be protected, a metal band that is about 24 to 30 inches in height can be placed around the trunk of a tree at about 3 feet off the ground. This band will prevent the tree from being climbed, and because porcupines are not good climbers and rarely cross from one tree to another above ground, it is likely to be quite effective. We do not recommend leaving these bands on trees for any longer period than necessary—insects may accumulate, lay eggs or overwinter underneath them, and the trunks of sensitive trees could scald if the bands were removed and the sun were to fall on the sensitive bark that was exposed. In protecting any fruit tree, it is important that exclusion take into account winter snow cover and that bands or other excluding devices be placed 3 feet above the expected maximum level of the snowpack.

REPELLENTS
There is one capsaicin-based hot sauce repellent (see Appendix 2) that is registered

for use against porcupine damage to plastic tubing (e.g., lines and fittings on maple syrup collection equipment). The effectiveness of the product holds out some hope for being equally effective in protecting car hoses or other devices that porcupines might find tasty and may be registered for such use in the future. Preservatives, such as copper napthanate and pentachlorophenol, used in the manufacturing of plywood also appear to have some repelling properties, even though they are not registered as animal repellents.

A Last Word

Keep your porcupine friends close, but not touching.

Additional Source

Dodge, W. E. 1982. "Porcupine." In J. A. Chapman and G. A. Feldhamer (eds.), *Wild Mammals of North America*. Baltimore: The Johns Hopkins University Press. 355–68.

24

Prairie Dogs and Ground Squirrels

Occur widely throughout the western and midwestern parts of the continent, ranging into the very far North.

Mostly a concern in and around large areas of open space; occasional to rare in developed areas.

Early settlers encountered a prairie dog town in the Texas Panhandle that measured 250 miles long and 100 miles wide, and contained upwards of 400 million animals.

PRAIRIE DOGS AND GROUND SQUIRRELS are fossorial animals. This does not mean that they are extinct and preserved as little lumps of stone, but simply that they spend a good deal of their time underground. Both build elaborate tunnel or burrow systems, live in fairly large to very large groups, are gregarious, have complex social lives and have adapted to occupy a wide range of different habitats. All tend to look somewhat alike, although there are plenty of differences when you look really close.

Near the end of World War I, California became the first state to officially declare a "ground squirrel week." The event, however, was not to honor these plucky little rodents, but to better organize forces for their destruction. Schools and shops were encouraged to close so that both children and adults could be mobilized into a workforce dedicated to killing as many of these animals as possible. Even though the official state holiday has disappeared, the effort to develop better, more efficient and more deadly technologies to destroy these animals has not.

Prairie dogs have fared even worse. Once they occupied more than 700 million acres throughout the Great Plains. Poisoning campaigns reduced that range to less than 2 percent of what it had been. For some people, that has not been enough, and virulent attempts to eradicate these animals continue. These strategies are extremely shortsighted, neglecting not only the evidence that shows their impacts not to be that great, as well as a misunderstanding of the positive and beneficial role these animals play as important parts of the ecosystem.

Natural History

Classification and Range

Prairie dogs (*Cynomys* spp.) and ground squirrels (*Sperophilus* spp.) include numerous species, which reside widely throughout North America. In the United States they occupy all regions except the mid-Atlantic and Northeast. All are members of the same group of animals (the *Sciuridae*) that includes tree squirrels and chipmunks. There are four or five species of prairie dogs and more than twenty different species of ground squirrels.

Of the two main types of prairie dogs, the black-tailed and the white-tailed, the black-tailed *(Cynomys ludovicianus)* is most likely to cause problems for people. Among the ground squirrels, the thirteen-lined *(S. beecheri)* is the species that is most widely distributed and most often comes into conflict with humans.

Ground squirrels and prairie dogs are medium-sized rodents, ranging about a foot or more in length and averaging about 2 to 3 pounds. Coat color varies widely but generally is brownish, with lighter and darker variants in both groups, faint spots in some

of the ground squirrels and distinctive white or black tips on the tail of the two types of prairie dogs.

Habitat

Black-tailed prairie dogs are grassland specialists, most commonly associated with open short-grass prairies. More than the other species in its group, the black-tailed prairie dog forms large social assemblages, based on a unit called the *coterie* and organized around family affiliations. Prairie dog "towns" were frequent phenomena of the Old West and still can be found in places today. None, however, will ever again approach the size of the town described at the beginning of this chapter. Ground squirrels are also found in prairie and grassland areas and also are tolerant of scrub and brushlands, deserts and even wooded places. One of the reasons there are so many species in this group of animals is that they have adapted to a wide variety of habitats.

Diet

Both prairie dogs and ground squirrels are *herbivores* (plant-eaters). Grasses and forbs are the mainstay of their diets, but may be supplemented by insects or an occasional small mammal. Prairie dogs not only eat grasses, but clip and maintain them, both for housekeeping purposes underground where dens are lined and for aboveground housekeeping as well. By maintaining short grass around the burrow entrances, the town sentinels, a duty in which all share, can keep a better eye out for approaching predators.

Burrows

Prairie dog towns are distinguished by the many burrow entrances, each obvious as a small mound of excavated earth that the prairie dogs sit on to scan for predators or other danger. Below ground the burrow may be anywhere from 2 to 6 feet deep and 15 feet long. Ground squirrel burrows are similar to the prairie dog's, and both can have several entrances to allow escape from predators such as rattlesnakes.

Public Health

Prairie dogs can play hosts to the ectoparasites (fleas) that are implicated in the transmission of bubonic plague (see Chapter 2).

Problems and Their Solutions

Problems

Agricultural crops, pasture and occasional garden crops are sometimes damaged by ground squirrels and prairie dogs, and complaints about burrows and possible injury to livestock, people and farm machinery are sometimes made.

Solutions

TOLERANCE

Sometimes the damage that we think animals do is actually much less than believed, and sometimes the "damage" is actually a benefit that goes unnoticed. This is the case with prairie dog and ground squirrel populations. Recent studies focusing on the overall impact and benefit of animals like these suggest that we have overlooked the critical role they may play in encouraging biological diversity, and have overestimated the impact they have on our own economic interests.

EXCLUSION

Fencing is generally not a practical means of excluding any of these animals except in special cases. Hardware cloth ($^1/_4$- or $^1/_2$-inch mesh) can be placed to a depth of 18 to 20 inches around small plots of individual ornamental plants and trees, or trunks can be wrapped in commercial tree wrap (see Figure 13, p. 37). One specialized

application of fencing in a municipal ballpark involved the horizontal application of woven wire mesh over an entire playing surface, which was then covered by soil. This method illustrates the imaginative thinking that can be applied to conflicts between people and wildlife. Another imaginative and possibly successful way to limit the presence and activity of animals such as prairie dogs can be accomplished by erecting visual barriers—short fencing of the sort used along construction sites to control runoff, for example. Because of the strong innate drive to clear vegetation and maintain open visual fields that these animals have, fences that are placed along the perimeter of colonies and obstruct this can be highly effective in limiting colony spread or even forcing existing colonies to relocate.

HABITAT MANAGEMENT

Habitat modification practices aimed at reducing cover, controlling weeds and limiting available forage may be helpful in limiting conflicts. Sometimes conflicts occur because people move into habitat occupied by these animals and force them to live in and around human settlements. If such areas are maintained with as much of the natural plant communities intact as possible, then conflicts with these animals will be minimized.

REPELLENTS

There are no repellents currently registered for use on these animals. Being essentially only slightly different models of tree squirrels, however, possibly some of the repellents commercially manufactured for use on these animals would be effective as well on ground squirrels and prairie dogs, and could at some time in the future be registered for use.

A Last Word

As discussed throughout this book, attempts to eradicate any wild animal through the use of widespread poisoning and trapping campaigns are simply bad ideas. Not only do they provide only temporary remission of the problem, but they invariably create environmental and ecological problems that extend damage far beyond the benefit of relieving damage to a specific resource. As we learn more about the role and function of individual species as members of the communities of living things that make up entire ecosystems, we learn how interconnected things are to one another and to ourselves. Fortunately, many people have already noted that when we poison wild animals we are also poisoning ourselves, both literally and figuratively.

Additional Source

Tomich, P. Q. 1982. "Ground Squirrels." J. A. Chapman and G. A. Feldhamer (eds.), *Wild Mammals of North America.* Baltimore: The Johns Hopkins University Press. 192–208.

25

Rabbits

Widespread throughout the United States, but of limited distribution in Canada.

Yards and gardens are rabbit hangouts.

Anywhere rabbits abound is called a *warren*—originally the word meant those places officially granted by the English king for raising rabbits.

"TIMID AS A RABBIT" people will say to characterize others who are not given to direct actions. This may not be that good an analogy, however, considering that timid people don't have to worry about being at the bottom of a long food chain. "Circumspect as a rabbit" might be more apt, because rabbits go to extremes not to advertise themselves as available to be eaten. Few animals are as content to sit unmoving for as long as rabbits are, as those who keep them as pets know. This is not to say that rabbits don't let their guard down once in a while. The observant homeowner may, if lucky, see rabbits on their lawn in the early morning or evening hours in spirited and spontaneous chases of other rabbits, a playful nature that is rare in other animals. Rabbits lead interesting lives, undoubtedly ones that are full of concern and fear, but sometimes of an apparent joy of living that we can envy.

Natural History

Classification and Range

Rabbits are commonly misunderstood to be rodents, but actually belong to their own order and properly are called *lagomorphs*. The evolutionary split between rabbits and other living mammals probably occurred about thirty million years ago. Lagomorphs are found in both the Old and New Worlds, with the New World forms distinguished between true rabbits, belonging to the genus *Sylvilagus*, and the hares or jackrabbits that belong to the genus *Lepus*. It is the cottontails that are primarily problems in yards and gardens, while the hares and jackrabbits are more problematic in agricultural and open-range settings.

The cottontails and their close relatives make up twelve species in the United States, with the eastern cottontail *(Sylvilagus floridanus)* being the most widely distributed and familiar to most people. Eastern cottontails have been introduced to Oregon and Washington State and are widespread enough throughout the South and Midwest to make the descriptor "eastern" somewhat misleading. Cottontails vary in color from gray to brown and have large ears and hind feet and short fluffy tails. Although cottontail species vary in size, they are all rather small animals, averaging about a foot in length and 2 to 3 pounds in weight.

Habitat

Cottontails are generally found in brushy hedgerows and the edges of wooded areas with dense cover, but they also do very well in suburbs and urban areas where lawns, gardens and shrubs meet their habitat requirements. Besides the plants essential to their diet, rabbits need resting and escape cover. The briar patch is a real attraction to them because the dense prickly growth of raspberry or other thorny shrubs provides excellent protection. The type of early successional habitat that rabbits favor is often characterized by the term *old field*.

Diet

Rabbits feed on leafy plants during the growing season and the buds and bark of woody plants in the winter. Both garden plants and ornamentals can be damaged, and smaller trees, including fruit trees, can be damaged significantly in bad winters or when high numbers of rabbits are present. Rab-

bits are most active just at dusk and dawn, an activity pattern described by the term *crepuscular*.

Reproduction

Famous for their reproductive abilities, cottontails breed from February through September farther north. Gestation is about twenty-eight days. Three or four litters of four or five young ("kittens") are born each year (litter sizes can be up to eight). Young are born helpless in a shallow depression lined with grass and mother's fur, but they grow rapidly and are weaned when less than half the size of the adult. Cottontails may live to two years in the wild, but where predators are numerous they seldom live more than one year.

Public Health

Rabbits can be infected with tularemia, which may be transmitted to people if they eat undercooked, infected meat, handle a sick animal or allow an open cut to contact the infected meat of a butchered rabbit. They may also serve as a host for the ticks that transmit Rocky Mountain spotted fever.

Problems and Their Solutions

Problems

Cottontail damage is usually the result of feeding activities. Flower and vegetable plants are eaten in spring and summer and fruit trees and ornamentals in the fall and winter. Damage may be distinguished from that caused by other animals by the cleanly cut plant remains (see Figure 22, p. 101) and the presence of nearly spherical pea-sized droppings scattered around the area, or sometimes left in small piles. Deer scat, although similarly shaped, is quite larger. The easily recognizable tracks of rabbits may also be found in soft soil or snow. Of course, the rabbits themselves may be seen; they tend to be active at dusk and dawn.

Solutions

EXCLUSION

The most effective permanent protection for gardens subject to rabbit damage is a well-constructed fence. Chicken wire supported by posts every 6 to 8 feet is strong enough to exclude rabbits. Such fences normally need to be only about 2 feet high. It is important to make sure the bottom is either buried 6 to 8 inches or staked securely to the ground to prevent rabbits from pushing their way underneath it. Some gardeners prefer to construct movable fence panels (see Figure 24) that can be stored as sections (2 x 8 feet being one recommended size) and set out to protect the garden right after first planting, when damage is likely to be most severe. Some years the panels may not be needed at all, given the ups and downs that occur with rabbit populations. When their presence is only sporadic or occasional, new plantings can be protected by using commercially sold cloches or 1-gallon plastic milk containers that have the bottom cut out and are placed over the seedling to provide protection both from rabbits and late frost (see Chapter 3).

TREE PROTECTION

Barriers such as commercial tree wrap (see Figure 13, p. 37) may be effective in preventing bark damage by rabbits. Cylinders of hardware cloth (usually self-supporting) or poultry wire (which may require some staking) can also be used. These barriers are placed around the trunks to a height equal to the expected snow depth plus 18 inches.

Young trees and saplings are more vulnerable than old trees with thicker, tougher bark. Low-hanging branches may also be within reach of rabbits and should be included inside the barrier if possible. Routine pruning done in the fall will provide a decoy food source for the rabbits if trimmings are left on the ground. Rabbits find twigs and buds more desirable than trunk bark and will concentrate their feeding on these.

REPELLENTS

If fencing is impractical, or damage is so slight that it is not cost effective, small plots and individual plants can be protected with chemical repellents. A variety of Thiram-based repellents are registered for use on inedible plants, as well as Hinder®, Ro-Pel®, Shotgun®, Rabbit-Scat®, Miller's Hot Sauce® and Get-Away™ (see "Chemical Repellents" in Chapter 3). Care should be taken not to use a repellent on plants that will be eaten (unless it specifies on the label that this can be done). Many homemade repellent strategies have been tried, with the usual varying results that taunt anyone trying to make real sense out of them. These include soap and hair as recommended sometimes for repelling deer. While we cannot endorse any of these procedures enthusiastically, they may be worth trying and certainly are an inexpensive form of entertainment if nothing else.

SCARE DEVICES

Some claim empty soda bottles buried up to their necks and placed along a garden perimeter repel rabbits by producing a wind-aided noise that scares them. What happens when it is not windy is unclear. Under some circumstances scare tape or balloons might frighten rabbits away from an area. The pinwheels sold to repel moles might provide a visual deterrent to rabbits as well.

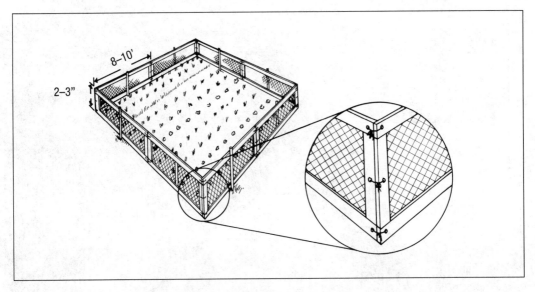

Figure 24. *Simple framed panels of chicken wire or other fencing material can be strung together and placed around a small vegetable or flower garden that needs protection from rabbits. If necessary, wooden stakes can be driven in at intervals to support the panels.*

HABITAT MODIFICATION

Some success with rabbit problems can be achieved through habitat management, but consideration must be given to the potential impact of any such actions on other desirable wildlife species, such as songbirds. Certainly, removing cover around gardens and orchards can help reduce damage from rabbits.

Predators

It is important to recognize the role that predation plays in keeping rabbit numbers in balance. Hawks and owls play important roles as avian predators, and foxes, raccoons, skunks and opossums as mammalian species that prey on rabbits. Domestic cats and dogs take a toll on local rabbit populations as well. Obviously, the role of predators is not to completely control prey populations, but to regulate them at levels where other techniques can be more effective in deterring them from causing serious damage.

A Last Word

The English rabbit, cousin to our own cottontail, was introduced to Australia many years ago with the thought that it might make a profitable side industry as a food source. The results were a population explosion that resulted in major changes in native vegetation. We are fortunate that our rabbits are native species and that no matter how much we alter our landscapes to favor their populations increasing, the natural checks and balances that have worked for millennia seem to prevent the sorts of things that happened in Australia from occurring. The moral of the story seems clear: the more careful we are to allow natural ecological processes to work, the more controllable potential conflicts with animals will be. This is true even (perhaps especially) in our cities and towns.

Additional Source

Lockley, R. M. 1975. *The Private Life of the Rabbit*. New York: Avon Books. 152 pp.

26

Raccoons

Widespread throughout the United States and Canada, where they continue to expand their range northward.

Can be found in attics, chimneys, crawl spaces, outbuildings, yards, gardens and wherever else humans provide something to peak their curiosity.

This "solitary" mammal has been found in winter dens containing more than twenty animals.

WITH THEIR BANDIT'S MASK and ringed tail, raccoons are recognized by just about everyone, even if not frequently seen due to their nocturnal habits. Raccoons are one of a very few species of wild animal that appears to have actually benefited from contact with humans, and they have shown no trouble adapting to suburban and even urban environments. Such *synanthropes* (animals able, or even preferring, to live with humans) are usually generalists, tolerating widely different habitats and eating many different foods. If the few studies that have been conducted on urban and suburban raccoons are representative, then the densities they achieve in urban areas can be up to twenty times that typical of rural environments. This inevitably leads to conflicts with humans because raccoons are smart enough to defeat any but the most determined defense of garbage cans or home gardens. It has also led to many cherished moments, as homeowners became enthralled by a glimpse of these fascinating animals. Among those who know them well, there is a strong sentiment that raccoons could easily share honors with the bald eagle by being declared our national mammal.

Natural History

Classification and Range

Raccoons *(Procyon lotor)* are truly New World animals, with only a debatable relationship to Asian animals such as the giant and red pandas. The fossil evidence suggests that essentially modern-looking raccoons ranged coast to coast throughout the United States as much as a million years ago. Today they are found in almost every major habitat *(biome)* throughout the forty-eight contiguous states and have made recent inroads into southern Canada as well. There are several species of raccoon found throughout the Americas, some of them restricted to small offshore islands. There are more than twenty subspecies living on the U.S. mainland, most being named back in the days when it was more fashionable to "discover" new types of animals than it is today. Whether there are real differences between any of them is something that still needs to be determined.

The raccoon may be as long as a small dog (2 to 3 feet from nose to end of tail), but actually weigh much less. The average adult male may weigh anywhere from 10 to 15 pounds and tend to be slightly larger than the female, who will weigh anywhere from 6 to 12 pounds. Raccoons in the northern parts of their range may be larger, and even exceed 60 pounds, as will animals that have been fed (or overfed) by humans. Coat color varies from dark, almost black, to sandy or pale. Although sometimes less noticeable on pale animals, the mask and ringed tail are the hallmarks by which we know them best. Raccoons are probably color blind, although they have excellent night vision. Their tapetum (the layer of the eye that reflects light) sometimes reflects light in a greenish glow.

Raccoons are at least as intelligent as cats or dogs and possess far greater manual dexterity. In fact their sense of touch may be as fully or more developed than their other senses. The scientific name of the raccoon refers to the "washing" behavior, once thought to be instinctive and mandatory in these animals. In truth, raccoons do not wash everything they eat. They manipulate food, dunking and soaking it when water is available, and so appear to be washing it. When water is not available, however, they use much the same motions in handling food, and the behavior probably more accurately reflects a need to tactually experience things than it does to clean them.

Habitat

Although they prefer mature woodlands, there are raccoons that thrive along seashores or that live in prairie grasslands. The range of this species has expanded quite recently into parts of Canada and deep into the American Midwest, largely through human beneficence in providing barns and outbuildings as shelter and crops as nourishment. Cities and suburbs provide both natural foods and abundant castoffs from human tables. Shelter can frequently be found in unused chimneys, in attics, under porches or in outbuildings along back alleys. Of course, the old standby hollow tree will be used if available, even if it is right next to a busy street. All cities provide extensive travel corridors for raccoons, who are quite at home using storm sewers when these are not too flooded.

Diet

The raccoon's diet is so highly varied that it almost seems easier to describe the foods they don't eat rather than those they do. Small pieces of tinfoil, newspaper and even an occasional cigarette butt in raccoon scats testify to the use of human refuse. The mainstays of the diet, however, are fruits, vegetables, high-energy mast foods, such as acorns, and earthworms in early spring when other foods are scarce. Fish and aquatic animals, such as crayfish, are eaten when available, but most urban streams are no longer of high enough quality to support these forms of life. Raccoons will eat small animals such as birds, amphibians and mice on an opportunistic basis, but are generally not regarded as effective or efficient hunters. Their appetite for foods such as grapes and sweet corn lead to frequent conflicts with home gardeners.

There is often a pattern to raccoon feeding activity. In the mid-Atlantic states, for example, an early-spring diet of insects and earthworms is followed by meals of mulberry, the first of the ripening fruits. Following that, the summer diet follows the order of ripening fruits: blackberries, cherries, grapes and, last, the persimmons that may not be available until late fall. Between September and the end of December raccoons gorge themselves on whatever fruits remain and acorns, which are a dietary staple. As much as 30 percent to the summer body weight can be added before the start of winter, and make up critical fat reserves that the animals live on during the coldest periods of the year. In severe cold or when deep snows are on the ground, raccoons will remain in dens in a state of general torpor for days on end. They do not, however, go into a state of true hibernation like bears and woodchucks.

Dens and Shelter

Raccoons are usually active at night, although along coastal areas they will often forego this to be active at low tide. By day, raccoons retire to denning or resting sites. Dens are made above ground in tree cavi-

ties, chimneys and attics, and underground in old woodchuck burrows, storm sewers or crawl spaces under buildings. When they feel secure enough, raccoons may simply lie up in thickets or swamps on open ground. Unusual day beds range from squirrel leaf nests to log and brush piles or, on occasion, even large bird nests such as those built by magpies. Sharing of den sites may be common in suburban areas among adult raccoons. Even in rural areas, wintertime dens with more than twenty animals have been found.

Reproduction

Breeding seasons vary from north to south, and in the far South breeding may occur year-round. If a line were drawn, bisecting the United States from east to west, raccoons north of it would generally mate from January to March. Below it raccoons would mate later, perhaps March through June. Whenever breeding occurs, births follow about sixty-three days later, around the same time as for a cat or dog. Occasional late litters occur in early fall, apparently to females that have lost a litter or had a failed pregnancy. In the North, these late births place young raccoons at a distinct disadvantage because in order to survive the winter, a certain amount of weight should be gained. These late-arriving young have trouble putting on the weight in time. Litter size ranges from one to seven, with three to five usual. Young are weaned at about two months and may remain with the mother through the first winter. The travel and exploratory activities of young that are moving out of the area in which they were born are formally known as *dispersion*. These movements often lead to conflicts with people, as the exploring young break into garages, occupy chimneys, get into the trash or engage in other behavior that draws human attention.

Public Health

The raccoon is one of four wild animals (including the fox, skunk and bat) considered to be primary carriers of the rabies virus in the United States, and classifiable as a rabies vector species (RVS). Most of the eastern United States is where raccoon rabies occurs. Racoon rabies was first documented in 1977 in West Virginia and Virginia, where it was apparently imported along with a shipment of animals from Florida brought in to repopulate a hunting area. Raccoon rabies has been known in Florida since at least the 1950s, and is now enzootic (present at low levels, but definitely within the population) there and in many eastern states. Raccoon rabies is spreading northward toward Canada and west toward Ohio.

A serious public health concern involving raccoons derives from the roundworm (*Baylisascaris procyonis*) that can infect humans who accidentally ingest or inhale eggs that are passed through raccoon feces. Raccoons are also hosts for the zoonotic disease leptospirosis and giardiasis.

Problems and Their Solutions

Problems

Raccoons can cause both real damage, as when they get into crops, or simply be nuisances, as when they occupy the family chimney or panhandle at campgrounds. They are often blamed for more damage than they really do, while the neighborhood dogs or crows that have scattered trash make off blameless.

Short of actually seeing the animals themselves, tracks are one of the best ways to identify raccoon presence. In gardens the characteristic hand and footprints will dis-play themselves if the ground is damp. On hard surfaces or in dry weather, flour, lime or other suitable powder can be used to record prints. Raccoons that are using attics or chimneys usually begin to make noise at dusk and just before dawn, while squirrels will be active by day and quieter at night (except when the less common flying squirrels, which are nocturnal, are involved). Even mice in or near chimneys can make considerable amounts of noise, and it is important to make sure what the source of any unknown scratching or tapping noises really is. One clue could be found in the noisy vocal exchanges of raccoons, especially family members, which are usually not to be mistaken for anything else.

Solutions

TOLERANCE

As with any human-wildlife conflict the first course of action is to decide what level of damage is occurring, how long it may be likely to persist and whether the damage requires an immediate response or can be dealt with on a non-emergency basis. Because they are generally secretive, raccoons do not often alarm people by their presence enough to cause them to seek immediate control measures. A careful and calm approach to encouraging a raccoon to abandon an attic or chimney is by far preferable to the excited and demanding first response people often have upon discovering these animals are present. On the other hand, the first observation of raccoon damage to crops such as sweet corn demands an immediate reaction because the animal can be expected to revisit the garden and to continue attacking the crop as long as it is available.

EXCLUSION

The only long-term, permanent means of coping with troublesome raccoons is to exclude them from areas where they are unwanted. Raccoons are intelligent animals with routines that are dictated by their needs; if they cannot get a meal at one place they will look elsewhere, and they will remember where they can and cannot expect to have their hunger satisfied. Tragically, unthinking individuals will feel the only solution is to put out a live trap, catch the raccoon and destroy or relocate it. Before too long, another raccoon moves into the area and the cycle begins all over again.

DEALING WITH RACCOON YOUNG

Many situations with raccoons in chimneys and attics involve raccoon families. Raccoons are born blind and helpless, but noisy, and frequently the first indication that raccoons are present is when these kits begin to make noise. They are entirely unable to fend for themselves for a long period of time after birth and usually do not even venture out of the den until eight or nine weeks of age. For many weeks after that the mother is the teacher and protector, and she must be allowed to remain with them. Like cats, mother raccoons will carry their young to a new den if the old is uninhabitable. In virtually all habitats, but especially cities and suburbs, raccoons have alternate den sites to which they will move if disturbed. The mother will move young even when not disturbed; as they become mobile she takes them to new places as part of their general education.

When a mother raccoon with young is present, the recommended course of action is to leave them alone for the few weeks that the young are helpless, monitor them to determine when they have moved on their own accord and deal with the issue of securing or preventing entry and use of the chimney or attic after the family has left. In emergencies, gentle harassment may cause the mother to relocate her young, but there is always the chance that one or more youngsters may be abandoned in this process. Trapping and moving the family will almost inevitably lead to separation and the probable death of the young. And invasive techniques, including the use of smoke or fire to drive animals out of chimneys, can lead to the mother's abandonment of the site and death of young, who are physically unable to climb.

CHIMNEYS

Raccoons will use uncapped chimneys for denning and to give birth and raise young. The fireplace flue, because it has a horizontal smoke shelf just above the damper, is usually preferred. All flues should be checked, monitored and secured preferably prior to their ever being occupied. The steps in inspecting and capping a chimney are described in Chapter 3. Because raccoons are nocturnal, the best time to use repellents or frightening strategies to get them out of a chimney is right before the animal would normally start its nightly routine. Driving an animal out of a chimney or attic during the day should be avoided. During the day, raccoons are more easily confused and more vulnerable than at night, as well as more likely to come into contact with people or their pets should they be evicted.

ATTICS

The attic should be inspected to determine where access is occurring, and the opening should be sealed once the raccoon is evicted or leaves the premises. Where raccoons have long been in residence and feces (scats) have accumulated in an attic or crawl space, care must be taken to avoid exposure to the eggs of the roundworm described previously. Protective clothing and a dust mask should be worn and scat material as little disturbed as possible until the raccoons have left. Then, a thorough cleanup is recommended, following the procedures described in Chapter 2.

INSIDE THE HOUSE

Occasionally, raccoons will enter a house through a pet door and be unable to find their way out. Because they can cause considerable damage when they are panicked, it is advisable upon encountering such a situation to keep both yourself and the raccoon as calm as possible. Move slowly, if it can be done safely, close doors providing access to other parts of the house, open windows and doors through which the raccoon could exit and wait quietly for the animal to make its escape. If for any reason the animal does not leave, call animal control for assistance. The capture and handling of live raccoons should be attempted only by properly equipped professionals.

YARDS

Besides eating plants, tipping over garbage cans and climbing on and around houses, raccoons can also damage lawns by digging in search of earthworms and grubs. The most easily damaged lawns are those that have been recently sodded. Because new lawns have to be well irrigated, lots of worms and grubs collect under the sod. This attracts raccoons and sometimes skunks. Often they may simply reach under the strips and feel around for their meal, pulling out the grubs and worms without any disturbance at all. Occasionally, they tear up the sod and cause significant damage. On a small area, an application of a hot sauce (capsaicin) repellent (see "Chemical Repellents" in Chapter 3) may be effective.

GARDENS

Raccoons often cause considerable damage to garden fruits and vegetables, such as grapes and corn. Attacks often occur just before foods are ready to be picked, so ex-

tra vigilance at these times (chasing animals away and using lights or radios to create disturbances) may drive them off long enough to harvest the crop. Single-strand electric fencing can be used effectively where damage is frequent and raccoons are numerous.

PONDS

With the increasing popularity of ornamental ponds in many yards, problems with raccoons are mounting. Naturally attracted to water, visiting raccoons will catch and eat fish, frogs or other aquatic life that a homeowner may be trying to raise. They will further tear up plants in search of food and generally make a mess of most small ponds once they have discovered them. Depending on the size of the pond, fish can be provided with protection by using stacking cinder blocks (the kind with the holes) next to one another in groups of three or four, piling rocks so that shelters are created or sinking sections of the ceramic tile that is used to line chimneys so that fish can take refuge when the raccoon visits. Ponds should be at least 3 feet deep at places in order for shelters to work effectively. Disturbance of plants and other unwanted activities can be deterred in extreme cases by erecting single-strand electric fencing around the pond at anywhere from 4 to 8 inches off the ground (see Figure 25, page 158).

RACCOONS AND DOMESTIC ANIMALS

On occasion raccoons will kill small animals housed outside, such as chickens and rabbits, and they will sometimes get into scraps with dogs and even cats. Pets such as cats and dogs should not be let out unsupervised and, preferably, should be kept on a leash and controlled. Encounters between raccoons and pets should be treated very seriously, with consultation with the animal's veterinarian and local animal control officials

Figure 25. *This homeowner has installed a single-strand electric fence to deter nightly visits from raccoons. Once the local raccoons have been exposed to it a time or two, the fence very likely can be deactivated until signs of new visits occur. A pile of rocks in the center of this pond also provides a refuge for the fish being kept there, which is always a good idea.*

to ensure that pets either have proper protection or that follow-up procedures to a potential exposure are adequate.

When rabbits or other small animals are housed outdoors, proper protection is absolutely necessary. Heavy-gauge welded wire (see Chapter 3) can be used to protect rabbit hutches if it is firmly enough attached with metal staples. Finer mesh wire should be laid on top of the welded wire wherever a raccoon could reach in. If possible, pets should be brought into the house or a secure outbuilding at night to avoid any chance of raccoon attack.

A Last Word

The advantage and success we have indirectly given raccoons by changing the landscape in their favor comes at a cost to them. Both rabies and canine distemper take a toll on urban raccoon populations. They currently have no protection against canine distemper, other than the gradual process of selection that undoubtedly will favor animals that have some degree of natural immunity. There is a vaccine that can be delivered to raccoons in the form of fish meal baits that will immunize them against rabies. It is being tried experimentally in a few places, but has not yet been considered for wide-scale use. The reason for this is partly economics, partly the sort of "who cares" attitude that exists toward urban wildlife and partly that our resources in the field of public health are urgently needed elsewhere at the current moment. Again, it is likely that some naturally immune raccoons will escape rabies and that their populations will rebuild quickly. Several future scenarios will tell where the interaction between this wild animal and the diseases might go, but none of these predict the demise of the raccoon. If any animal is here to stay, it is this one.

Additional Source

MacClintock, D. 1981. *A Natural History of Raccoons.* New York: Charles Scribner's Sons. 144 pp.

27

Rats

Widespread throughout North America, but most prevalent where humans and their buildings abound.

Found both inside and outside buildings, at landfills, waste sites and in industrial areas.

The second most successful mammal on the planet— undoubtedly trying for first.

OUR CONFLICTS WITH RATS are as old as civilization itself. No animals have been greater objects of vilification by more human cultures past and present than rats, and no animal has more successfully held its own in the face of determined attempts to eradicate it. Members of one of the most diverse and successful mammalian families, rats are hardy, intelligent and (like humans) accomplished in adapting to changing circumstances. Unknowing carriers of disease and invaders of stored grains, rats do at times present real threats to humanity. Accordingly, with damage worldwide running into hundreds of millions of dollars annually and countless billions of dollars over the long term, it is amazing that so few resources have been invested in the study of environmentally and ecologically sound ways to deal with these animals.

It's disturbing that the usual means of controlling rat problems involve brute force: trapping, poisoning or, as is done periodically in parts of China, mobilizing thousands into a workforce to drive rats into the open and club them to death. The usual consequence of such acts is the return, shortly, to the condition that prevailed before, or one slightly worse. If nothing is done to address the root ecological cause of problems with rats, then we will forever be locked in a hopeless cycle of short-term *non*solutions.

Natural History

Classification and Range

There are several types of animals people commonly call rats that are found in North America, including woodrats and packrats (*Neotoma* spp.) found mostly in the East and West and the cotton rats (*Sigmodon* spp.) of the South. The two that most concern humans are the Norway or brown (*Rattus norvegicus*) and black or roof (*R. rattus*) rats, which were introduced from the Old World. Both belong to the family *Muridae*, which comprises fifty-one species, including seven that are of economic concern to humans. Black rats probably arrived in the United States as stowaways with the first permanent European settlers. Norway rats are said to have first arrived in the New World around 1775, when they started their own revolution by displacing their less aggressive cousins (black rats) wherever the two met. Today, the Norway rat has become established almost continent-wide, while the black rat is mostly restricted to coastal areas of the southern, southeastern and western United States.

Physically, rats do not appear more imposing than many mammals, but they are incredibly hardy and capable of physical feats that would seem beyond the ability of creatures so small. An opening no larger than a quarter is sufficient to allow an adult rat to gain entry to a building, and both species climb well enough to use a pipe or conduit within 3 inches of an outside wall to gain access at any level. Rats are capable of vertical leaps of as much as 3 feet and horizontal leaps of 4 feet. They are excellent swimmers and the tales of Norway rats emerging in toilet bowls after swimming up through plumbing, while rare, appear to be true. The Norway rat is slightly larger than the black rat, averaging 10 to 16 ounces, while its smaller cousin runs between 8 and 12 ounces. Black rats are more slender than Norway rats and have more pointed muzzles and larger eyes relative to body size. The Norway rat's tail is shorter than its head and body combined, while the black rat's is longer.

Habitat

Norway rats are found almost everywhere humans are but are most common in older denser settlements where food and shelter are abundant. Neither species apparently copes well with natural grass or woodlands, where predators abound and competition from native species is keen. In cities, Norway and black rats favor small municipal

Rat Tracks

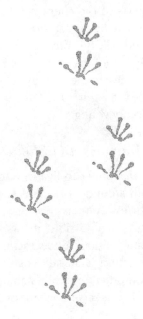

parks where humans inadvertently leave food in refuse containers. Older industrial areas, rail yards and back alleys provide excellent habitat. The common Hollywood image of hordes of rats in sewers or abandoned warehouses is not realistic unless highly unusual environmental conditions exist, including superabundant food resources provided by humans through improper trash management.

Diet

Rats are *omnivorous*—they will eat a wide range of plant and animal foods. Adults require about 1 ounce of food a day and need access to some supply of water. In the winter, seed spilled from bird feeders can be an important source of food, as can pet food left outside. Norway rats tend to eat more animal matter than do black rats, and will consume insects, meat refuse, bird eggs and even pounce on small mammals such as mice.

Reproduction

Rats breed year-round, although peak breeding in parts of the country with dramatic seasonal changes probably occurs during the spring and fall. Breeding age is reached at two to three months, and litter size averages eight to twelve in the Norway rat and five to six in the black rat. One female can wean about twenty young a year.

Dens, Burrows and Shelter

Norway rats prefer to live in burrows that are usually around 18 inches deep and 3 feet long. Burrow systems may have multiple openings that, if possible, are placed so that the entrance abuts a solid structure—building foundation, sidewalk edge, rock, tree root or any other physically stable platform. Some entrances serve as escape or bolt holes and may be loosely closed with soil or located in dense vegetation to foil easy detection. The main entrances are usually marked by a well-worn path that leads up to them. In buildings, Norway rats will live inside walls, under stacked lumber or other construction material and anywhere human clutter is allowed to build up. Black rats are accomplished climbers and are found in the upper levels of buildings more often than Norway rats. They often build loose spherical nests of shredded material in trees or vines well above the ground.

Behavior

Rats are wary of new objects (neophobic) in their environment, which makes them difficult to trap. We are just beginning to realize how complex the behavior and social organization of rats is. Little is known about their home range preferences and the ways in which they utilize their habitats, but what we do know is intriguing. Norway and black rats utilize areas of about 75 to 500 feet in diameter as a typical home range, although this might vary greatly depending on the location and availability of necessary resources such as food. We know that Norway rats will travel a half mile or more in a single night to use a reliable source of food. Black rats live more off the ground than do Norway rats, nesting in trees and other structures above ground and using electrical and telephone wires to move about as squirrels do. Both species are largely nocturnal, although, as is true for other urban species, this may largely be a conventional adoption of a behavioral routine to avoid humans. Rats seen during the day are said to reflect a high population density, and usually are juveniles that must take the risk of exposure because they cannot compete with adults.

Public Health

Rats are implicated as carriers or transmitters of more diseases of importance to humans than any other organism, except possibly the mosquito. Physical attacks in the form of rat bites exceed fifteen thousand annually in the United States and often involve very young, old or incapacitated people. Rat bites should be treated by a physician.

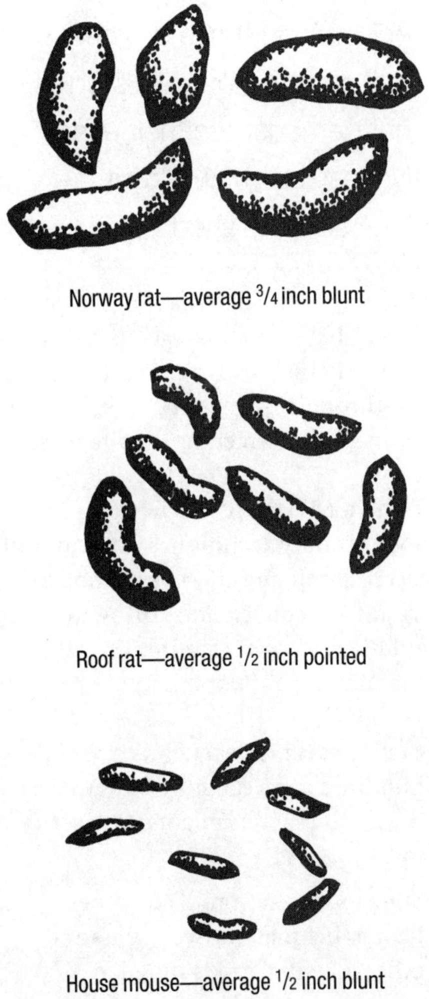

Norway rat—average $3/4$ inch blunt

Roof rat—average $1/2$ inch pointed

House mouse—average $1/2$ inch blunt

Figure 26. *Droppings, or scats, of rats and mice can help homeowners tell which is present.*

Among the diseases that can be spread from rats to humans are bubonic plague, salmonella, leptospirosis, hantavirus and tularemia.

Problems and Their Solutions

Problems

Rats damage human food more through contamination with their urine and feces than by consumption, and can cause structural damage and disfigurement in many ways. Burrowing is potentially damaging, although usually the problem is more cosmetic than structural because burrow systems are instinctively built to remain stable and to not allow water to enter. Gnawing can be a dangerous problem when electrical wires are attacked. Rats can and do gnaw through materials as dense as lead pipe, meaning that most woods are not impediments to them at all.

Identifying Rat Signs

It is important to recognize the signs rats make and what the evidence of their presence says about their possible abundance. Inside buildings, rats may make their presence evident from droppings (see Figure 26). Gnawed holes in baseboards or at door frames up to 2 inches wide and smudge marks left from body oils when the rat rubs along walls are also signs of their presence. (Rats are thigmotaxic—they feel secure when pressed against something and will move about a room pressed to the wall whenever possible.) In heavy infestations, rats are often heard in walls and attics or observed during daylight hours, and the excitement of a cat or dog can be the first sign of their presence. Outside, burrows are an indicator, although these could be confused with the burrows of other animals such as ground squirrels and chipmunks. Sometimes "burrows" turn out to be just holes in the ground put there by some other source. Loosely filling any suspected burrow entrance with soil or leaves and checking it within a day or two to see if it is reopened will determine current use.

Solutions

The key to managing rat populations lies in reducing the availability of shelter, food and water. It is problematic whether this can be done without killing animals, but it is beyond a certainty that killing should *never* occur without ensuring that the chance of rats returning to be a problem is minimized and the killing occurs humanely. The practice of good sanitation, removal of cover and the exclusion of rats from buildings ideally should occur *before* they invade structures or establish a presence on property where they are not wanted. Direct removal by lethal means comes as the unfortunate consequence of inattentiveness and letting things go too far.

EXCLUSION

Rats can access buildings through holes as little as 1 inch wide—about the size of a quarter. All such holes and openings should be sealed with heavy-weight material ($1/4$-inch hardware cloth or heavy-gauge screening is recommended). Heating vents often are overlooked as points of entry, and they should be checked to ensure that access through them by rats is not possible. Anywhere electrical conduits, utility or air conditioning lines enter a building, the hole that has been made needs to be checked for gaps that will allow entry. Wire mesh (see Chapter 3) can be used to plug openings in walls and floors through which rats might gain entry. Aluminum window screen can be

---

Ultrasound: Does It Work?

Ultrasonic devices are widely advertised in aggressive presentations that purport to relieve homeowners of everything from mice and rats to silverfish. The Humane Society of the United States will not recommend these devices until scientifically valid studies that demonstrate their effectiveness in real-world situations are published.

---

wadded and stuffed in openings to deter rat entry. Caulking or foam sealants can be used to seal openings also, but because rats can gnaw through them, they are best when combined with screening or wire mesh.

HABITAT MODIFICATION

Proper sanitary techniques constitute the most economic and effective method to limiting rat presence. The following steps should be followed to minimize attracting or maintaining rat populations:

- Mow grass and clear debris close to buildings to reveal burrows as well as openings that rats might use to get inside.

- Store food in rat-proof containers. Remember that birdseed, grass and other potential foods stored in garages and buildings frequently attract these animals.

- Store and dispose of garbage properly so that rats cannot gain access.

- Do not leave pet food outside. If pets are fed outside, leave the food out for twenty minutes and then remove it.
- Remove old wood or debris piles if rats are a problem—these are frequent havens for these animals.

Where rat infestation has been and continues to be a problem around buildings, the long-term solution to preventing burrowing along foundations can be addressed by creating an L-shaped footer of either hardware cloth or concrete. Bury the footer about 12 inches and extend it from the foundation about another 12 inches (see Figure 11, p. 35). Although rats may begin to dig at the foundation, they will encounter this obstacle, dig down and, frustrated, give up.

A Last Word

The war between humans and rats will go on for some time. The discovery of effective and economic alternatives to the traditional short-term displays of force used to control rats will not occur spontaneously. Only by a better understanding of their natural history and their dependency on environments created by humans are we likely to discover ways of minimizing the damage they do and the problems they cause.

Additional Source

Hart, M. 1973. *Rats*. New York: Allison and Busby. 712 pp.

28

Skunks

Found throughout almost all of North America; absent only from the far North.

Conflicts occur in yards and when skunks take up residence under buildings.

Chicago is a term deriving from a Fox Indian word for "place of the skunk," suggesting, for reasons unknown, that these animals were once abundant there.

SKUNKS, OF COURSE, ARE KNOWN to most people as the producers of an odor so powerful that it brings everything from elephants to comic book characters to an abrupt and humorous stop. "Don't mess with me" is the message these animals communicate. Their primary defense is a complex chemical substance that includes sulfuric acid and can be "fired" from either one of two independently targetable anal glands. A person or animal hit in the eyes will experience an intense discomfort that reminds them long after the pain is gone that they have crossed a skunk. The efficiency of this defense means that skunks inherently will stand and face a threat rather than try to escape it. This works when the enemy is another animal that can be dissuaded from completing an attack, but is useless against nonrational contrivances such as automobiles. Consequently, many skunks die on roadways, and their kind may possibly disappear entirely from areas with a lot of traffic. This is unfortunate because skunks are placid and retiring animals that try hard not to get in harm's way.

They deserve much better press than they usually get and are beneficial to humans because they eat many insect pests.

Natural History

Classification and Range

There are four general kinds of skunks found in the United States. All are members of the group of animals termed *mustelids* that includes weasels, martens and badgers. The spotted *(Spilogale putorius)* and striped *(Mephitis mephitis)* skunks are the most widely distributed and most likely to be involved in skunk-human conflict situations. The hooded *(M. macroura)* and hog-nosed *(Conepatus mesoleucus* and *C. leuconotus)* skunks are mostly limited to the southwestern states of Arizona, New Mexico and Texas. There are, as for many mammalian groups, ongoing debates about taxonomic relationships. The spotted skunks may parse into eastern and western *(S. gracilis)* species, and some who have studied skunks feel the hog-nosed and spotted are essentially the same animal. Whatever the case, all skunks are about cat-size or smaller and have long fur, long bushy tails and black and white coloration that tells the viewer that this animal is, indeed, to be treated with respect.

Habitat

In the East, the spotted skunk is thought to have a preference for agricultural landscapes and spends much of its life in or near farmyards, but the other species are adaptable to a variety of open, scrub, wooded and developed habitats. Normally, skunks do not engage in long movements and have home ranges that encompass a few hundred acres at most. Skunks are primarily nocturnal and usually solitary, except when mothers appear with offspring in tow. Skunks can be active all year, although they remain in dens through the coldest spells in the northern parts of their range.

Diet

Skunks are primarily *insectivorous*, and of the many kinds of insects they eat, a fair number are pests to humans. Some plant material is eaten, primarily wild fruits, and apples and corn are occasional dietary items. In winter and spring, skunks may consume small vertebrates, such as mice, and the eggs of ground-nesting birds.

Reproduction

Not as much is known about reproduction in the other skunk species as is the striped skunk, but apparently all skunks are capable of delayed implantation, meaning that after mating, the female can store the male's sperm and delay initiating pregnancy for some weeks. Breeding usually occurs in late winter or early spring (probably between February and March for striped and between March and April for spotted). Gestation also varies in length, but averages about sixty to seventy-five days, meaning that young usually are born in May or June. Second litters and late births do occur, and the western spotted skunk appears to breed in fall and early winter but not give birth until the following spring. Litters range from three to as many as ten young, who remain in the burrow or nest for about two months, after which they begin to follow their mother as she forages.

Dens and Shelter

All skunks seem able to dig their own burrows, but when some other animal or humans have done the work for them, they appear content with what is at hand. Favorite den and resting sites include abandoned groundhog burrows, hollow logs, wood or rock piles, under buildings, stone walls, hay or brush piles and (occasionally) trees or stumps. A den may be used only for brief periods before the skunk switches to another.

Public Health

Skunks can carry rabies, and one of the main strains of this disease in skunks occurs throughout the states of the Midwest. Skunks have also been known to carry leptospirosis.

Problems and Their Solutions

Problems

Skunks are usually announced more by smell than sight, although if neither of these cues gives them away, sometimes their scat does. These are more or less indiscriminately deposited and usually show high concentrations of insect parts that impart a dark shiny appearance. Musk odor may linger for days in the area where a skunk has sprayed. Persistent, faint musk smells associated with a 4- to 6-inch diameter hole under a building or woodpile indicates that a skunk may have taken up residence. While foraging for grubs, skunks may dig many shallow holes in the lawn, similar to those made by both gray squirrels and raccoons. Long black or white hairs or a faint skunky odor will suggest skunks but not confirm them. Long-haired cats can leave long black or white hairs, and foxes have a musky odor. Skunks occasionally raid chicken houses for eggs or young chickens and all too frequently are encountered when they become trapped in window wells.

Solutions

TOLERANCE

It may be hard for people to tolerate skunks once it has been found that they are, indeed, living under the deck or piled in a communal den underneath the old shed out back. But this is exactly what skunks have to do when they are most vulnerable (during the winter and when raising young). The nocturnal habits of skunks, their nonaggressive and retiring ways and the generally beneficial role they play in consuming harmful insects all give them enough credits to make it worth leaving them alone until they have moved on their own accord (which they readily do) or can safely be harassed away from an area where they are not wanted.

HABITAT MODIFICATION

Occasional skunk sightings in a neighborhood need not be cause for alarm. Preventive measures, such as removing attractants from the vicinity of houses, will decrease the likelihood of an unpleasant encounter. Attractants include garbage and pet food left out at night and convenient denning sites such as wood and rock piles, elevated sheds, openings under concrete slabs and porches and access to crawl spaces under houses.

EXCLUSION

Discovery of a den suspected to harbor a skunk should first be checked to determine if the occupancy is current. This may be done by loosely filling the hole (or holes) with soil, leaves or material such as straw. If a skunk is present, it will easily push its way out that night and reopen the hole. If the plug remains undisturbed for two or three nights (and it is not winter), it is safe to assume that the hole is unoccupied and can be permanently closed. If a skunk (or any other animal) *is* present, either harass-

---

One-Way Doors

Do not install a one-way door in May or June when there may be babies left behind in the den. The babies will starve and possibly discharge their spray before succumbing to this unpleasant fate. Instead, either wait for the skunk family to move or use mild harassment to try to accelerate that process. The mother skunk will, under the right circumstances, carry her babies to a new den. Do not permanently seal the opening until the plug remains undisturbed for several nights.

---

ment or eviction using a one-way door system is recommended.

HARASSMENT

When it is safe to displace skunks, mild harassment can be very effective. This can consist of an approach as simple as repacking the hole it is using with the leaves or straw or other material to see if the skunk gets the message and moves elsewhere, or using mild repellents, such as ammonia-soaked rags, placed near or inside the burrow to one side so that the skunk has to pass them in getting out. In all cases such as this, make sure the skunk is not close by before placing the disturbing stimulus.

EVICTION

A skunk may be evicted from an active den by installing a one-way door over the entrance to allow it to leave but prevent reentry (see Figure 10, page 33). Care must be taken to ensure that the door can open without hitting an obstruction. Leave the door in place for two or three nights to be sure that the skunk has left. Be sure that no new holes appear nearby. Remove the door and close the opening as described under "Exclusion" on page 169.

Exclusion is also the only long-term solution to skunk predation on chickens or eggs. In this case skunks must be excluded from the chicken house, and the chickens must be securely enclosed in the coop at night. All openings must be repaired, and fencing around the coop should be extended 6 to 8 inches underground to prevent skunks from digging underneath.

SKUNK IN A WINDOW WELL

If a skunk becomes trapped in a window well (the basement window area), the best method of freeing it is to provide it with a means of escape. In the well, place a rough board (or one with cleats) that is long enough to act as a ramp to the top (see Figure 27). The board should lean no steeper than a 45° angle. The board should be slowly and carefully placed by approaching the well low enough to be out of sight of the skunk. If possible, a second person with a vantage point high enough to see the skunk can warn of any signs of its becoming agitated, indicated by the skunk raising its tail or stamping its front feet. If this happens, an immediate retreat and reanalysis of the situation is recommended. Another method of placing the board is to tie it to the end of a long pole and lower it by holding the opposite end of the pole. Once the board is

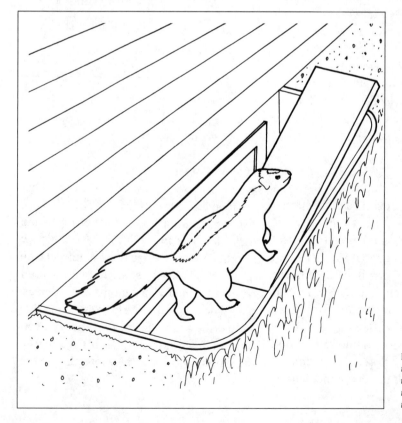

Figure 27. A ramp can help a trapped skunk out of a window well. It's a good idea not to let the family dog get involved in this procedure!

What Smell?

Skunk odor on pets may be neutralized with liberal amounts of vinegar or tomato juice. This will make the odor tolerable— only time will eliminate it. A reported deodorant recipe for skunk spray that can be used on animals and clothes is

> 1 quart of 3% hydrogen
>   peroxide
> 1/4 cup baking soda
> 1 teaspoon liquid soap
>   (laundry or
>   dishwashing soap)

Chlorine bleach, ammonia or commercial products containing neutroleum alpha may be used on inanimate objects (do not use this on any living thing). Carbolic soap and water are safe to use on skin. Liberal flushing with cold water will ease the discomfort of skunk spray in the eyes. And at least two commercial products are available (see "Odor Control" in Appendix 2).

placed, keep people and pets away from the area until nightfall, when the skunk should leave on its own. To prevent this situation from reoccurring, place exit ramps or tight-fitting covers at each window well.

A Last Word

People remember encounters with skunks, whether or not they are sprayed. It is common knowledge among those who work closely with these animals that it actually takes a lot to get sprayed, although those who do undoubtedly consider it no sort of honor. How many skunks are killed each year in the United States just because someone's afraid of being sprayed is not known but is surely a large number. Hopefully, we will become better educated and more tolerant of these animals in the future, and recognize their role and place as part of the natural scene, even in the town and city.

Additional Source

Rosatte, R. C. 1987. "Striped, Spotted, Hooded and Hog-nosed Skunk." In M. Novak, J. A. Baker, M. E. Obbard, and B. Malloch (eds.), *Wild Furbearer Management and Conservation in North America*. Ontario: Ministry of Natural Resources. 599–613.

29

Snakes

Snakes are widely
distributed throughout
North America and are found
in almost every habitat except
the Arctic tundra.

Usually encountered in yards;
occasionally enter buildings in
search of mice or insects.

Rattlesnakes will move more
than a mile in the fall to
traditional hibernation dens
shared year after year with
dozens, sometimes hundreds,
of other rattlesnakes.

SNAKES INSTILL SUCH DEEP-ROOTED FEAR in so
many people that it may be the feeling is instinctive.
In fact, many wild animals clearly recognize snakes as
threatening, and some birds and monkeys even have
special vocalizations for sounding alarm when a snake
is sighted. Small mammals have reason to fear snakes,
and all but the very largest animals would do well to
be cautious around the few snakes that are poisonous. But the persecution of these animals and the acts
of violence often committed when even the most innocuous of them
is sighted have a lot more to do with societal and cultural prejudices
than anything else. Learning to accept snakes may take a while, but
learning to tolerate an occasional crossing of paths and to use the
simple and expedient methods available to deal with any problems
these animals might pose is currently within our grasp.

Natural History

Classification and Range

Snakes are reptiles and belong to the group of animals that do not
produce heat internally as mammals do but must rely on outside
(ambient) temperatures to reach a certain minimum before they can
be very active. There are about 250 species and subspecies of snakes

in the United States, each with its own distinct markings, life history and habitat requirements. Snakes always try to avoid contact with people. Of those that share human habitats, the vast majority are harmless.

There are four types of poisonous snakes in the United States: the copperhead, the coral snake, the rattlesnake and the water moccasin. Only rattlesnakes are likely to be of much concern in urban and suburban areas, and then only in parts of the West and Southwest. Reptile field guides and local nature centers can tell you which poisonous and common nonpoisonous snakes occur in your area and how to identify them.

Senses

Snakes cannot hear airborne sounds, but they are very sensitive to substrate vibrations. They have what amounts to an auxiliary sense of smell by which they use their tongue and specialized organs in the mouth to detect chemical changes. Some poisonous snakes have special heat receptors that help them locate warm-blooded prey. Vision is poor in some species while good in others. All snakes are carnivores, eating small mammals such as mice, insects, small birds or even other snakes.

Habitat

Each species of snake has a unique natural history and set of habitat requirements. Snakes must have access to cover, and many species prefer to be close to standing and running water. Wood and brush piles, stone walls and unmowed fields all provide snake habitat. Because food draws most snakes into contact with humans, places where mice and insects abound are most likely to be where human-snake encounters occur.

Public Health

Snakes are not known to transmit any disease to humans. Nonpoisonous snakebites that break the skin should be treated like any puncture wound with a potential for infection, preferably with the consultation of a physician. Victims of poisonous bites should stay calm and inactive, if possible, and should seek a doctor immediately. Physicians now urge people not to administer first aid for a snakebite—procedures such as cutting open the bite sites and bleeding the wound can do more harm than good. Snakebites from poisonous snakes are rarely fatal, and if transport to a hospital can occur quickly after a bite is received, this is now considered the best response possible.

Problems and Their Solutions

Problems

Snakes do not cause damage to structures or other property, nor do they eat any plant or crop foods that humans raise. On occasion, some of the larger species cause problems around poultry houses and might take chicks or eggs, but, except for the poisonous varieties, human pets are invariably more of a threat to snakes than snakes are to them.

Solutions

TOLERANCE

Most encounters with snakes are fleeting; people who enjoy seeing snakes are often denied for years the satisfaction of this actually happening. The first rule for dealing with any encounter with a snake is to leave it alone, identify it by species and then continue to leave it alone as long as it is not poisonous and isn't inside a house or building where not wanted. Virtually all outdoor encounters with nonpoisonous snakes should be resolved by letting the animal go its own way. The chances that the snake will ever be seen again are fairly small, and if it does reappear this only means that the mice or insects that attract it are still present, and it is doing the homeowner a service. Poisonous snakes, on the other hand, should not be left in residential yards. Encounters with these species should be taken seriously and the snakes removed to ensure that children, pets or even adults do not come to harm. *This does not mean the snake has to be killed.* In many places, animal and pest control operators, and sometimes even police or fire departments, will remove and relocate poisonous snakes to places where they are not likely to come into contact with humans.

EXCLUSION

Exclusion of snakes usually refers to keeping snakes out of buildings. There are designs published for snake "fences" that can be used to surround yards, gardens or any other outside area, but the need for such structures is questionable. Snakes in houses fall into two categories: those that entered accidentally and will be attempting to escape because they find the habitat unsuitable and those that have entered to find prey or shelter and would take up permanent residence if allowed. The former includes most of the very small snakes that may be considered trapped and will likely die from lack of food or moisture if not captured and removed. Snakes that may become residents include rat, king and black snakes that often follow mouse trails into buildings. Some snakes may hibernate in older houses with leaky cellars or crawl spaces with dirt floors. The presence of shed skin usually indicates that a snake has been living in the house for some time.

When a snake is discovered in a house, remain calm and avoid any act that might disturb it and drive it into hiding. It may be possible to carefully open a nearby door and use a broom to gently, but quickly, herd it out. Or, it may be possible to place an empty pail or wastebasket slowly over a small or coiled snake and then put a weight on it to trap the snake until an experienced handler can come to remove it (which should be as soon as possible, both for the snake's benefit and for the homeowner's peace of mind). If the snake can be confined in a room or corner with barriers such as boards or boxes, it will be available to be captured when the expert arrives.

Once the snake has been captured, the homeowner can proceed to snake-proof the property. Snakes usually enter a house or other building at ground level, the smallest individuals perhaps through a tiny crack or hole no more than $1/8$ inch wide. An intensive inspection of the foundation for unsealed wire or pipe conduits or basement windows or doors that do not seal tightly will usually reveal the snake entrance. All such openings should be sealed immediately. The techniques used to deter snakes from entering houses are exactly the same used to deter rodents from entering.

Resident snakes may be extremely difficult to locate and capture, even by an expert, because they are capable of retreating for long periods (weeks) inside walls or in other inaccessible locations in the building. Also, there may be more than one snake inhabiting the same house. After the discovery of a snake in a house, the entire house should be inspected inside and outside to evaluate the situation. The interior inspection should be concentrated on the basement and first floor, but without neglecting the attic (larger snakes will often climb inside the walls and emerge in an unfinished attic). The purpose of the inspection is not only to look for snakes but also for potential openings that allow snakes to enter into rooms.

Next, inspect the exterior of the house for possible entrances, particularly at or near ground level. Keep in mind the size of the snake that was discovered and look for any opening large enough for the snake's head to pass through. Many snakes are also good climbers, so check for plantings that may give access to the roof. A fieldstone wall or chimney may also be climbed by a snake. If such access is present, check for openings around the eaves and roof. Another common place of entry is behind concrete porches or steps or where decks attach to the house.

Once the entire exterior has been inspected and one or more openings have been discovered, decide which opening is likely to be the main snake entrance. To determine the snake's route of travel, consider the size of the openings, ease of access by the snake and clear penetration into the area of the house where the snake was discovered. Seal all the openings except the suspected main entrance. On that opening, install a one-way door for snakes that is made from a piece of aluminum window screen rolled into a cylinder about 10 inches long and with a slightly larger diameter than the entrance hole. With the outlet end of the tube suspended off the ground, the returning snake will not be able to find the opening and will be forced to find another hiding place. It may be left in place for a month or longer to allow time for the snake to leave. If it is fall when the tube is installed, leave it in place until well into the following spring. After removing the tube, permanently seal the opening.

Habitat Management

Homeowners can minimize the chance of a snake taking up residence in the yard by making the area less attractive to it. This means removing potential hiding places for snakes and their prey, such as piles of rocks, wood or other debris, tall grass and undergrowth, cracks around concrete porches and sidewalks and storage sheds with space under the floor. Pet foods and household garbage left outside overnight attract rodents, and, in turn, the presence of rats or mice may attract snakes.

Repellents

There is currently one commercially marketed repellent for snakes (Snake-A-Way®) (see "Chemical Repellents" in Chapter 3) and a long list of home repellents, ranging from sisal rope to sulfur, have been claimed to be effective.

To our knowledge, no scientific studies have been conducted to prove the effectiveness of any product to humanely repel snakes.

A Last Word

In addition to the persecution they experience routinely at human hands, snakes have suffered greatly from the habitat alterations we have created. They and their amphibian cousins fare poorly when we break up natural lands for urban and suburban development and isolate animals that cannot easily move across inhospitable terrain. Many species are either already gone or are rapidly disappearing from urban and suburban environments, and the issue of human-snake conflicts has essentially become moot in many places. Whether some species adapt to the changing conditions wrought by humans remains to be seen. Certainly they will not do so as long as our irrational fears about them dominate us so unmercifully.

30

Starlings

Widespread throughout all of North America; common in cities.

Yards and houses; frequently build nests where people don't want them.

Starling song is quite complex, including a series of whistling notes, chatter and a clear wolf whistle that is somewhat scandalous.

STARLINGS WERE INTRODUCED INTO NORTH AMERICA in 1890, when an enterprising New Yorker named Eugene Schieffelin had about a hundred of these birds brought over from England to be released into Central Park. It seems Mr. Schieffelin and a small group of like-minded friends had a passionate interest in introducing into this country all of the animals mentioned in the works of Shakespeare. They started with birds, but attempts with types such as the lark ended in failure. Not so with the starling. From the initial hundred, their population numbers are in the hundreds of millions now. Starlings join with native grackles and blackbirds at certain times of the year to form huge flocks that can be serious problems to agriculture. It is the built environments of cities and towns that seem to be the ideal habitat for these birds, however. There they outcompete many native birds and alter the balance of nature so much that we really have no idea what it might be like without them.

Natural History

Classification and Range

The European starling *(Sternus vulgaris)* is about 8 to 8 1/2 inches in length, with a relatively short tail and a bold orange-yellow beak. Starlings are members of a very large and diverse group of *passerine* (song) birds found throughout the Old World. The family, which includes the vocal mimics known as myna birds, has some strikingly beautiful members. In fact, a close look at starlings in their best winter plumage reveals them to be fairly attractive birds (once the viewer gets past the learned prejudices that dictate that all starlings are ugly). Juveniles are a uniform mousy brown color, but the adult plumage is a glossy green and purple with white tips on each feather. During the winter, these tips wear away, revealing the iridescent plumage below. The beak is brown in winter but turns brillant yellow with the coming of spring. Females and males are quite similar, with the only good distinguishing mark being a spot at the base of the bill that is reddish in females and bluish in males.

Habitat

Starlings are adept at exploiting urban and suburban environments but also do quite well in agricultural settings. Their original habitat is less well known than some of the other introduced bird species such as the house sparrow and pigeon. Currently, they are one of only a few birds that tolerate areas of high human density and disturbance. Starlings are found in otherwise barren human landscapes around industrial areas and heavily settled commercial zones.

Most of the spring and summer is spent by paired birds in nesting and raising young. The juvenile birds may collect in small flocks soon after they fly from the nest *(fledge)*. Winter flocks of starlings create noisy roosts sometimes numbering more than a million birds.

Diet

Starlings have wide-ranging food tolerances, typical of most urban generalists. They are probably more *insectivorous* than house sparrows and pigeons, as a close look at the bill suggests. Spring flocks of starlings often descend on lawns, much to the dismay of homeowners who feel they are doing damage. The truth is that they are probably doing the homeowner a favor by consuming insect pests. They can do damage, however, by eating fruits people are trying to raise, such as grapes, cherries and raspberries. It is common to see starlings around dumps and landfills, and many seem to specialize in

Starling Tracks

picking through the open dumpsters common around apartments, grocery stores and restaurants. Household trash placed unprotected at the curb is just a snack compared to these steady sources of food, but can attract starlings who think nothing of tearing bags open with their strong bladelike bills. Starlings will visit bird feeders, depending on their hunger and motivation, and will even consume sunflower seeds when millet, suet or other preferred foods are not available.

Reproduction

Starlings court and mate in the early spring and can even be heard in song at this time. Surely, most people do not find this somewhat strident and monotonously repetitious vocalizing to be true song, but to the starling it undoubtedly is. Anywhere from three to eight eggs are laid in each clutch, and a successful pair of adults can nest three times in a year. The young fledge at between two and three weeks of age, but it is not known whether they breed the first year or not.

Nests

Starlings are cavity nesters and will exploit any hole into a suitably sized interior cavity to transport nesting material and set up shop. An ideal nesting site for starlings, and an important problem for people, are dryer, range and bathroom vents. Even when protected by a metal flap, many starlings have learned how to approach and hover or perch while raising covers to these areas to gain access to the interior. The nesting material they pack into such cavities not only impairs the function of the vent but could present a fire hazard as well.

Public Health

The infectious diseases associated with starlings are much the same as those found in pigeons and house sparrows and include histoplasmosis, chlamydiosis and salmonellosis. As for the other urban species, there is little direct evidence linking starlings to disease problems in humans, but the potential for this should not be dismissed.

Problems and Their Solutions

Problems

Outside of the problems they cause in agricultural settings, probably the biggest issue with starlings in urban and suburban areas has to do with their nesting habits. The potential problem with vents has been mentioned, but starling nests built into any house cavity can accumulate material that is unsightly and could represent a fire hazard. The nests built by these birds can be accumulative in that they do not remove material previously brought in but keep adding year after year to what is there. Starlings also cause complaints by getting into the trash, competing with desirable birds at feeders and getting stuck in chimneys and metal flues. Larger environmental problems occur with flocks, which can involve tens of thousands of birds.

Solutions

TOLERANCE
Much of the time, starlings can be tolerated by understanding that their transgressions are only temporary, or that permanent solutions can be carried out once the timing

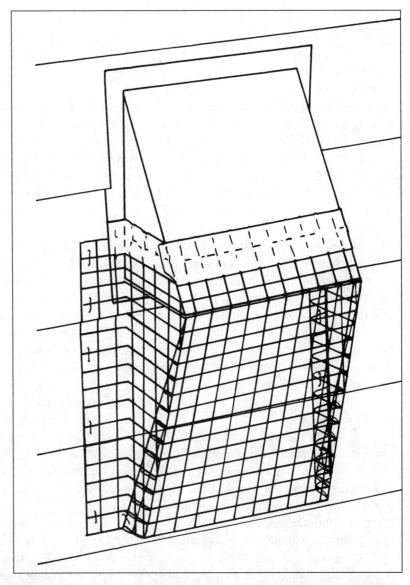

Figure 28. *Dryer vents or exhaust vents from kitchen hoods are often invaded by starlings who build nests in interior cavities. Screening may be one way to prevent this. Here, a rigid, heavy-gauge (1/4 inch) hardware cloth has been fitted around a dryer vent, leaving the bottom open (about a 1/2-inch slot) so that lint can escape. Screening used around a vent should be checked periodically to make sure it is not blocked.*

is right. One example of when starlings should be tolerated comes in the spring, when visiting flocks work over lawns, probing for grubs and cleaning up any insects found among the new growth. They undoubtedly perform a beneficial service to the homeowner. Nesting starlings should be tolerated until the young have fledged. The nest site can then be cleaned and sealed to prevent reuse. Large winter flocks that repeatedly reuse an area to roost may not be tolerated but should not be dispersed without using coordinated intervention strategies under the guidance of bird control experts.

EXCLUSION

As always, exclusion is the method of choice. Starlings that are discovered early in the nesting process, before eggs are laid, can be evicted and the openings they were using sealed with hardware cloth or metal flashing to keep them from being reoccupied. Lighter material, such as plastic netting or window screening, is rarely effective in keeping determined starlings out of a cavity. With their strong bill, they can simply tear lighter material open. Nests that contain young can often be located by the sound of begging nestlings or the characteristic fan-shaped trail of smeared droppings that spot a wall below a corner joint or other sites where a cavity is present. Dryer and range vents can be screened with hardware cloth as illustrated in Figure 28 on page 179.

SCARE DEVICES

Both visual and auditory frightening tactics offer viable approaches to solving problems with starlings. There are a variety of noise-making devices as well as taped-recorded alarm calls sold to frighten these and other birds (see "Bird Distress Calls" and "Acoustical Alarms" in Chapter 3). Visual stimuli such as mirrors, pie tins, revolving lights, colored flags, scare tapes and balloons (see Chapter 3) can also be effective in frightening starlings away from resources to be protected.

REPELLENTS

Polybutenes are registered for use on starlings, but not recommended because of the danger to birds from accumulating the material on their feet and feathers to a point where it can incapacitate them. Avitrol® is widely promoted as a frightening or flock dispersal agent, but is not recommended for the reasons explained under "Toxicants" in Chapter 3.

HABITAT MODIFICATION

The availability of food and nesting cover are elements that can be modified directly in places where starlings are a problem and, ultimately, are essential approaches to try to limit the numbers of these birds. Places where roosting is occurring and found to be intolerable can also be addressed by practices that modify the site to make it less accessible and/or acceptable to the birds. Refuse can be an important source of food for a local population of starlings, and both homeowners and businesses should share in the obligation to control access to dumpsters and household trash to prevent these birds from gaining easy access. Making sure that dumpsters are covered after trash is placed in them and are not routinely overfilled is a great step to limiting access to food, and household trash in covered containers rather than in plastic bags placed along the roadway goes a long way toward limiting starling access.

ROOSTS

Liberal trimming (removing at least 1/3 of all interior branches) of trees at sites where starlings have established roosts can help disperse birds and may be especially effective in conjunction with the use of frightening tactics and other strategies. Generally, large roosts should be controlled by experienced professionals to ensure that birds are effectively dispersed and remain that way. Problems with starling roosts can be very difficult (if even possible) to solve using a single method of control applied over a short period of time.

A Last Word

Consider starlings for their entertainment value. Many of us spend more of our lives than is good for us stopped at traffic lights. The next time you are at a major intersection, look around at the poles, transformers, lights and other structures and see if you can find the starlings using them. There they are, sitting on the wires, flying from pole to pole and occasionally disappearing altogether after they land. Look closely and there are small ports or access hatches that were left ajar or never closed in the first place, and which now make an ideal nesting site for these cavity-loving birds. In the spring, the adult birds can be seen diligently bringing food to nestlings, and at times, the clamor of the young can even be heard over traffic. No predator would ever have access to these nests. The great risk must come when the young are ready to fledge and take that first flight into the void. How many survive this and how many fall into traffic below is unknown, but enough survive to ensure that starlings appear under no threat of diminishing in numbers.

Additional Source

Welty, J. E. 1975. *The Life of Birds.* Philadelphia: W. B. Saunders. 623 pp.

31

Tree
Squirrels

Found throughout most of the United States, excepting the treeless Great Plains and Great Basin areas and into southern Canada.

Commonly associated with yards and homes; will get into attics if given the chance.

Squirrels will not bury acorns with insect parasites in them—their sense of smell is so keen that they recognize these as spoiled and reject them.

WHERE PUBLIC OPINION HAS BEEN POLLED regarding suburban and urban wildlife, squirrels generally rank first as problem makers. Where they don't hold this status it is usually been because there are no squirrels in that part of the country. Even then, it almost seems that their reputation is good enough to pull down at least a few votes. Interestingly, squirrels almost always rank first among preferred urban/suburban wildlife species as well. Such is the paradox they present: we want them and we don't want them, depending on what they are doing at any given moment. Tree squirrels are certainly one of the most successful mammals in accommodating to human-altered environments.

Tree squirrels owe their success to a variety of things, not all of which make good objective sense. Because they have bushy tails and large eyes relative to the size of their heads, squirrels present an image, or *gestalt*, that some animal behaviorists liken to that presented by young animals, including humans. Put simply, they all look like babies, puppies, etc. The relative *neonatal* appearance of squirrels may unconsciously warm people to them. Their close relative—the Norway rat—has a naked tail and small, beady eyes that help evoke a strong negative reaction in people. Of course, there is more to it than that, and squirrels have many engaging and fascinating behavioral traits that help endear them to us. Squirrel watching can be an educational and enriching experience, and thanks to the fact that these animals are active by day, an easy thing to do.

Natural History

Classification and Range

There are an astonishing number of squirrels worldwide, and many are strikingly attractive animals. In North America there are several species that are regarded as "tree" squirrels, in contrast to an even greater variety of "ground" squirrels. The fox squirrel (*Sciurus niger*) and eastern (*S. carolinensis*) and western (*S. griseus*) gray squirrels usually are the species involved in homeowner conflicts. Northern and southern flying squirrels (*Glaucomys volans* and *G. sabrinus*) may also nest in buildings near wooded sites and can occasionally be problems, but not so frequently as their larger cousins. The eastern gray squirrel is about 8 to 10 inches long and has a bushy tail that's almost the same length. Frequently, squirrels sit with the tail arched over the back, allowing the viewer to see that it provides almost complete cover for the body. The gray squirrel can actually be highly varied in coloration and range from a rufous tint to almost pure white, or even an all black or *melanistic* form. The western gray squirrel is a little longer on average, and heavier than the eastern gray, weighing almost 1 3/4 pounds, while the eastern form rarely weighs that much. The fox squirrel, though, is the big-gest of all, and can be as much as 15 inches with a tail almost as long, and weigh up to 3 pounds. The coloration of fox squirrels is as varied as that of the grays but predominantly a rusty yellowish color with a pale yellow or orange belly. In the East some fox squirrels are a striking pure steel gray color.

Habitat

Both fox and gray squirrels traditionally depend on trees, especially oak trees, as places to bear and raise young, take shelter from the weather, find food and escape from predators. As part of their adaptation to human-wrought changes to the landscape, almost anything that looks like a tree can now be used, including the pilings around marinas, nest boxes set out for woodpeckers or kestrels and many places on and in houses. Squirrels have fluidly adapted to the planted and landscaped "forest" of urban and suburban parks and can usually maintain themselves quite well there. They also do well in both urban and suburban neighborhoods, although wherever they are found, they rarely turn down handouts from people.

Diet

The diet of squirrels varies with the seasons and the availability of the plant material that almost entirely makes up their larder. Acorns and other nuts are both eaten and stored underground in the fall and early winter, with the underground storage making up a substantial portion of the winter diet. In the spring, the flowers and growing buds on the terminal ends of branches are eaten, and it is common to see squirrels busily working high in yet leafless trees at this time of the year. In summer, fruits such as mulberry, raspberry and wild cherries are eaten. Some feel that this is actually the hardest time of the year for squirrels, more than spring when buds are a mainstay and fall and winter when mast is collected and consumed. Squirrels do occasionally take bird eggs or nestlings and may even pounce on and kill small birds at feeders, much to the dismay of human witnesses who might have assumed they were passive vegetarians.

Reproduction

The eastern gray and fox squirrels usually have two litters a year. The first breeding period usually begins in December or early January, with young born between February and April after a gestation period of a little more than forty days. A second breeding period begins in early summer, with that litter born in August or September. The western gray squirrel has only one breeding season a year, and young are born between February and June. Courtship is characterized by frantic chases, often with several males pursuing one female. After mating, the female drives the males away and raises the two to five young by herself. The babies are born naked and helpless and do not venture out of the nest for about seven or eight weeks. They are weaned at ten to twelve weeks. The spring litter is usually driven away by the mother shortly after weaning and as the next breeding cycle begins. The fall litter may stay with the mother in the nest through the winter until well after the winter courtship season. Flying squirrels are strictly nocturnal, may share a den with up to twenty other adults (particularly in winter) and breed twice a year in a pattern similar to that of the gray squirrel.

Dens and Shelter

Squirrels use two basic types of natural dens—tree cavities and leaf nests—and take liberal advantage of shelter provided by humans in attics and crawl spaces along the upper floor of buildings. Leaf nests, called dreys in England, need constant repair and do not provide as much protection from weather extremes as do tree cavities.

Seasonal Activity

Both fox and gray squirrels are active during the day *(diurnal)*. Fox squirrels may spend more time on the ground than grays and have been found to use larger home range areas (2 to 30 acres), while grays generally use a much smaller home range (less than 4 acres), but there is a lot of variability to this. Squirrels become active at first light and usually rest in the middle of the day before becoming active again later in the afternoon. These patterns vary, however, depending on weather conditions and other factors. The most remarkable yearly event for gray squirrels from a human perspective is the "fall reshuffle" during which the seasonally frenetic activity of collecting, eating and burying nuts is accentuated by the dispersal of both adults and juveniles, perhaps in search of that "perfect" homesite. Automobiles kill many squirrels at this time of the year.

Public Health

Squirrels can carry disease organisms of potential consequence to humans but rarely, if ever, are documented as transmitting these. Rabies can occur in squirrels, as in any mammal, but squirrel-to-human transmission of the disease is not documented. If anything, the value of squirrels in regard to pubic health may be positive because they have been shown to be "indicators" of environmental quality in some studies, telling us when and perhaps where harmful concentrations of industrial by-products and pesticides may lurk in urban and suburban environments.

Problems and Their Solutions

Problems

Squirrels cause damage by nesting in buildings, digging in lawns, eating ornamental plants and bulbs and stealing food from bird feeders. The most serious problems with squirrels probably involve adult females entering a building to establish nests. They will explore any likely looking opening while searching for a den site and often enter chimneys or attics through unscreened vents or openings left by loose or rotten boards. Squirrels invariably enter a building somewhere high on the structure and exploit an existing hole, though they may enlarge the hole by gnawing. A homeowner's first sign of the squirrel's presence is usually the sound of scampering in the attic or above the fireplace.

Squirrels entering chimneys are often unable to climb back out and, if possible, may emerge from a fireplace or follow a stovepipe to the furnace and get loose in the basement. A squirrel found inside the living area of a house probably entered in this way and will characteristically seek windows to escape. Frustrated, trapped squirrels can do a surprising amount of damage to windowsills and furniture.

Squirrels nesting in attics will usually gather insulation into a nest near the entrance and may gnaw on adjacent boards and electrical wires. Typically, people hear the squirrel during daylight hours as it comes and goes on foraging trips. Juvenile squirrels, and occasionally adults, roaming around the attic may fall into wall cavities and be unable to climb out, making persis-

tent scratching noises as they attempt to escape and eventually dying if they are unsuccessful. Unpleasant odors and fly problems may ensue.

Squirrels often become nuisances at bird feeders, where they consume large quantities of birdseed or gnaw feeders into unusable shards of plastic. Squirrels can also damage ornamental plants or fruit and nut trees by feeding on bark, buds and fruits. Spring bulbs, especially tulips and crocus, may be dug up and consumed or the plants clipped and eaten just as they start to flower. Squirrels occasionally gnaw on outdoor furniture, wooden decks and wood trim on buildings for reasons unknown to us, but probably clear to the squirrels.

Solutions

TOLERANCE

Sometimes it is easy for people to accept, tolerate and enjoy squirrels, and sometimes it is not. No one is expected to be pleased when one of these animals is loose in their house, and continuous visits to bird feeders can likewise go beyond what normal patience and endurance permit. It is important to remember, however, that these animals are only doing what is natural to them—seeking release from entrapment and looking for a meal at a time of the year when shortages are critical and death is always imminent. The first approach to dealing with squirrels is to establish limits of tolerance, accept them for what they are and be patient enough so that if they need to be excluded from an attic or prevented from stealing bird food, this is done in a way that does them and their young no harm.

EXCLUSION—ATTICS

Thoroughly inspect inside the attic to find the opening(s), where the nest is and to determine whether there are any babies present. Concentrate the search in the area where noises were heard. If there is no access to the attic, inspect the outside of the eaves, vents and roof until the opening is located.

If the nest can be seen and there are no immature squirrels, attempt to frighten the squirrel outside by banging on the rafters inside the attic, or wait until you are sure all squirrels have left as they usually do during the day. Then seal up the opening with $1/4$- or $1/2$-inch mesh hardware cloth or sheet metal flashing, securely fastened. Extend the metal patch at least 6 inches beyond the hole in all directions to prevent the squirrel from gnawing around the patch. Seal any other weak spots or potential entrances in the same way. Listen carefully for the next day or so to be sure no squirrel is trapped inside or has regained entry. Watch closely to see if the squirrel is persistent in attempts to regain entry. Mothers will go to extreme lengths to reunite with their young and can cause extensive damage to houses when doing so.

If, for any reason, it cannot be determined if the squirrels are outside, *do not seal the entrance.* Instead, install a one-way door (see Chapter 3) and leave it in place until no more sounds are heard inside the attic for several days. The door can then be removed and the opening patched as described above.

If the nest is inaccessible or out of sight and there is the likelihood of babies (the squirrel has been in the house for more than a couple of days and it is March through May or August through October), wait until the young are grown enough to come out on their own. At that point, a one-way door may be installed over the opening and left in place until no more sounds are heard inside the attic for several days. The door can then be removed and the opening patched.

In all cases, once the squirrels are known to be gone, the opening should be permanently sealed by whatever carpentry work is necessary. This is simply good housekeeping and not only prevents squirrels from regaining entry at a future date but keeps weather and insects out to help maintain an orderly house.

EXCLUSION—
CHIMNEY WITH A FIREPLACE

It can be assumed that the squirrel heard scrambling in a chimney is trapped unless there is clear evidence it is able to climb out on its own. *Do not try to smoke a squirrel out of a chimney*—a trapped squirrel or babies may be killed. If the squirrel is not trapped, proceed the same as with a nest in the attic as described above.

If the squirrel is above, or has access to, the flue damper, a means of escape may be provided by hanging a $3/4$-inch or thicker rope down the chimney. Be sure to tie one end of the rope to the top of the chimney before lowering the other end, and make certain that it reaches the damper or smoke shelf. If a rope is unavailable, a series of boards or sticks may be securely attached end-to-end to sufficient length. Be careful not to lower anything into the chimney that cannot be easily retrieved. The squirrel will climb up the rope and escape, usually within a few (daylight) hours. After it is certain that the squirrel has escaped, remove the rope and screen the chimney, preferably with a commercially made chimney cap (see "Chimney Caps" in Appendix 2).

If a squirrel is down in the fireplace (presumably behind the fireplace doors or screen), try tapping on the door and scaring it back up above the damper. If successful, close the damper and proceed as above. If the squirrel cannot or will not leave the fireplace, the next best option is to obtain a suitable live trap, bait it with peanut butter and set it very carefully inside the fireplace. Normally, the squirrel will retreat to a back corner of the fireplace as the doors are opened and stay there if the trap is placed, slowly and quietly, just inside the doors. Close the doors and leave the room to wait for the squirrel to enter the trap. As a precaution, before opening the doors of the fireplace to set the trap, close any interior doors in the room and open an exterior door or window in line of sight from the fireplace. In the event that the squirrel gets out of the fireplace, do not chase it; just sit quietly, and it will instinctively head for the light of the open door and go outside. After the squirrel has been removed, screen the chimney as described above.

SQUIRREL LOOSE IN HOUSE

A squirrel that has entered a house has done so by accident and does not want to be there. If its exact location is known, close interior doors to limit its movement and open a window or exterior door in the room. The squirrel will find the opening if it is left alone and it will even readily jump from a second-story window onto a lawn (not onto concrete) without harming itself. If for some reason it is not possible to give the squirrel an exit, set a baited live trap on the floor near the squirrel and leave it alone for a few hours. Squirrels can be captured in a blanket if trapping is not an option. Approach the squirrel with the blanket covering your body, so that it does not see a human form but rather a large and indistinct mass. Drop the blanket on the squirrel and roll it up, taking care not to put too much weight or pressure on the animal. Then, take the blanket and squirrel immediately outside and unfurl it, letting the animal escape. Once the squirrel has escaped or has been captured, it is important to discover how it

got in the house and prevent it from happening again. Look for tracks in soot or dust around the fireplace or furnace that may indicate that it came down the chimney, and check the attic for evidence of a nest or entrance hole that may need attention.

HABITAT MANAGEMENT— BIRD FEEDERS

The agility of squirrels makes it difficult to prevent them from reaching bird feeders. Various types of specialized feeders are available from wild bird supply centers or catalog sales that keep *almost* all squirrels at bay. Several designs respond to the greater weight of squirrels and large birds by closing a metal cover over the birdseed when they climb onto the feeder. These feeders are usually very effective, but cost more than traditional feeders.

One step up in the battle is to keep squirrels away from the beginning, when the feeder is first put out. Once a squirrel becomes accustomed to finding food, it will persistently try to overcome any obstacles that are placed in its way. Feeders on a pole can be rigged with a baffler (see Chapter 3) that prevents them from climbing. As long as they cannot leap from a nearby tree onto the feeder, they generally have to content themselves with whatever the birds spill.

Squirrels will have difficulty raiding a feeder hung from a tree branch on a wire that is more than 10 feet long. The feeder should be positioned at least 8 feet away from any limbs or structures from which the animals might leap. If a squirrel does slide down the support wire, a plastic or metal umbrella-shaped commercial or homemade baffle can be mounted over the feeder.

DAMAGE TO PLANTS

Squirrels rarely do significant damage to plantings. So, when damage is observed, the

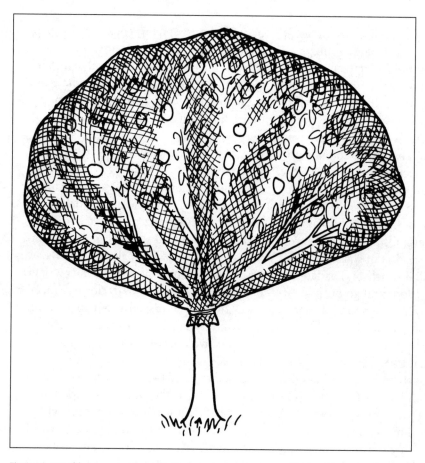

Figure 29. *Dwarf fruit trees can be covered with netting to prevent access to squirrels and birds while fruit is ripening. Local garden centers and plant nurseries often carry this netting, or it can be ordered directly from suppliers (see "Netting" in Appendix 2).*

first step is to make sure it's not being caused by another animal. Squirrels are only active during the day, so it should be possible to observe the damage happening. Once a squirrel has been implicated, consider the possibility of preventing access to the affected plant. For instance, one or several fruit trees that are isolated from surrounding trees may be protected by wrapping a 2-foot band of sheet metal around the trunk about 6 feet off the ground. Branches growing below 6 feet also may have to be trimmed. Squirrels show a preference for certain varieties of ornamental plants and leave others alone. Small fruit and nut trees can be protected by netting the entire tree for the short period of time

when squirrel (or other animal) damage is most likely to occur (see Figure 29).

REPELLENTS

There are several commercial repellents (see Table 2, pages 48 and 49) that are registered for use with squirrels. Some, such as the products with Thiram, can be used to soak bulbs before planting. Other are intended to be sprayed on ornamental plants squirrels are attacking. We have encountered at least one product that uses capsaicin, with the recommendation that birdseed be dusted with it to repel squirrels but not birds. The concept is that birds do not have the same sensory reception of this chemical as mammals do—a questionable assumption. We do not recommend this method of protecting birdseed from squirrels.

A Last Word

There are volumes written about squirrels, some of which have focused entirely on the squirrel-human warfare conducted every year in our neighborhoods. In the space allocated here, we can only suggest the extent of some of the battles that have raged across the American landscape, and we recommend that readers consult advanced texts for details of the more complex maneuvers. The battles will go on into the foreseeable future, with humanity continuing to win the minor skirmishes, while the squirrels seem to have their sights on the strategic, rather than tactical, victory. All we can recommend for those who feel completely frustrated by the struggle is to take another, closer look at the enemy.

Squirrels are fascinating animals to watch, photograph and study. They make themselves available for observation in a way that few other animals do and have a rich and complex enough repertoire of behaviors to award both the novice and expert with the challenge of deciphering what it is they really are about. For those willing to be patient, to learn and to watch, squirrels have a lot to offer.

Additional Sources

Gurnell, J. 1987. *The Natural History of Squirrels*. New York: Facts on File. 201 pp.

Long, K. 1995. *Squirrels: A Wildlife Handbook*. Boulder, Colo.: Johnson Books. 181 pp.

32

Voles

Voles occupy virtually all of North America.

They live outside in yards and gardens but by far prefer open grassy fields.

Never weighing more than 2 ounces, these little animals are nevertheless a critical part of the food chain where they are found.

ALTHOUGH RARELY SEEN, voles are surprisingly common in many cities. In downtown Washington, D.C., these little mouselike creatures have made a name for themselves by presenting vexing problems in some years when they attack the large planted beds of ground cover. The White House even has a resident population of voles that periodically make their presence felt in the large euonymus beds out back, sometimes leaving large brown areas of dead vegetation by girdling stems. Voles are far more likely to be a serious concern to commercial agriculture than to homeowners, and most of the strategies that have been developed to deal with them reflect that. Perhaps they are a latent urban wildlife issue, waiting for the more highly visible issues involving geese, raccoons, deer, beavers, pigeons and other species to die down some before claiming their place. If so, they may be in for a long wait.

Natural History

Classification and Range

Voles, also known as meadow mice, are members of a large and complex group of rodents called arvicolids. There are around twenty species in the genus *Microtus* alone, depending on the latest consensus of the experts, but only some six or seven are generally considered to cause significant problems for humans. All are mouse-sized (6 to 8 inches) animals that weigh about 4 to 5 ounces and have stocky compact bodies. Their ears and eyes are small relative to other mouselike animals commonly seen. The physical feature that is most distinguishing is a short tail, which is less than 3 inches long. Both house

(Mus musculus) and deer *(Peromyscus* spp.) mice, with which voles are often confused, have tails that are at least as long as their bodies.

The voles that most often cause damage in different regions of the country are the prairie vole *(Microtus ochrogaster)*, meadow vole *(Microtus pennsylvanicus)*, pine or woodland vole *(Microtus pinetorum)*, montane or mountain vole *(Microtus montanus)*, Oregon vole *(Microtus oregoni)* and California vole *(Microtus californicus)*. Meadow and prairie voles cause surface damage, while woodland voles cause damage beneath the soil. The pine and Oregon voles, for example, spend almost all their time underground. Because control methods would be different based on such considerations and because there is extensive range overlap of some species, exact species identifications in situations where damage is occurring is important.

Habitat

With so many different types of voles distributed throughout North America it can hardly be surprising to find them in a wide variety of habitats. Even within a given habitat, different species of voles may overlap, avoiding direct competition through separation into specialized niches. Several species are major agricultural pests, having moved into commercial fruit orchards, planted crop fields and pastures in easy transition from traditional habitats. The affinity of some voles for forest edges with moist loose soil high in organic matter easily brings them into residential areas and conflicts with homeowners.

Diet

Voles are primarily *herbivores* (plant-eaters) and are not to be confused with moles.

Voles forage on grasses, flowers, vegetables, fruits, bulbs and roots, although they will occasionally consume animal matter such as insects and snails. In winter, voles make tunnels beneath the snow, under the protection of which they gnaw the bark from trees and shrubs. They will also horde food in underground caches of as much as a gallon of stored nuts and berries. (These were often raided by American Indians to supplement their own winter diet.)

Reproduction

Like many small rodents, voles are short-lived but prolific breeders. In the wild, there can be four or five litters each summer, and even more in warm climates where breeding can occur year-round. Depending on the species and geographic region, the average litter size varies from two to five young. Within three weeks of birth, females may begin breeding, with gestation a short twenty to twenty-three days. With this kind of reproductive potential, populations rapidly expand. Populations in commercial and home orchards can attain high concentrations because optimal vole habitat is inadvertently created by landscaping practices such as mowing (which leaves a protective layer of thatch) and by fertilization, which results in dense ground cover. Vole populations are cyclical. During spans of about three to six years, vole populations experience dramatic fluctuations. Years in which populations grow rapidly are sometimes called "mouse years."

Nests and Runways

While all species of voles do some burrowing, certain specialists such as the pine and Oregon vole are almost entirely subterranean. Others, including the meadow vole, construct obvious runways on the surface of the ground, clipping and mowing in their own fashion to maintain a network of maintained trails partly covered by overlapping vegetation. Nests are usually well built and provide refuge from environmental extremes, as well as places to rest and raise young. Voles may spend the bulk of their day in these, coming out to feed for short periods during both day and night.

Public Health

Voles are not considered to be a significant source for any infectious disease that can be transmitted to humans, companion animals or livestock. They are known, however, to be the hosts for such communicable diseases as tularemia and bubonic plague.

Problems and Their Solutions

Problems

The worst damage done by voles is associated with agricultural crops, and the operators of large orchards are most likely to suffer damage. Debarking of fruit trees occurs under the cover of snow and can be fatal when trees are completely girdled. Voles also feed on the roots of fruit trees, primarily during the winter. This spurt in damage may be a result of the diminished food supply during this dormant season. Apple tree roots contain more sugar and starch during the winter than any other season, possibly making them more attractive to voles. Moreover, in winter voles spend more time close to their nests to avoid cold temperatures and predators. Because the nests are frequently located near tree trunks, roots are a convenient source of food. Typical vole damage occurs within the first decade after an orchard has been planted because as trees mature they are better able to sustain and fend off damage.

Voles will use mole tunnels to reach plant roots and bulbs and often cause damage for which moles erroneously are blamed. Homeowners may experience damage similar to agriculturalists but on a lesser scale. Fruit trees or shrubs such as blackberries and raspberries and occasional garden vegetables may be badly damaged or ruined. Plants in growing frames and greenhouses may be badly damaged, as might certain shrubs and bulbs in the ornamental garden.

Solutions

HABITAT MODIFICATION

The control of damage by voles should focus on the management of the habitat to make conditions less favorable for these animals. Populations can be reduced through soil cultivation, a tactic that destroys burrows and reduces ground cover. Frequent, close mowing will reduce both cover and carrying capacity for these animals and is an important part of an integrated approach to population management. Orchards should be mowed four times a year: after trees bloom, just before cropping limbs, prior to harvest and in late fall.

Clearing vegetative debris from grassy areas adjacent to gardens and crops is a useful prevention measure. Clearing vegetation from a 3-foot radius around the base of a tree or shrub can force voles to relocate. However, because woodland voles remain below ground, this tactic may not affect their activities. In northern climates snow may provide cover for voles at the time of year when plants are most likely to incur damage. Clearing snow away from the base of trees may be helpful when just a few need to be protected. Deep beds of mulch also encourage voles by facilitating their movement through tunnels created between the mulch and the ground. Reducing the layer of mulch to 1 to 2 inches may discourage voles.

Kill Them All?

The eradication of any animal from the landscape is rarely possible, and in the few cases it is achieved, it is at best a temporary remission. Using proper methods of wildlife damage control, a property owner can curb problem behavior or reduce the problem to a tolerable level.

Individual plants or flower beds can be partially protected with a subterranean barrier composed of hardware cloth (^{1}/4-inch mesh or less) buried 6 to 8 inches into the soil. By sinking the barrier to a depth of at least 6 inches, the property owner will assure that animals do not burrow under the obstacle. This tactic may offer the best permanent solution to problems with voles in the residential yard. A barrier of gravel on paths also discourages voles from moving around yards because they prefer to excavate soft soil.

Tulips and hostas are favorite foods of voles and may occasionally sustain high damage. Homeowners whose plants are repeatedly assaulted by voles should consider substitute plants, such as daffodil, which are less palatable. Crown imperial (*Fritterlaria* spp.) is another showy plant that has a reputation for repelling voles. Plastic, metal or cloth barriers (see "Tree Protectors" in Appendix 2) may be wrapped around the trunks of individual trees to prevent voles from gnawing on their bark. Tar paper also is used for this purpose.

REPELLENTS

Voles can cause serious damage to ornamental flower beds by destroying the bulbs of plants such as lilies and tulips. Soaking bulbs before planting in one of the many commercially available bittering agents containing Thiram (see "Chemical Repellents" in Chapter 3) can be effective in limiting damage to new plantings.

PREDATORS

Voles are an important component in the diet of many predatory species including foxes, bobcats, snakes and hawks. One of the best ways to ensure that other forms of control work well is to encourage natural predation. Predators do not, of course, eliminate prey species. Natural predation, however, can help keep numbers of animals, such as voles, down to a point where other management strategies become far more effective. Raptors can be particularly effective, and nesting boxes for barn owls and kestrels can encourage their presence. It is also possible to attract hawks and owls by erecting perches constructed of wood or metal and shaped into a "T" that will serve as observation posts to scan fields for voles and other small mammals.

A Last Word

The average homeowner is unlikely to encounter problems with voles of the sort that commercial orchardists and agriculturalists do. On the rare occasions they do, it is likely that the damage comes as a result of one of those cyclical periods when vole numbers are peaking. Certainly, protection of valued plants is merited at those times, but lethal control of vole populations is unlikely to yield any significant results, because the natural population cycle will lead to reduction in vole numbers regardless of the attempts to eradicate animals.

33

Waterfowl

Found throughout all of North America; increasingly common in urban areas.

Most conflicts are restricted to open space and parklands, including corporate lands and golf courses. Occasional problems in private yards.

The subspecies of Canada goose so common now in many cities was thought to have been extinct as recently as the 1960s.

FOR AS LONG AS SPRING has come for people it has been heralded by geese calling overhead on their way north to breeding grounds. The opposite turn of season is signaled by their return voyage, which also introduces the newly arrived members of the flock to the tradition of the group's flight path. What the first humans on this continent saw were already ancient patterns. What later arrivals saw were dwindling numbers overhead as more and more land was taken that once supported an enormous variety of species.

Not so long ago it looked as if the sky might not be occupied by migrants at all. Strictly enforced laws and, finally, some effort to conserve diminishing wetlands helped bring them back from the brink, but still the outcome for many species remains critical. In the face of the changes we imposed on them, some species of waterfowl began to adapt in remarkable ways. "Resident" ducks and geese have become noticeable only recently, and already are one of the most controversial wildlife issues in many parts of the country. Books may be written about the human-waterfowl conflicts of these times, the reasons for it and the deep irony of what has happened. These birds, so heavily hunted for so long, have not been driven to hide in some remote vastness. They have literally embraced humanity and settled underfoot in cities and towns throughout the country. Ironically, by only trying to adjust to the situation people have imposed on them, they have been declared a "problem."

Natural History

Classification and Range

"Waterfowl" is a generic term that applies to dozens of different types of birds. The main species that are of concern in urban areas, and which are addressed here, include geese, ducks, coots and swans. Although there are several species of goose in North America, it is the Canada goose (*Branta canadensis*) that causes by far the majority of problems in urban and suburban areas. The large size, black head and prominent white cheek patch of this bird make identification easy for most urbanites, as the only other large bird commonly found on urban ponds is the swan. At least ten subspecies or races of Canada geese have been identified, with the "giant" form (*B. c. maxima*) being the one that has settled most comfortably on a year-round residency among people. These large birds (about 12 pounds on average) were actually considered extinct in the 1950s, only to be rediscovered in 1965. Since then, their populations have risen steadily.

The mute swan (*Cygnus olor*) is an Old World species that has been introduced into North America. These swans are common in many municipal parks in the East, always standing out because of their great size and the gracefulness of the curve of the neck, which is what most people think of when they conjure a mental image of a swan. The American coot (*Fulica americana*), or mudhen, is a small aquatic bird that is distributed almost nationwide. Many different species of ducks use urban and suburban ponds as stopovers when migrating. The mallard (*Anas platyrhynchos*) is by far the most common and the one that is present year-round in many urban ponds. The brown female is drab in comparison to the male, who has a green head, white neck band and rusty chest. The muscovy duck (*Cairina moschata*) is an introduced species that is found in many towns and cities as a result of intentional releases. It is a large, bulky bird ranging from blackish to all white; males are characterized by the pronounced knob at the end of the bill. Confusing the issue of what duck is what duck is the frequent hybridization of mallards with domestic species, so that a sometimes perplexing combination of wild and domestic ducks appears on our ponds.

Habitat

Although traditionally associated with lakes and ponds, most waterfowl spend time on land and even nest some distance from water if the site seems safe. Artificial ponds and lakes, storm water impoundments and, especially, the vast expanses of good grazing surfaces typical of municipal parks, corporate developments, golf courses and other human-built environments are ideal habitat for geese, swans and ducks. This is the main reason they have settled in year-round residency and have grown in numbers in municipal areas.

Diet

Geese derive more food from terrestrial sources than their more aquatic relatives, the ducks and swans, although all seem to benefit from agricultural practices. Waste corn and other agricultural crops are especially important for migrating flocks, which can be seen foraging in fields as migration progresses. Geese are predisposed to use short grasslands, and these have become a major source of food that remains available throughout the spring and summer because we humans cut, water and fertilize vast areas of this sort. The human love affair with the lawn is, doubtless, the key element in sustaining goose populations in cities and towns. Ducks can satisfy themselves with a more aquatic fare, eating submerged vegetation and aquatic insects, but, of course, are always willing to take advantage of human handouts.

Reproduction

Geese are strongly monogamous and do not usually pair until a rather advanced age (for birds) of about three years. Strong family attachments complement the pair-bonding of the adults; a vigorous defense of both nest and chicks is one characteristic of these birds leading to conflicts with people. This defense is also characteristic of swans. Most waterfowl will make new nests if a clutch is lost and the season is still early. Removal of eggs stimulates continued laying. Molting occurs in early summer (usually between late June and mid-July), and it may take up to a month to regain the ability to fly.

Mallards are renowned for their tendency to build nests in strange places. Flower boxes, building alcoves and other areas far from water are all used. Spraying of the national Christmas tree that stands on the ellipse across from the White House is periodically delayed because a mallard is discovered nesting underneath it. Whether prompted by competition for favorable sites or just a natural inclination to test different

sites, the hatchlings are usually led to water immediately, provoking many of the sorts of scenes immortalized in *Make Way for Ducklings*, a favorite childhood storybook.

Public Health

Waterfowl are not implicated in any serious public health threat to humans, although their droppings are increasingly cited as a cause for concern in controlling water quality in municipal lakes and ponds. Some waterfowl species are primary carriers of chlamydiosis. Botulism outbreaks in waterfowl involve a strain that is not transmitted to humans.

Problems and Their Solutions

Problems

The primary conflict between waterfowl and humans occurs over maintained lawns (or lawnscapes) and is an aesthetic, cosmetic, convenience and (some say) sanitary issue. The actual grazing done by geese is seldom an issue because they do not disturb or physically damage turf. Most often, it is the fecal deposits and the aggregation of numbers of birds that produce conflict. Droppings can accumulate at considerable rates, and on lawns that people use frequently, this can be regarded as a nuisance. On a large corporate headquarters with its acres of mown but unused lawn surface, geese may not be a problem at all. Occasional problems occur with geese guarding their nests. Protective responses are strong in these birds, and they are known to sometimes confront and even physically challenge people who come too close. As rare as these occurrences are, they usually make news when they do occur.

Coots

Most people think of coots as grumpy old men, but another sort of coot is a small and retiring member of the bird family that includes rails and cranes. Like ducks and geese, coots inhabit ponds around human residences and recreational areas and come ashore to forage. Coots can be more destructive than geese when grazing on lawns because they also forage for insects and worms, damaging turf with the strong claws of their hind feet. In California where these birds have long been regarded as agricultural pests, many are shot annually because people are unwilling to work toward nonlethal solutions.

buttons. Geese are intelligent birds who learn quickly and remember what they learn. With a little consistency in our behavior, there is every reason to assume that if we impose "rules" on them, they will follow them. As with other urban wildlife species, compatibility and mutual benefits are more the norm than the exception. It seems always the exception that gets the attention, however. People demand immediate solutions or quick fixes, and those responsible for providing services are forced to take an expedient rather than a prudent course of action. Part of this is a bureaucratic decision in which resources, time and attention are targeted at some things but not others. Working out reasonable wildlife solutions is very low in the pantheon of bureaucratic responses and rarely approached through the sort of planning process that other municipal issues are. Public calls for responsible and humane solutions and the efforts of individuals and organizations to expand the message that this planning is not only possible but preferable will help to address this issue.

FEEDING

Both geese and ducks can be attracted to and held at municipal parks by the "generosity" of humans. Handouts may allow them to maintain numbers greater than those that might be expected under natural conditions. While the occasional handout is of little consequence, sustained feeding is not recommended.

Solutions

TOLERANCE

The adaptation of geese to a nonmigratory way of life is of such recent origin that we can certainly say that more time is needed for people to get used to living with geese, and geese to become used to living with people, before anyone pushes any panic

HABITAT MODIFICATION

The use of habitat modification strategies to exclude geese from areas where they are viewed as problems, or (better yet) to maintain them at acceptable levels is clearly the most farsighted and reasonable approach we currently have to solving conflicts between these animals and humans. It is foolish to claim that the formulae for such solutions have already been worked out, with a packaged remedy ready to apply to all situations. Even when they are known, it is often difficult to get people to accept changing the appearance or management of a landscape they have grown used to. This is an issue for the future; for now we clearly have to continue to experiment with the changes themselves.

The most important tool in managing habitat to deter geese and, to a lesser extent, ducks involves vegetation management around the edge or berm of any body of water that they are using. Geese not only prefer to walk between water and land, but have to walk when molting or escorting goslings. They dislike and will avoid walking through tall (18 inches and up) vegetation because this both impedes their movement and can hide predators. Natural vegetation that is allowed to grow along ponds is not only a deterrent to geese (and to a lesser extent ducks) but also lessens the amount of mowing necessary, filters the runoff of fertilizer and herbicides from lawn surfaces, increases habitat for other wildlife species such as songbirds and has an aesthetic appeal to many that is more satisfying than the homogenous and neatly trimmed lawn that runs down to water's edge. Where access is necessary, desirable walkways can be designed or small areas of lawn set aside for humans. If geese use these to move back and forth to lawns, simple fencing as described in the following section can block these areas off as well.

Vegetation management also extends to modifying the vast expanses of highly fertilized and closely cropped lawns that dominate the suburban landscape. Geese prefer the tender grasses and other succulent vegetation that are diligently maintained for

them by humans, at great expense and far-reaching environmental consequences. Anywhere that a lawn can be turned to meadow will serve a host of environmentally beneficial purposes, including the removal of preferred grazing areas from access to geese.

EXCLUSION

Fencing acts like an artificial vegetation barrier, and while it lacks many of the other desirable characteristics, it can be put out and taken up once nesting has begun (elsewhere) and a site is not so attractive to geese. To be effective, fences or natural barriers need only be 18 inches tall. Chicken wire is sufficient, but not as durable or practical as other types of fencing. Nylon or plastic fencing works best. The solid nylon silt fences used in construction to prevent or channel runoff is an excellent material, as are other types of construction fencing, which are moderately priced, reusable and easy to install. These barriers should *not* be put up *after* nesting has begun—they will deprive goslings of the access back and forth from water to land that they will need to survive. They could be installed to only allow geese access to certain areas where they would be tolerated, while keeping them away from places that receive a lot of use by people.

Another tactic that may be effective is the use of stone riprap along shorelines. Riprap is coarse (4 inches and up) stone that is laid around the perimeter of ponds and along stream channels to help control erosion. Geese are often hesitant to cross this material, and it has the added benefit where muskrats might be a problem of deterring their burrowing into banks. Actual exclusion of geese and other waterfowl from ponds has been attempted using a line grid system that creates a physical barrier to prevent birds from landing on the water. Monofilament line, originally used in such applications, is

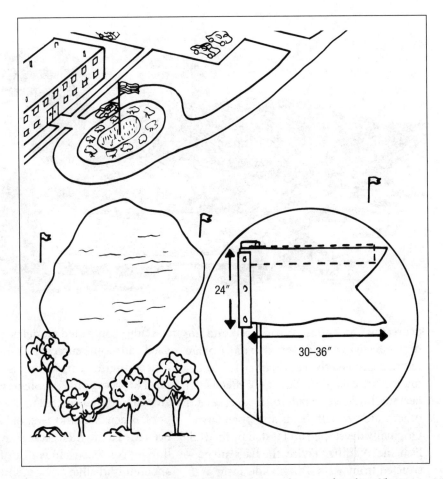

Figure 30. *A simple plastic flag system has been used very effectively in some settings to deter geese from areas of open lawn. Like any scaring or frightening strategy, this works best if combined with other techniques.*

not recommended because under usual light conditions, the birds do not see it in time to avoid collisions. Any heavy-gauge durable metal or darker line material can be used, but the obvious initial expense and maintenance costs of such barriers make their use problematic in all but unusual settings.

Netting is sometimes used over ponds or small impoundments, but is fairly expensive and difficult to maintain. Hollow plastic bird balls (see Appendix 2) have been tried in some industrial waste pond settings to keep waterfowl away from water that is contaminated with toxic material. Dozens, or hundreds, of these balls are floated on the surface of the pond to prevent access to waterfowl. While not yet tried in many other settings, it might be possible to float enough of these on the surface of small ponds to harass geese or ducks away at certain times when they are not wanted there.

HARASSMENT

A variety of techniques can be used to harass or scare geese and other waterfowl away from areas where they are causing damage, with the greatest effectiveness usually achieved when a combination of these techniques with other strategies is used.

Scarecrows and effigies work well and are most effective when designed to move or are relocated frequently (see Chapter 3). Home-made plastic flags can be highly effective in keeping birds, especially ducks, geese and other waterfowl, off fields and open lawns. Originally developed and tested by the U.S. Fish and Wildlife Service, the flags are constructed from a 2 x 3-foot wide sheet of 3-mm plastic that is attached to a 4-foot lath or post (see Figure 30, p. 199). Usually, black plastic is used, but any solid color is believed to be effective. The 3-foot side is wrapped and fastened to the lath, which is then sunk in the ground (usually one to five per acre is the recommendation). Sometimes a V-shaped notch is cut in the free end to enhance its movement in slight winds. This system is easily made from locally obtained materials and may be one of the least expensive and most efficient ways of deterring unwanted waterfowl. Like any other system intended to produce negative conditioning, it is something birds will get used to, so it is best when altered frequently (by moving flags around) and combined with other strategies.

Radio-controlled model boats have been used with some success to harass geese and other waterfowl from ponds and may be ideal for occasional problems with the mis-guided bird that wanted to use a swimming pool. Beach balls and eyespot balloons have been used to frighten geese away from shore-line property as well as from fields. Geese apparently dislike walking under objects, and a large helium-filled balloon (30 inches in diameter) tethered on a 40- to 50-foot monofilament line of at least a 50-pound test can be effective in keeping them off a field or lawn of 1 to 2 acres. Mylar tape in rows can be highly effective against water-fowl but does have a high maintenance com-ponent and prevents free access and use of the protected area. Probably the best appli-cation of this product would be in lieu of line strung over small impoundments to keep waterfowl out.

HAZING

Hazing can be an effective tactic when ap-plied at the right time, practiced consistently and used in combination with other proce-dures, such as repellents. Hazing should occur early in the season, prior to nesting. Techniques range from having a human simply approach and shoo geese away whenever they are seen out of water to intense and full-time disruptive harassment using pyrotechnics and even special human-dog teams of breeds such as border collies, whose natural herding instinct can keep geese continually in the water and frustrate them so much that they abandon a site. This kind of harassment can be particularly effective on facilities such as golf courses.

REPELLENTS

The recent approval of the repellent methyl anthranilate (see "Chemical Repellents" in Chapter 3) offers promise of an important and useful chemical deterrent for waterfowl that has application in a variety of situations. Made from the extract that flavors grape soda and candy, methyl anthranilate can be sprayed on lawns or introduced directly into bodies of water (currently, those without fish; the product is in line for approval in fish-bearing waters) to cause extreme irritation in any bird that comes into contact with it. Alone or (even better) in combination with other strategies, this product has great promise as a useful goose repellent.

DESTROYING EGGS

A more drastic, short-term and problematic solution to goose population control is the process of shaking eggs to render them unhatchable, known as addling. Removing eggs before they are two weeks old will re- sult in the female simply laying another clutch. Destruction of older eggs means the destruction of developed embryos and is considered inhumane. Consultation with FWS and USDA APHIS-ADC staff (see Appendix 1) should occur prior to adopting any egg addling program. *A permit from the U.S. Fish and Wildlife Service must be obtained to addle eggs.*

A Last Word

The recent increase in resident goose populations is yet another indication of how decisions humans make regarding the management of land can inadvertently lead to change in other areas. Geese are not to blame for occupying the optimal habits we have built for them—they are simply following a natural pattern that their course had dictated long before humans were even present. Like all problems, there are many ways that it can be settled. It will say much about not only our relationship to geese and other wildlife but to the land itself as to how solutions are crafted as well as imposed.

Additional Sources

Johnsgard, P. A. 1975. *Waterfowl of North America.* Bloomington: Indiana University Press. 575 pp.

Nielsen, S. 1992. *Mallards.* Stillwater, Minn.: Voyageur Press. 143 pp.

Ogilvie, M. A. 1978. *Wild Geese.* Vermillion, S. Dak.: Buteo Books. 350 pp.

34

Woodchucks

The woodchuck is distributed throughout the eastern and mid-western parts of the United States and most of Canada.

Can live in yards and gardens; sometimes take up residence under outbuildings, patios or decks.

Recent research suggests that these animals would not chuck any wood even if they could chuck wood.

MANY PEOPLE KNOW WOODCHUCKS by the name "groundhog," and the two terms seem to be used with about equal frequency. "Whistle pig" is also used but less heard. It is, in fact, better descriptive of these animals who will apparently never chuck wood and rarely hog ground, but will issue a shrill whistling signal when taken by surprise. "Chuck" is another convenient name to use that doesn't take as long to say as the others. All of these animals are guaranteed to make the news at least once a year on Groundhog Day. February 2 has been recognized as the day on which a representative of this species, resident of a small town in Pennsylvania, Punxsutawney, traditionally captures the attention of the country by prognosticating on the duration of the winter. Punxsutawney Phil, as the chosen chuck is known, is expected to emerge from hibernation to check whether or not "his" shadow is visible. If it is, we have six more weeks of winter; if not spring is on its way. Modern science cannot explain the reason for this event to be predictive of climate, reminding us that there are still many mysteries on this planet remaining to be solved. As with many other species of wild animals that enter into conflict with humans, the woodchuck is one that has greatly benefited from human alteration of the landscape. In this case it has been agricultural lands that provided benefits for this species, but where farmlands are converted to subdivisions, woodchucks have often made the transition from rural to suburban as well.

Natural History

Classification and Range

The woodchuck *(Marmota monax)* is a large bulky rodent, weighing 5 to 10 pounds and measuring 16 to 20 inches, with a short tail of 4 to 8 inches. Coat color ranges from light to dark brown. The several recognized subspecies range from New England, south through parts of Georgia and Alabama and into the Midwest. Woodchucks are for the most part absent from states west of the Great Plains, but the species does range north throughout much of Canada and into Alaska. Their rather odd distribution finds the species absent from western parts of the United States, but present in many colder climates. The close relative of the woodchuck, the yellow-bellied marmot *(M. flaviventris)*, ranges throughout much of the area from which its larger cousin is absent, and it is likely that a comparison of the adaptations of the two would reveal why they occupy mostly separate ranges.

Habitat

Woodchucks are traditionally associated with agricultural areas where open fields and croplands provide food, woodlots and hedgerows needed cover. Suburban and even urban habitats are colonized when open fields suitable for their needs can be found in conjunction with areas of cover. Woodchucks often establish their burrows along the grassy strips of land paralleling highways and can be seen grazing right up to the road's edge.

Diet

Woodchucks are herbivores and primarily eat grasses and forbs. (A *forb* is any plant, other than a grass, with growth that dies back after flowering and seeds set [usually

Woodchuck Tracks

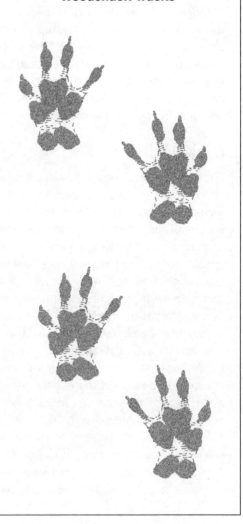

over winter] to emerge with new above-ground growth when the next reproductive cycle begins [usually in the spring].) Common forbs that are eaten by woodchucks include clover and dandelion. Although numerous types of vegetables have been cataloged as foods utilized by woodchucks, there is a surprising scarcity of studies that document which nonagricultural plants are eaten. It is the taste for vegetables and fruits grown in home gardens that leads to the battles between woodchucks and humans—of which gardening legend is made.

Reproduction

Woodchucks breed in March and April, and the usual litter of four to six young are born about a month after mating. The young mature rapidly and are usually on their own by midsummer. Woodchucks are true hibernators and will sleep for up to five months after the onset of cold weather.

Dens and Burrows

The burrows that woodchucks excavate are almost as good a sign of their presence as seeing the animal itself. One main entrance is generally used with the greatest frequency and can be told by its open and well-kept appearance and the fan of excavated soil that extends out from its front. One, two, three or sometimes more secondary entrances will be constructed in a well-managed burrow system and often hidden so well in tall grass that even a careful search may overlook them. These are used as escape or "bolt" holes when the woodchuck is threatened by any of its numerous enemies, including dogs and humans that might try to dig it out. The tunnels are usually rather shallow (2 to 3 feet deep), and burrow systems range from single tunnels leading to a chamber to complex systems over 30 feet long that have

multiple chambers off of them. Complexity probably depends on the length of occupancy and the number of chucks in residence. The entrances are often structured around a large rock, tree root, wall or other structure that provides support and may discourage predators from trying to dig their way in. Some burrow systems will be inhabited for decades by successive generations of woodchucks and may be occupied by many other species of wildlife both during and between periods of occupancy by chucks.

Public Health

Woodchucks are not considered to be a significant source for any infectious disease that can be transmitted to humans. They can get rabies and may be boldly aggressive when this disease has taken its final hold on them. And for this reason, unprovoked attacks by woodchucks must be treated very seriously as potential rabies exposures.

Problems and Their Solutions

Problems

Woodchucks will occasionally damage garden or field crops, and in a small garden, they can cause extensive damage in a very short period of time. Because they hibernate, woodchuck damage will typically not be seen between early November and late February, and damage done during this time is more likely to be caused by deer or rabbits. In fact, the damage done by deer and woodchucks is often confused. Damaged plants should be carefully examined for the clipped neat appearance of browse typical of woodchucks and rabbits as opposed to the ragged appearance of deer browse (see Figure 22, p. 101), and for browsing that occurs above the 24 to 30 inches that woodchucks can reach. Distinguishing woodchuck or rabbit damage may be even harder and requires other information, such as the amount of damage done and the type of plants attacked.

Solutions

TOLERANCE

People and woodchucks can coexist for years without conflict. Where buildings, lots and houses have sprung up on old farmlands and woodchucks have burrows in the remnant woodlots, the only contact may be an occasional early morning or evening sighting of chucks grazing at lawn edges. The animals do no recognizable harm and are simply a part of the natural scene. Then, a perennial bed or a vegetable garden suffers damage and the presence of woodchucks becomes an issue. Sometimes not even this stimulus is necessary for people to issue a call for action. To many, woodchucks may be simply "vermin," unusable animals that do humans no obvious service and are thus worthy of persecution. Just the possibility that woodchucks might cause problems for residents at some time in the future is used as an excuse to attempt to "control" them. Those who advocate such an ideology are wrong, or at least wrongfully informed. It is never appropriate to brand entire species as worthy of destruction simply because they occasionally cause problems. Where conflicts occur, it is the individual animal, individual human(s) and the specific problem that must be addressed. The level at which the problem and its potential solutions should be considered is that of the individual case—not through the indiscriminate pursuit and persecution of entire populations.

HABITAT MODIFICATION

Woodchucks are cautious animals. Novel stimuli, such as a beach ball left to move with the wind across a lawn or open area or scarecrows, may temporarily keep them out of an area. A simple change in human activity or use of an area (e.g., more frequent visits to the garden) may disturb and unsettle them and discourage their return. Removal of cover around burrows can create insecurity and, with other methods applied simultaneously, help cause them to abandon a burrow system—especially one that has not been used for long. During the course of the year there is a lot of movement between burrow systems as a part of normal routine anyway. Frequently a burrow is abandoned or unoccupied for weeks and even months before it is reopened. A highly developed sense of smell allows woodchucks to locate places where others have been living for months (and maybe years) after the occupants have left, even when the entrance is partly filled and full of vegetation. It's only a few minutes' work for the average chuck, and the tunnel system is open and usable again.

EXCLUSION

Where woodchucks have burrowed under houses or outbuildings, or when burrows located close to gardens mean that depredations are inevitable, exclusion is the recommended course of action. Woodchucks can be driven from burrows by harassment or alteration of conditions to disturb them, or by using one-way doors that let them out but not back in (see Figure 10, p. 33). Their formidable digging skills require that a more substantial area surrounding the door be protected than would be the case if skunks or opossums were involved. Hay or similar material loosely packed into the entrance will indicate if the burrow is currently vacant. After three to five days when the entrance has not been disturbed, the burrow can be assumed unoccupied and permanently closed. Heavy-gauge welded wire (3-inch squares) is available at most large hardware and home supply stores and recommended for the job of closing burrows. This wire should be cut in about 3-square-foot sections and buried at least 1 foot deep after excavating a suitable area around the entrance.

Kicking Them Out

Exclusion should take place only after young are weaned (in the late summer). Like many burrowing animals, woodchucks are not always present in a burrow system. When they are not, and sometimes even when they are present, other animals may use the burrow system as well. It is important to recognize this possibility and act responsibly to ensure that no animals are present when a burrow system is closed.

If the burrow system is occupied, attempts may be made to repel the residents by partially digging the entrance out, clearing vegetation away from entrances, using strong-smelling substances such as ammonia-soaked rags placed just inside the entrance or any other general form of harassment that would displace not only the woodchuck but any nontarget species using the burrow system as well. Remember that several entrances may be present in a given burrow system and all should be located and treated. Frequent monitoring of the closed burrow to make sure a new resident is not trying to establish itself is recommended as a follow-up procedure.

Removal of undergrowth and grass cover by mowing may be effective around buildings and residences. Woodchucks are good climbers, and fences are only likely to be effective if the area to be protected is small. The fence should be buried about 1 foot underground to prevent tunneling under it and be 3 to 4 feet high, protected by a single strand of electrified wire placed immediately in front of it at a height of 4 to 5 inches.

Gas cartridges are frequently used by professional animal damage personnel and are lethal to anything inhabiting a burrow system. It is futile to kill woodchucks in a burrow system and not permanently close the burrow entrance to prevent reoccupancy.

REPELLENTS

There are no repellents registered for use on woodchucks. Undoubtedly those registered for use on such other species as rabbits, squirrels and deer will have some repelling effect on chucks, and where a homeowner is uncertain about the species causing damage or has more than one species involved, they could be effective. We often hear of people who, in an act of ignorance, will pour gasoline down a burrow entrance and expose themselves and others to the safety hazard this represents. Beyond that, this type of act is extremely cruel and certainly foolish.

A Last Word

It is a paradox that we can make a celebrity out of a woodchuck over a fictitious relationship between shadows and springtime and a villain of it a few weeks later when thinking that it is snacking in the garden. There are ways to deal with these animals that make it possible to live with them more or less in harmony, even when the potential for conflict is high. In places or at times when woodchucks must be removed from an area, please recognize that this is only the first step in a process that must be followed to manage the factors that caused a problem to occur in the first place. These factors, then, should be altered to prevent reoccurrence of the problem in the future.

Additional Source

Lee, D. S., and J. B. Funderburg. 1982. "Marmots." In J. A. Chapman and G. A. Feldhamer (eds.), *Wild Mammals of North America*. Baltimore: Johns Hopkins University Press. 176–91.

35

Woodpeckers

The numerous species of these birds are spread throughout North America.

Most, if not all, conflicts are restricted to wood-sided buildings that are attacked by woodpeckers.

The special anatomical structures woodpeckers have to prevent brain injury when they drill wood may provide insight into protecting humans from head injuries.

WOODPECKERS RARELY ENGAGE in activities that bring them into conflict with humans, but sometimes when they do, it is in a fashion that can be regarded as quite newsworthy. In May 1995, a pair of flickers delayed launch of the space shuttle *Discovery* when they would not stop knocking holes in the foam insulation of the shuttle's external propellant tank.

Less expensive but more frequent conflicts involve the drumming and feeding on wood-sided houses. Some people are driven to distraction as the woodpecker starts right at dawn and continues every day for what seems to (and sometimes even can) stretch into weeks. Nerves are frayed, tempers are roused to incredible heights and the homeowner becomes desperate for what to do. The federal laws that protect woodpeckers and other migratory birds mean they can only be killed under a special permitting process, and even the launching of the space shuttle must comply with the rules. Besides, nonlethal methods work in almost every case and probably only fail when people are unwilling to extend an effort.

Natural History

Classification and Range

There are twenty-two species of woodpeckers in the United States, although one of these (the ivory-billed) is almost certainly no longer found, and another (the red-cockaded) is on the endangered species list. Most woodpeckers are year-round residents, but a few, notably the sapsuckers, are migratory. Woodpeckers are members of the taxonomic family *Picidae*, and all species share certain characteristics that are well suited to their remarkable lifestyle. Their bills and tongues are adapted to drilling and probing under tree bark, while their strong claws and stiff tail feathers help prop them to the tree trunks or branches they work. Their skulls have special sacs that cushion the brain from impact, while the tongue of most woodpeckers raps around the skull and enables them to probe deep into the cavities of trees and dead wood. The feathers around the woodpecker's nostrils filter wood dust.

Each species of woodpecker has distinctive markings and is found within a defined geographic range. A field guide is invaluable in distinguishing among field marks and plumages. Twelve species are most likely to be involved in conflicts with humans. These are the red-headed woodpecker *(Melanerpes erythrocephalus)* found in the East; the acorn woodpecker *(Melanerpes formicivorus)* of the West; the golden-fronted woodpecker *(Melanerpes aurifrons)*, which is confined almost exclusively to Texas; the red-bellied woodpecker *(Melanerpes carolinus)*, a bird of the eastern and central states; the ladder-backed woodpecker *(Picoides scalaris)* of the Southwest; the downy woodpecker *(Picoides pubescens)*; the smallest and most common woodpecker in the United States and the almost as widely distributed hairy woodpecker *(Picoides villosus)*, which is very similar to the downy; the endangered red-cockaded *(Picoides borealis)*, a resident of the southeastern United States; the northern flicker *(Colaptes auratus)*, also widely distributed; the pileated woodpecker *(Dryocopus pileatus)*, our largest woodpecker and a resident of the eastern United States and the Pacific Northwest; the yellow-bellied sapsucker *(Sphyrapicus varius)*, primarily a winter resident of the eastern and southeastern United States and Williamson's sapsucker *(Sphyrapicus thyroideus)*, a western species.

Habitat

As with most groups of animals, woodpeckers occupy a variety of niches in the natural world. Lewis's woodpecker, for example, behaves like a flycatcher, darting from its perch to catch flying insects. The northern flicker feeds on the ground, probing the soil for insects. Sapsuckers, as their name suggests, feed on the sap flowing from the orderly rows of small holes that they drill in trees. Most woodpeckers are residents of mature open woodlands. Woodpeckers do most of their foraging on dead or dying trees.

Diet

Most woodpeckers feed primarily on wood-boring insects, such as carpenter ants and bark beetles, which they can dig out with their powerful beaks. They also consume gypsy moths, tent caterpillars and grasshoppers. Some species favor a diet consisting primarily of plant material such as nuts, fruit, berries or tree sap. The acorn woodpecker is a species that caches food for winter consumption. It will pound acorns into small holes excavated in trees. While the pounding may seem detrimental, woodpeckers keep trees alive and healthy. Many woodpeckers are readily attracted to bird feeders stocked with sunflower seeds. Suet is a preferred food and often used to attract these birds in winter.

Dens

Woodpeckers also use their beaks to excavate cavities in trees for nesting sites. Depending on the species, nests may be up to 2 feet deep beneath the entry hole. Woodpeckers carefully position the entry holes to their nest cavities. In the spring, woodpeckers lay their eggs and raise their young in their nest cavities. Both parents usually help to dig the nest cavity and care for the young.

Public Health

Woodpeckers are not considered to be a significant source for any infectious disease that can be transmitted to humans.

Problems and Their Solutions

Problems

Problems with woodpeckers are most likely to occur in the spring, with most damage falling into three categories: drumming, feeding and nesting. Many species rhythmically "drum" on resonating objects with their beaks as a territorial advertisement. Occasionally, drumming "stations" are set up on utility poles, gutters, chimney caps and other places on buildings that seem to have good resonance. Typically, drumming is con-

centrated in one area of the house, occurs persistently, is confined primarily to spring months and does not result in damage. Feeding can cause extensive damage to the exterior of buildings. Once they have established a feeding pattern on a house, woodpeckers can be very persistent. Nesting involves the largest hole-making activity, but is also the rarest of the three problems.

Solutions

TOLERANCE

While a property owner may be quite frustrated by attacks on siding or by other woodpecker activity around the house, the environmental benefits and enjoyment people derive from the presence of these birds certainly outweigh any damage or inconvenience they cause. Any problems a woodpecker may cause should be immediately addressed and solved with nonlethal methods. The key to effectively using nonlethal methods to resolve problems is to recognize woodpecker activity early in the damage cycle and respond appropriately to it.

EXCLUSION

Whether attacking a house for food or to drum, there are some simple techniques that can be used to exclude woodpeckers. Usually, exclusion is all that is needed, and the problem birds will move to another drumming site or seek food elsewhere. It's important to maintain the care and upkeep of the exterior of wooden houses to keep insect infestations at bay and to secure loose boards or to use filling behind those that do sound hollow and attract woodpecker drumming. Smaller boards and chimney caps may be covered with cloth or foam rubber padding until the habit is broken, taking care not to enclose the cap completely. It may be possible to hang bird netting, plastic sheeting or screen from the eaves and suspend it several inches from the affected wall to prevent access. When panels must be replaced, it may be helpful to add additional insulation to deaden the resonance.

The root cause of the problem is insect infestation, and the woodpeckers are doing the homeowner a favor by drawing attention to it. Insect control may necessitate hiring a professional exterminator. After the insects are controlled, the damaged siding should be repaired or replaced. Keep plastic in place for two to three weeks. Putting out suet may distract birds that are searching for insects on the house.

As a temporary measure, the homeowner can cover the part of the house under attack with a sheet of heavy plastic, nylon webbing or plastic storm window material. The material should be fastened to rain gutter or eaves so that it stands away from the wall at least 3 inches so that birds cannot grasp the wall through it. If there is nothing to fasten the screen to, then temporarily fasten a board along the top of the wall to attach it.

Woodpeckers excavate cavities for nesting, roosting and, in some species, for food storage. These holes will be round and deep and often occur at loose knots in the siding. The birds often start a hole and then abandon it and start another. In some cases, they may be confused when the hole penetrates the board and insulation is encountered. Sometimes the cavity is completed and nesting proceeds in the wall of the building. If the cavity is not used by the woodpecker, it may be used by other species, such as starlings or house sparrows.

This may be the most difficult problem to control, but several techniques have been successful. One thing to keep in mind is that the bird building a nest or roosting cavity is passing through a seasonal behavior pattern, and if it can be discouraged from completing a cavity in a building for a few days or weeks, it will probably fulfill its need elsewhere and stop trying to use the building. (There is no guarantee that the bird will not return next year, however.) Therefore, a combination of prompt repair of the damage as it occurs and a program of scare tactics usually works. Shallow holes can be quickly repaired with caulking or wood filler, which is usually available from building suppliers in a variety of matching colors. Larger holes (if no birds are inside) may be filled with wooden plugs or wadded window screen and then caulked. While repairing holes, also caulk any loose knots that may be in the area. Small mesh hardware cloth or welded wire can be used to cover damaged areas and protect them from further damage.

HABITAT MANAGEMENT

A few homeowners leave dead trees standing as habitat for wildlife, taking down only as much of the limb structure as might be hazardous to people. Perhaps this way of managing habitat can encourage woodpeckers not to "misbehave"—we don't know. There are nest boxes built to attract woodpeckers, and these might satisfy the needs of birds causing damage and eliminate their attraction to houses or outbuildings.

Sapsuckers are woodpeckers that drill rows of small holes in live trees to make sap flow. They then eat the sap as well as any insects caught in it. They rarely damage trees in doing this, but if protection is necessary, netting (see Chapter 3) the tree (see Figure 29, p. 188) can be effective. If the homeowner wishes, the affected area could be wrapped with hardware cloth or material such as burlap, but this often provides harborage for insects.

FRIGHTENING

A number of the devices described in the "Scare Devices" section of Chapter 3 are known to be effective against drumming or feeding woodpeckers, as well as homemade standbys such as wind chimes, aluminum pans and plastic streamers. The least expensive alternatives should be tried before going to the trouble and expense of employing other tactics. Hanging strips of aluminum foil, scare tape or cloth that flutters in the wind from the eaves may also frighten the offending bird off. Scare balloons can be used, or mylar party balloons tried. All are hung from the gutter or eave to cover the area under attack and scare birds off. One-inch (or greater) tape hung in strips 2 to 3 feet long are recommended. The strip should hang loosely and twist in the wind above the damaged area. Strips of aluminum foil might work in some cases.

Equip each end with a tape tab, using a tear-resistant tape such as duct tape or nylon packing tape. Nail one tab to the outer end of the roof soffit just under the guttering. Attach the other tab to the side of the house directly below the soffit tab. Before nailing the bottom tab, turn it over six times (three complete revolutions). Pull the tape downward until it is taut and then provide approximately $1/4$ inch of slack. The slack and twisting are necessary to produce the shimmering effect as the tape flutters in the wind.

Several tape strands should be mounted parallel at intervals of 2 to 3 feet. Even though the damage may be localized, put out at least five strands of tape with the center strand over the damage site. Within limits, the more tape installed the greater the chances for successful results. The ends of the house or multistory houses might be protected in much the same manner; longer lengths of tape will be required. Twist the tape at the rate of two turns (one revolution) per linear foot of tape.

A pinwheel with a reflective surface may also startle woodpeckers. The pinwheel is attached to siding with tape or industrial staples. To be effective, the vane must turn freely. An aluminum pie pan may be effective. Punch a small hole near the rim of the pan and then thread 2 feet of twine or monofilament line (fishing line) through the hole. Suspend the pan from a small nail hammered into the siding, or fasten the twine around a protrusion such as a tree branch. The pan should be positioned immediately above the area attacked by the woodpecker. The pie pan will spin or swivel in the breeze, clatter against the house and, on a clear day, it will also reflect sunlight. It is also possible to hang pie pans horizontally along a rope or thick section of twine. Run one end of the rope to a convenient window and fasten it to an object inside the house. Whenever you hear drumming, jerk on the string to make the pans move. A small mirror tied to a string and suspended from a nail may scare woodpeckers away even after damage has begun. When hung beside an excavation, the mirror enlarges the reflected image of the bird and frightens it with the threat of a large adversary.

Harass the bird by shouting, banging on a pot or gently squirting water from a hose. Homeowners must be persistent and consistent if they hope to dissuade the bird from causing damage. A woodpecker may be scared away by simply opening a nearby window or door and shouting or banging. If the homeowner is patient, in time the bird will get discouraged and move to another location.

REPELLENTS

No chemical has been found to deter woodpeckers from human-made structures. In general, chemical treatments are not an option for property owners. Some have been able to repel woodpeckers by treating wood siding with wood preservatives containing pentachlorophenol, but this has not been rigorously tested.

A Last Word

Individual birds vary in their susceptibility to methods of wildlife damage control. Timing, the availability of food and shelter and previous exposure to tactics will influence success. The property owner must weigh the trouble and expense of control against the scope of the damage caused by woodpeckers.

Afterword:
Looking Back toward the Future

The turn of the millennium will be a very interesting place from which to look back on this book. We will be looking "back" also from a world in which our wildlife will have returned to a time like the one before the turn of the last century—the time of the greatest exploitation and destruction of wildlife in our history. Hopefully, the techniques and approaches we so painstakingly have extolled will be outdated by then. And, hopefully, our understanding and compassion for wild animals will be much greater than they are now, as we experience them simply as a part of our lives that is expected and constant. Hopefully, books like this will not be needed.

It won't take much for us to achieve a greater understanding of urban and suburban wildlife because so little of it exists now.

Greater compassion comes from greater understanding. We have seen the gap between us and other living things shrink to a point where arguments promoting human superiority rarely (if ever) fit in any system of logic. The great uncertainty is what will happen with technology. Undoubtedly humanity's strongest suit, it could become a very potent weapon in the hands of those who seek to resolve human-wildlife conflicts by destroying rather than by understanding it. If we do not teach ourselves and teach our children what it means to be a member of a community of living things, then our technology will be used to destroy. Education, the weight that balances all of technology's advances, must be used to foster understanding, respect and compassion. To this end, we all have to be teachers—and students.

Appendix 1:
Sources of Information

Wildlife Damage Control Books

The Nebraska Handbook (S. E. Hyngstrom, R. M. Timm, and G. E. Larson. 1994. *Prevention and Control of Wildlife Damage.* University of Nebraska Extension Service. 2 vols.) is now in its second edition and is expanded to include two volumes and appendices. This is the most comprehensive guide to wildlife damage published anywhere. It covers agricultural, livestock, commercial and urban/suburban contexts. It does include, and sometimes even emphasizes, lethal control procedures, but for many groups of animals (e.g., bats) and in places where urban and suburban wildlife is discussed this handbook does appropriately focus on nonlethal control. It is available from

The University of Nebraska
Wildlife Damage Handbook
202 Natural Resources Hall
University of Nebraska
Lincoln, NE 68583-0819
(402) 472-2188

The two-volume copy retails for about $40 + shipping. A CD-ROM version is also available.

The Florida Wildlife Resources Handbook (F. Mazzotti, J. Schaefer, C. N. Huegel, and B. Kern. 1995. University of Florida, Institute of Food and Agricultural Sciences) is a comprehensive guide to Florida wildlife and the problems of suburban and urban residents; it includes many species also found throughout the Southeast. The guide is several hundred pages of information in a loose-leaf format that allows the owner to subscribe to additions and updates. It contains species accounts, information on techniques, names and addresses of private control operators and a lot of other information on how to address wildlife problems. It can be ordered from

Cooperative Urban Wildlife Program
Department of Wildlife Ecology
  and Conservation
P.O. Box 110430
Gainesville, FL 32611-0430

and currently sells for about $30.

Living with Wildlife (Sierra Club Books. 1994. The California Center for Wildlife with Diane Landau and Shelley Stump) is an engaging book that combines many sensible and reasonable nonlethal approaches to wildlife problem solving with information on appreciation and wildlife viewing opportunities. It is available in many bookstores or from the Center and currently retails at about $15.

Two books by Bill Adler (*Outwitting Squirrels.* 1988. Chicago Review Press and *Outwitting Critters.* 1992. HarperPerennial) provide enjoyable, insightful and often humorous insights into coping with conflicts with wild animals around the home.

Extension Service Literature

Several states have brochures series that focus on human-wildlife conflicts. Some are heavily geared toward agricultural and rural issues, but some address urban solutions as well. Wildlife series are published by

Kansas State University
Kansas Wildlife & Parks
127 Call Hall
Manhattan, KS 66506-1609

The University of Kentucky
College of Agriculture
Cooperative Extension Service
Lexington, KY 40546

Missouri Department of Conservation
P.O. Box 180
Jefferson City, MO 20240

Cornell Cooperative Extension
Department of Natural Resources
Cornell University
Ithaca, NY 14853

Additional Books on Urban and Suburban Wildlife

Adams, L. 1994. *Urban Wildlife Habitats: A Landscape Perspective.* Minneapolis: University of Minnesota Press. 186 pp.

Baines, C. 1986.*The Wild Side of Town.* London: BBC Publications and Elm Tree Books. 186 pp.

Gilbert, O. L. 1989. *The Ecology of Urban Habitats.* London: Chapman and Hall. 369 pp.

Harris, S. 1986. *Urban Foxes.* Biddles of Guilford, England: Whittet Books. 128 pp.

Harrison, K., and G. Harrison. 1985. *America's Favorite Backyard Wildlife.* New York: Simon and Schuster. 320 pp.

Kinkead, E. 1978. *Wildness Is All around Us: Notes of an Urban Naturalist.* New York: E. P. Dutton. 178 pp.

Landry, S. B. 1994. *Peterson's First Guide to Urban Wildlife.* Boston: Houghton Mifflin. 128 pp.

Long, K. 1995. *Squirrels: A Wildlife Handbook.* Boulder, Colo.: Johnson Books. 181 pp.

Mitchell, J. H. 1985. *A Field Guide to Your Own Back Yard.* New York: W. W. Norton. 288 pp.

Mohrhardt, D., and R. E. Schinkel. 1991. *Suburban Nature Guide.* Harrisburg, Pa.: Stackpole Books. 252 pp.

Swanson, D. 1995. *Coyotes in the Crosswalk.* Stillwater, Minn.: Voyageur Press. 72 pp.

Tuttle, M. D. 1988. *America's Neighborhood Bats.* Austin: University of Texas Press. 104 pp.

Books on Wildlife Law

King, S. T., and J. R. Schrock. 1985. *Controlled Wildlife.* Vol. III: State Wildlife Regulations. Washington, D.C.: The Association of Systematics Collections. 315 pp.

Littell, R. 1993. *Controlled Wildlife.* Vol. I: Federal Permit Procedures. Washington, D.C.: The Association of Systematics Collections. 264 pp.

Musgrave, R. S., and M. A. Stein. 1993. *State Wildlife Laws Handbook*. Rockville, Md.: Government Institutes. 840 pp.

Newsletters and Periodicals

Urban Wildlife News is a newsletter published in the United Kingdom under the auspices of UNESCO's Man and the Biosphere Project No. 11. For copies, send name and address to George Barker, English Nature, Northminster House, Peterborough PE1 1UA, England. (There is no charge.)

The Urban Open Space Manager Newsletter is published quarterly by Urban Wildlife Resources, 5130 W. Running Brook Road, Columbia, MD 21044; (410) 997-7161 or (fax) (410) 997-6849. Available by subscription at $15 per year.

Urban Nature Magazine is published by Urban Environment, 40 Milford Road, Harborne, Birmingham B17 9RL, England. Contact the publisher for up-to-date subscription prices.

The IPM Practioneer and *Common Sense Pest Control Quarterly* are published by the BioIntegral Resource Center (BIRC) in Berkeley, California. Both address a variety of strategies and techniques for controlling wildlife problems in environmentally responsible and harmonious ways. Subscription rates are currently $25 a year for each of the publications. Contact BIRC at P.O. Box 7414, Berkeley, CA 94707; (510) 524-2567.

The National Wildlife Federation publishes the *Conservation Directory* and *Backyard Habitat Program Newsletter*. The *Conservation Directory*, published annually, is the most comprehensive guide to governmental, state and private organizations that deal with conservation issues. The Backyard Wildlife Program of the NWF is a long-standing series of resources that encourages people to enhance the value of their yards for wildlife. Contact NWF at 1400 16th Street NW, Washington, DC 20036-2266; (202) 797-6800.

Associations and Organizations

Bat Conservation International
P.O. Box 162603
Austin, TX 78716
(512) 327-9721
(512) 327-9724 (fax)

Beaver Defenders
Unexpected Wildlife Refuge
P.O. Box 765
Newfield, NJ 08344
(609) 697-3541

Beaver, Wetlands & Wildlife
P.O. Box 591
Little Falls, NY 13365
(518) 568-2077

BioIntegral Resource Center (BIRC)
P.O. Box 7414
Berkeley, CA 94707
(510) 524-2567
(510) 524-1758 (fax)

The California Center for Wildlife
76 Albert Park Lane
P.O. Box 150957
San Rafael, CA 94915-0959
(415) 456-7283

Driftwood Wildlife Association
1206 West 38th, Suite 1105

Austin, TX 78705
(512) 266-2397

The Fund for Animals
200 W. 57th Street
New York, NY 10019
(212) 246-2096

National Animal Damage
Control Association
Route 1, Box 37
Shell Lake, WI 54871
(717) 468-2038

The National Wildlife Federation
1400 Sixteenth Street NW
Washington, DC 20036-2266
(202) 797-6800

Tufts Center for Animals and Public Policy
Tufts University
School of Veterinary Medicine
200 Westboro Road
North Grafton, MA 01536
(508) 839-7991

Urban Wildlife Resources
5130 W. Running Brook Road
Columbia, MD 21044
(410) 997-7161
(410) 997-6849 (fax)

HSUS Regional Offices

CENTRAL STATES REGIONAL OFFICE
800 West Fifth Avenue, Suite 110
Naperville, IL 60563
(630) 357-7015
(630) 357-5725 (fax)
(SERVES: TN, KY, NC, IL, MN, WI)

GREAT LAKES REGIONAL OFFICE
745 Haskins Street
Bowling Green, OH 43402-1696

(419) 352-5141
(419) 354-5351 (fax)
(SERVES: OH, IN, MI, WV)

MID-ATLANTIC REGIONAL OFFICE
Bartley Square
270 Route 206
Flanders, NJ 07836
(201) 927-5611
(201) 927-5617 (fax)
(SERVES: DE, NJ, NY, PA)

MIDWEST REGIONAL OFFICE
Argyle Building
306 East 12th Street, Suite 625
Kansas City, MO 64106
(816) 474-0888
(816) 474-0898 (fax)
(SERVES: MO, KS, NE, IA)

NEW ENGLAND REGIONAL OFFICE
Route 112
P.O. Box 619 (mailing address)
Halifax Jacksonville Town Line
Jacksonville, VT 05342-0619
(802) 368-2790
(802) 368-2756 (fax)
(SERVES: CT, MA, ME, NH, RI, VT)

NORTHERN ROCKIES
REGIONAL OFFICE
490 North 31st Street, Suite 315
Billings, MT 59101
(406) 255-7161
(406) 255-7162 (fax)
(SERVES: MT, WY, ID, SD, ND)

SOUTHEAST REGIONAL OFFICE
1624 Metropolitan Circle, Suite B
Tallahassee, FL 32308
(904) 386-3435
(904) 386-4534 (fax)
(SERVES: FL, AL, GA, SC, MS)

SOUTHWEST REGIONAL OFFICE
3001 LBJ Freeway, Suite 224
Dallas, TX 75234
(972) 488-2964
(972) 488-2965 (fax)
(SERVES: AZ, UT, CO, NM, AR, LA, OK, TX)

WEST COAST REGIONAL OFFICE
5301 Madison Avenue, Suite 202
P.O. Box 417220 (mailing address)
Sacramento, CA 95841-7220
(916) 344-1710
(916) 344-1808 (fax)
(SERVES: CA, OR, NV, WA)

Federal Agency Offices

Centers for Disease Control
and Prevention
Atlanta, GA
　　General information: (404) 639-1075
　　Rabies hotline: (404) 332-4555
　　Hantavirus hotline: (800) 532 9929

U.S. Environmental Protection Agency
Prevention, Pesticides and Toxic
Substances
　　Pesticide programs: (202) 305-7090
　　Pollution prevention and toxics: (202) 260-3810
　　Compliance monitoring: (202) 260-4543

U.S. Department of Agriculture Animal and Plant Health Inspection Service (APHIS-ADC)

P.O. Box 96464
Animal Damage Control Program
Room 1624, South Agriculture Building

Washington, DC 20090-6464
Operational Support Staff
(301) 734-8281

Denver Wildlife Research Center
Information and Technology Transfer
P.O. Box 25266, Building 16
Denver Federal Center
Denver, CO 80225-0266
(303) 236-7874

Regional Offices

ALABAMA
See Mississippi.

ALASKA
See Washington.

ARIZONA
1960 W. North Lane
Phoenix, AZ 85021
(602) 241-2537

ARKANSAS
55 Post Office Building
600 W. Capitol Avenue
Little Rock, AR 72201
(501) 378-5382

CALIFORNIA
Federal Building
Room E-1831
2800 Cottage Way
Sacramento, CA 95825
(916) 978-4621

COLORADO
Independence Plaza, Suite B-107
529 25 $^1/_2$ Road
Grand Junction, CO 81505-6122
(970) 245-9618

CONNECTICUT
See Massachusetts.

DELAWARE
See Maryland.

DISTRICT OF COLUMBIA
See Maryland.

FLORIDA
227 N. Bronough Street, Suite 1022
Tallahassee, FL 32301
(904) 681-7459

GEORGIA
School of Forest Resources
University of Georgia
Athens, GA 30602
(404) 546-2020

HAWAII
See Washington.

IDAHO
4696 Overland
Boise, ID 83705
(208) 334-1440

ILLINOIS
Federal Building, Room 104
600 E. Monroe Street
Springfield, IL 62701
(217) 492-4308

INDIANA
Entomology Hall, Room B-14
Purdue University
West Lafayette, IN 47907
(317) 494-6229

IOWA
See Missouri.

KANSAS
See Oklahoma.

KENTUCKY
See Tennessee.

LOUISIANA
P.O. Box 25315
University Station
Baton Rouge, LA 70893-5315
(504) 389-0229

MAINE
Federal Building, Room 506A
40 Western Avenue
P.O. Box 800
Augusta, ME 04330-0800
(207) 622-8262

MARYLAND
1825 Virginia Avenue
Annapolis, MD 21401
(301) 269-0057

MASSACHUSETTS
463 West Street
Amherst, MA 01002
(413) 253-2403

MICHIGAN
108 Spring Street
St. Johns, MI 48879
(517) 224-9517
(517) 224-9518 (fax)

MINNESOTA
see Wisconsin.

MISSISSIPPI
Mississippi State University
P.O. Drawer FW, Dorman Hall,
Room 316
Mississippi State, MS 39762
(601) 325-3014

MISSOURI
Federal Building, Room 259-C
601 E. 12th Street
Kansas City, MO 64106
(816) 426-6166

MONTANA
P.O. Box 1938
Billings, MT 59103
(406) 657-6464

NEBRASKA
437 Federal Building
Lincoln, NE 68508
(402) 437-5097

NEVADA
4600 Kietzke Lane
Building C
Reno, NV 89502
(702) 784-5081

NEW HAMPSHIRE
P.O. Box 2398
Concord, NH 03302-2398
(603) 225-1416

NEW JERSEY
RD #1, Box 148-A
Pleasant Plains Road
Basking Ridge, NJ 07920
(201) 647-4109

NEW MEXICO
10304 Candelaria NE
Albuquerque, NM 87112
(505) 275-5220

NEW YORK
P.O. Box 97
O'Brien Federal Building, Room 126
Albany, NY 12201
(518) 472-6492

NORTH CAROLINA
Federal Building, Room 624
P.O. Box 25878
Raleigh, NC 27611
(919) 856-4132

NORTH DAKOTA
1500 Capitol Avenue
Bismark, ND 58501
(701) 250-4405

OHIO
Federal Building, Room 622
200 N. High Street
Columbus, OH 43215
(614) 469-5681

OKLAHOMA
2800 N. Lincoln Boulevard
Oklahoma City, OK 73105-4298
(405) 521-4039

OREGON
727 NE 24th Avenue
Portland, OR 97232
(503) 231-6184

PENNSYLVANIA
See New Jersey.

RHODE ISLAND
See Massachusetts.

SOUTH CAROLINA
Federal Building
Strom Thurmond, Room 904
1835 Assembly Building

Columbus, SC 29201
(803) 765-5957

SOUTH DAKOTA
See Nebraska.

TENNESSEE
441 Donelson Pike, Suite 340
Nashville, TN 37214
(615) 736-5506

TEXAS
P.O. Box 830337
San Antonio, TX 78283-0337
(512) 229-5535

UTAH
P.O. Box 26976
Salt Lake City, UT 84126-0976
(801) 524-5629

VERMONT
See New Hampshire.

VIRGINIA/WEST VIRGINIA
105 Wilson Avenue
Blacksburg, VA 24208
(703) 552-8792

WASHINGTON
3625 93rd Avenue, SW
Olympia, WA 98502
(206) 753-9884

WEST VIRGINIA
See Virginia.

WISCONSIN
750 Windsor Street, Room 207
Sun Prairie, WI 53590
(608) 837-2727

WYOMING
P.O. Box 59
Casper, WY 82602
(307) 271-5336

U.S. Department of the Interior U.S. Fish and Wildlife Service Regional Offices

United States Fish and Wildlife Service
1849 C Street, NW
Washington, DC 20240
(202) 208-4717

Region 1

PACIFIC REGIONAL Office—
CA, HI and Pacific Islands, ID NV, OR, WA
Eastside Federal Complex
911 NE 11th Avenue
Portland, OR 97232-4181
(503) 231-6118

Region 2

SOUTHWEST REGIONAL Office—
AZ, MN, OK, TX
500 Gold Avenue, SW, Room 3018
Albuquerque, NM 87102
(508) 248-6282

Region 3

GREAT LAKES/BIG RIVERS
REGIONAL Office—
IA, IL, IN, MI, MN, MO, OH, WI
1 Federal Drive
Federal Building
Fort Snelling, MN 55111
(612) 725-3563

Region 4

SOUTHEAST REGIONAL Office—AL,AR,
FL, GA, KY, LA, MS, NC, PR, SC, TN, VI
1875 Century Boulevard
Atlanta, GA 30345
(404) 679-4000

Region 5

NORTHEAST REGIONAL Office—
CT, DC, DE, MA, MD, ME, NH, NJ, PA, RI,
VA, VT, WV
300 Westgate Center Drive
Hadley, MA 01035
(413) 253-8200

Region 6

MOUNTAIN/PRAIRIE
REGIONAL Office—
CO, KS, MT, ND, NE, SD, UT, WY
134 Union Boulevard
P.O. Box 25486
Denver, CO 80225
(303) 236-7920

Region 7

ALASKA REGIONAL Office—AK
1011 East Tudor Road
Anchorage, AK 99503
(907) 786-3542

Appendix 2:
Sources of Products

This section lists manufacturers and distributors of products discussed throughout this book. No endorsement of specific brands or any product line by The Humane Society of the United States is implied or intended by inclusion here or elsewhere in this work.

We have tried to make this list a comprehensive reference to providers of materials and products that are humane and that can be considered appropriate for use in nonlethal animal control under proper circumstances. We know that the list is not complete, and we regret any omissions. In some cases, companies that purport to market "humane" products are omitted because they also manufacture and distribute products that The HSUS considers inhumane. In some cases, a product is considered potentially humane if used under exacting and rigorous circumstances, but is felt by us to present too great a risk to animals to be included in this list. (As an example, we have chosen not to list *any* solid metal live traps although there are several marketed. We simply feel there is too great a risk for animals caught in these devices to suffer from extreme exposure to both cold and heat to warrant their use.)

The resources listed here are comparable, to the extent possible, with the sections in Chapter 3, "Tools and Tactics," as well as in the individual species accounts. Some companies have several lines of products, and although we have tried to be as inclusive as possible, we have undoubtedly missed some of these. We would appreciate hearing from anyone with information not included here, as we will continue to update and periodically publish revisions of this list. Such information can be sent to Urban Wildlife Program, HSUS, 2100 L Street, NW, Washington, DC 20037.

General Supplies

Ben Meadows Company
3589 Broad Street
Atlanta, GA 30341
(800) 241-6401
(800) 628-2068 (fax)

Forestry Suppliers, Inc.
P. O. Box 8397
Jackson, MS 39284-8397
(800) 647-5368
(800) 543-4203 (fax)

The Hugé Company
P.O. Box 24198
St. Louis, MO 63130
(800) 873-4843
(314) 725-2555 (fax)

Lakeshore Enterprises
2804 Benzie Highway

Benzonia, MI 49616
(616) 882-9601

Wildlife Control Technology, Inc.
2501 N. Sunnyside, #103
Fresno, CA 93727
(800) 235-0262
(209) 294-0632 (fax)

or

P.O. Box 151245
Cape Coral, FL 33915-1245
(941) 549-4625
(941) 549-4625 (fax)

Wildlife Management Supplies
K.D. Clark Services, Inc.
640 Starkweather
Plymouth, MI 48170
(800) 451-6544
(313) 453-6395 (fax)

Acoustical Alarms

Falcon Safety Products, Inc. (air horns)
25 Cubbway Road
P.O. Box 1299
Somerville, NJ 08876-1299
(908) 707-4900

Reed-Joseph International Company
P.O. Box 894
Greenville, MS 38702
(800) 647-5554
(601) 335-8850 (fax)

Weitech, Inc.
(Birdgard® AVA; Birdgard® GNB™)
P.O. Box 1659
310 Barclay Way
Sisters, OR 97759
(800) 343-2659
(503) 549-8154 (fax)

Animal Care and Handling

Animal Care Equipments & Services, Inc.
(ACES)
P.O. Box 3275
613 Lee Bert Way
Crestline, CA 92325
(800) 338-2237
(800) 338-2799 (fax)

Animal Management, Inc.
P.O. Box 957
Mechanicsburg, PA 17055-9786
(800) 745-8173
(800) 745-8193 (fax)

Ketch-All Company
Dept. AC
4149 Santa Fe Road #2
San Luis Obispo, CA 93401
(805) 543-7223
(805) 543-7154 (fax)

Animal-Proof Trash Containers

Capital Industries, Inc.
5801 Third Avenue South
Seattle, WA 98108
(206) 762-8585

Cubic Container Manufacturing (bear-proof dumpsters and lids)
11619 Pendleton Street
Sun Valley, CA 91532
(818) 504-7022

McClintock Metal Fabricators, Inc.
(Hid-a-Bag® bear-proof containers;
Hyd-a-Meal™ food storage lockers)
455 Harter Avenue
Woodland, CA 95776-6105
(916) 666-6007
(916) 666-7071 (fax)

Beaver Bafflers

DCP Consulting, Ltd.
*(Cory Beaver Stop®) (culvert beaver
excluders)*
3219 Coleman Road NW
Calgary, Alberta T2L 1G6
Canada
(800) 565-1152
(403) 220-9591 (fax)

Bird Distress Calls

Bird-X, Inc.
300 North Elizabeth Street
Chicago, IL 60607
(800) 662-5021
(312) 226-2480 (fax)

Margo Supplies, Ltd.
P.O. Box 5400
High River, Alberta T1V 1M5
Canada
(403) 652-1932
(403) 652-3511 (fax)

Reed-Joseph International Company
P.O. Box 894
230 Main Street
Greenville, MS 38701
(800) 647-5554
(601) 335-8850 (fax)

Sutton Agricultural Enterprises, Inc.
746 Vertin Avenue
Salinas, CA 93901
(408) 422-9693
(408) 422-4201 (fax)

Bird Wires

Bird Barrier America, Inc.
*(Bird Barrier Coils; Bird Barrier Birdpoint™;
Bird Barrier Birdwire™; Daddi Long Legs)*
1312 Kingsdale Avenue
Redondo Beach, CA 90278
(800) 503-5444
(310) 793-1732 (fax)

Birdmaster
International Bird Control Systems, Inc.
32 Cummings Park
Woburn, MA 01801
(800) 562-2473
(617) 937-0958 (fax)

Bird-X, Inc.
(Bird-X Spikes™)
300 North Elizabeth Street
Chicago, IL 60607
(800) 662-5021
(312) 226-2480 (fax)

Cat Claw®, Inc.
(Cat claw®)
P.O. Box 3778
Johnston, PA 15904
(800) 832-2473
(814) 269-3800 (fax)

Nixalite® of America, Inc.
(Nixilite®)
1025 16th Avenue
P.O. Box 727
East Moline, IL 61244-0727
(800) 624-1189
(309) 755-0077 (fax)

Caulking and Foam Sealants

Wildlife Management Supplies
K.D. Clark Services, Inc.
(Todol Foam Gun Kits)
640 Starkweather
Plymouth, MI 48170
(800) 451-6544
(313) 453-6395 (fax)

Chimney Caps

Chim Cap Corp.
120 Schmitt Boulevard
Farmingdale, NY 11735
(800) 262-9622
(516) 454-7535 (fax)

HY-C Company, Inc.
2107 N. 14th Street
St. Louis, MO 63106
(800) 325-7076
(314) 241-2277 (fax)

Disinfectants

Jeffers
P.O. Box 100
Dothan, AL 36302-0100
(800) 533-3377
(334) 793-5179 (fax)

Door Curtains

Consolidated Plastics Company, Inc.
8181 Darrow Road
Twinburg, OH 44087
(800) 362-1000
(216) 425-3333 (fax)

Effigies and Scarecrows

Bird-X, Inc.
300 North Elizabeth Street
Chicago, IL 60607
(800) 662-5021
(312) 226-2480 (fax)

W. Atlee Burpee & Company
300 Park Avenue
Warminster, PA 18974
(800) 333-5808
(800) 888-1447 (to order catalog)

Electric Fencing

Advanced Farms Systems
(Techfence®)
RD 1, Box 364
Bradford, ME 04410
(207) 327-1237

Gallagher Power Fence, Inc.
18940 Redland Road
P.O. Box 708900
San Antonio, TX 78270
(800) 531-5908
(512) 494-5211 (fax)

Grassland Supply *(Speedrite®)*
1126 Old Highway 56
Council Grove, KS 66846
(316) 767-5487
(316) 767-6679 (fax)

Jeffers
(Parmark®; Dare™)
P.O. Box 100
Dothan, AL 3630-0100
(800) 533-3377
(334) 793-5179 (fax)

Kiwi Fence Systems, Inc.
(Kiwi Fence®)
1145 East Roy Furman Highway
Waynesburg, PA 15370
(412) 627-5640
(412) 627-9791 (fax)

Live Wire Products, Inc.
(Stafix)
1127 East Street
Marysville, CA 95901

(800) 272-9045
(916) 743-0609 (fax)

Margo Supplies, Ltd.
P.O. Box 5400
High River, Alberta T1V 1M5
Canada
(403) 285-9731
(403) 652-3511 (fax)

Multi-Tech Industries, Inc.
(Techfence®)
Tech Fence Division
P.O. Box 159
Marlboro, NJ 07746-0159
(908) 462-6101
(908) 409-6695 (fax)

Premier Fence Systems
(Maxishock™)
2031 300th Street
Washington, IA 52353
(319) 653-6631
(319) 653-6034 (fax)

Waterford Corporation
(Shock Tactics®)
P.O. Box 1513
Fort Collins, CO 80522
(800) 525-4952
(970) 482-0934 (fax)

West Virginia Fence Corp.
(Maxflex®)
U.S. Route 219
Lindside, WV 24951
(800) 356-5458
(304) 753-4827 (fax)

Garden and Yard Supply

Alsto's Handy Helpers
P.O. Box 1267
Galesburg, IL 61401
(800) 447-0048
(800) 522-5786 (fax)

A.M. Leonard
P.O. Box 816
Piqua, OH 45356-0816
(800) 543-8955
(800) 433-0633 (fax)

Gardener's Eden
P.O. Box 7307
San Francisco, CA 94120-7307
(800) 822-9600
(415) 421-5153 (fax)

Gardener's Supply Company
128 Intervale Road
Burlington, VT 05401
(800) 863-1700
(802) 660-4600 (fax)

Plow & Hearth
P.O. Box 5000
Madison, VA 22727-1500
(800) 627-1712
(800) 843-2509 (fax)

W. Atlee Burpee & Company
300 Park Avenue
Warminster, PA 18974
(800) 333-5808
(800) 888-1447 (to order catalog)

High Tensile, Woven Wire, Polypropylene Fencing

Bekacet
(Tightlock™ Game Fence)
1395 South Mariette Parkway
Building 500, Suite 100
Mariette, GA 30067
(800) 241-4126
(770) 421-8521 (fax)

Benner's Gardens
6974 Upper York Road
New Hope, PA 18938
(800) 753-4660
(215) 477-9429 (fax)

Kiwi Fence Systems, Inc.
(Kiwi Fence®, Spider Systems)
1145 East Roy Furman Highway
Waynesburg, PA 15370
(412) 627-5640
(412) 627-9791 (fax)

Highway Reflectors

Streiter Corporation
(Strieter-Lite®)
2100 Eighteenth Avenue
Rock Island, IL 61201
(309) 794-9800
(309) 788-5646 (fax)

Lights

Bird-X, Inc.
300 N. Elizabeth Street
Chicago, IL 60607
(800) 662-5021
(312) 226-2480 (fax)

Reed-Joseph International Company
P.O. Box 894
230 Main Street
Greenville, MS 38701
(800) 647-5554
(601) 335-8850 (fax)

Netting

Bird Barrier America, Inc.
(Bird Barrier StealthNet™)
1312 Kingsdale Avenue
Redondo Beach, CA 90278
(800) 503-5444
(310) 793-1732 (fax)

Birdmaster
International Bird Control Systems, Inc.
32 Cummings Park
Woburn, MA 01801
(800) 562-2473
(617) 937-0958

Bird-X, Inc.
300 N. Elizabeth Street
Chicago, IL 60607
(800) 662-5021
(312) 226-2480 (fax)

J.A. Cissel Mfg. Co.
(Toprite® Netting)
P.O. Box 2025
Lakewood, NJ 08701
(800) 328-8456
(908) 901-1166 (fax)

Internet, Inc.
2730 Nevada Avenue North
Minneapolis, MN 55427
(800) 328-8456
(612) 541-9692 (fax)

Margo Supplies, Ltd.
P.O. Box 5400
High River, Alberta T1V 1M5
Canada
(403) 285-9731
(403) 652-3511 (fax)

ProSoCo, Inc.
P.O. Box 171677
Kansas City, KS 66117
(913) 281-2700
(913) 281-4385 (fax)

Quadel Industries
200 Tory Street
Coos Bay, OR 97420
(541) 267-2622
(541) 269-7300 (fax)

Sutton AG Enterprises, Inc.
746 Vertin Avenue
Salinas, CA 93901
(408) 422-9693
(408) 422-4201 (fax)

Valentine, Inc.
4259 S. Western Boulevard
Chicago, IL 60609
(800) 438-7883
(312) 650-9099

Wildlife Control Technology , Inc.
2501 N. Sunnyside #103
Fresno, CA 93727
(800) 235-0262
(209) 294-0632 (fax)
or
P.O. Box 151245
Cape Coral, FL 33915-1245
(941) 549-4625
(941) 549-4625 (fax)

Odor Control

G. G. Bean, Inc.
P.O. Drawer 638
Brunswick, ME 04011-0638
(800) 238-1915
(207) 725-6097

Drs. Foster & Smith
2253 Air Park Road
P. O. Box 100
Rhinelander, WI 54501-0100
(800) 826-7206
(800) 776-8872 (fax)

NoStink, Inc.
(Odorzout™)
6020 W. Bell Road, # E101
Glendale, AZ 85308
(800) 887-8465

One-Way Doors

Tomahawk Live Trap Company
(Tomahawk® Excluders)
P.O. Box 323
Tomahawk, WI 54487
(800) 272-8727
(715) 453-4326 (fax)

Plant Covers

Gardener's Supply Company
128 Intervale Road
Burlington, VT 05401
(800) 863-1700
(802) 660-4600 (fax)

W. Atlee Burpee & Company
300 Park Avenue
Warminster, PA 18974
(800) 333-5808
(800) 888-1447 (to order catalog)

Pyrotechnic Devices

H.C. Shaw Company
P.O. Box 31510
Stockton, CA 95213
(800) 221-2884
(209) 983-8449 (fax)

Margo Supplies, Ltd.
P.O. Box 5400
High River, Alberta T1V 1M5
Canada
(403) 285-9731
(403) 652-3511 (fax)

Reed-Joseph International Company
P.O. Box 894
Greenville, MS 38702
(800) 647-5554

Sutton AG Enterprises, Inc.
(Bird Bombs®, Bird Whistlers®)
746 Vertin Avenue
Salinas, CA 93901
(408) 422-9693
(408) 422-4201 (fax)

Repellents

Bird Shield® Repellent Corporation
(Bird Shield®) (methyl anthranilate)

P.O. Box 785
Pullman, WA
(509) 332-1989
(509) 334-1552 (fax)

Bonide Chemical Company
(TKO®, Shotgun®)
2 Wurz Avenue
Yorkville, NY 13495
(315) 736-8231

Burlington Bio-Medical
& Scientific Corporation
(Ro-Pel®) (bittering agent)
222 Sherwood Avenue
Farmingdale, NY 11735-1718
(516) 694-9000
(516) 694-9177 (fax)

Deer-Off, Inc.
(Deer-Off®)
(putrescent egg solids, capsaicin, garlic)
58 High Valley Way
Stamford, CT 06903-2714
(203) 968-8485
(203) 968-2882 (fax)

Dr. T's Nature Products
(Dr. T's Snake-A-Way® Repellent)
(sulphur, napthalene)
The Repellent Company
P.O. Box 682
Pelham, GA 31779

Earl May Seed & Nursery Company
(Rabbit-Scat®)
208 North Elm
Shenandoah, IA 51603
(712) 246-1020
(712) 246-1760 (fax)

Gustafson, Inc.
(Thiram 42-S)
P.O. Box 220065
Dallas, TX 75222

(800) 527-4781
(214) 931-8899

IntAgra, Inc.
(Deer-Away®; GET-AWAY™)
(putrescent egg solids; capsaicin and oil of mustard)
8500 Pillsbury Avenue South
Minneapolis, MN 55420
(800) 468-2472
(612) 881-7002

Miller Chemical and Fertilizer Corp.
(Miller's Hot Sauce®)
P.O. Box 333
Radio Road
Hanover, PA 17331
(800) 233-2040
(717) 632-9638

Mole-Med, Inc.
(Mole-Med®) (castor oil)
P.O. Box 333
Aurora, IN 47001
(800) 255-2527
(812) 537-9750

Nott Manufacturing
(Chew-Nott™)
P.O. Box 685
Pleasant Valley, NY 12569
(914) 635-3243
(914) 635-3243 (fax)

Pace International, Ltd.
(Hinder®)
Leffingwell Division
500 Seventh Avenue South
Kirkland, WA 98033
(800) 247-8711
(206) 822-8261

Plant Pro-Tec, Inc.
(Garlic)
P.O. Box 902

Palo Cedro, CA 96073
(800) 572-0055
(916) 547-5450 (fax)

RJ Advantage, Inc.
(ReJeX-iT®) (methyl anthranilate)
501 Murray Road
Cincinnati, OH 45217
(513) 482-7320
(513) 482-7377 (fax)

Safety and Personal Protection

Gall's, Inc.
2680 Palumbo Drive
P.O. Box 55268
Lexington, KY 40555-5268
(800) 477-7766
(800) 944-2557

Gemplers
211 Blue Mounds Road
P.O. Box 270
Mt. Horeb, WI 53572-0270
(800) 382-8473
(800) 551-1128 (fax)

Nasco Farm & Ranch
901 Janesville Avenue
Fort Atkinson, WI 53538-0901
(800) 558-9595
(414) 563-8296

Scare Balloons

Bird-X, Inc.
300 North Elizabeth Street
Chicago, IL 60607
(800) 662-5021
(312) 226-2480 (fax)

Reed-Joseph International Company
P.O. Box 894
230 Main Street
Greenville, MS 38701

(800) 647-5554
(601) 335-8850 (fax)

Scare Tape

Bird-X
300 North Elizabeth Street
Chicago, IL 60607
(800) 662-5021
(312) 226-2480 (fax)

Reed-Joseph International Company
P.O. Box 894
230 Main Street
Greenville, MS 38701
(800) 647-5554
(601) 335-8850 (fax)

Sutton AG Enterprises, Inc.
746 Vertin Avenue
Salinas, CA 93901
(408) 422-9693
(408) 422-4201 (fax)

Sprinklers

Contech Enterprises, Inc.
(Scarecrow™ Motion Activated Sprinkler)
P.O. Box 115
Saanichton, British Columbia V0S 1M0
Canada
(800) 767-8658
(250) 652-5351 (fax)

Traps, Live

Hancock Traps
(Hancock Beaver Trap)
P.O. Box 268
Custer, SD 57730
(605) 673-4128

H.B. Sherman Traps, Inc.
P.O. Box 20267
Tallahassee, FL 32316

(904) 575-8727
(904) 575-4864 (fax)

Kness Manufacturing Company, Inc.
(Kage-all live traps)
Highway 5 South
P.O. Box 70
Albia, IA 52531-0070
(515) 247-5062
(515) 932-2456 (fax)

Mitlyng Development
(Minnesota Plastic-catch™)
P.O. Box 43A
Darwin, MN 55324
(612) 275-2523
(612) 275-2523 (fax)

M.S.I. Tru-Catch
(Tru-Catch Traps)
P.O. Box 816
Belle Fourche, SD 57717
(800) 247-6132
(605) 892-6327

Mustang Manufacturing Company
(Mustang Live-Catch Traps)
P.O. Box 920947
Houston, TX 77292
(713) 682-0811

National Live Trap Corporation
(National Live Trap)
P.O. Box 302
Tomahawk, WI 54487
(715) 453-2249
(715) 453-4326 (fax)

Safe-N-Sound Live Traps
(Safe-N-Sound)
P.O. Box 573
Hutchinson, MN 55350
(800) 795-8093
(612) 864-6956 (fax)

Tomahawk Live Trap Company
(Tomahawk® Live Traps;
Bailey Beaver Trap)
P.O. Box 323
Tomahawk, WI 54487
(800) 272-8727
(715) 453-4326

Tree Protectors

Davlyn Manufacturing Company, Inc.
(Tree Tender™)
P.O. Box 626
Chester Springs, PA 19475
(215) 948-5050

Forestry Suppliers, Inc.
P.O. Box 8397
Jackson, MS 39284-8397
(800) 647-5368
(800) 543-4203 (fax)

Tree Pro
3180 West 250 North
W. Lafayette, IN 47906
(800) 875-8071

Treessentials Company
(Supertube® tree shelters)
Riverview Station
P.O. Box 7097
St. Paul, MN 55107
(800) 248-8239
(800) 809-5818 (fax)

Wire Mesh

Allen Special Products, Inc.
(Stuf-fit® copper mesh)
P.O. Box 605
Montgomeryville, PA 18936
(800) 848-6805
(215) 997-6654

Getting to Know
The Humane Society of the United States

Animals depend on us to protect them in a world that seems to have less and less regard for them. Whenever we encroach on animals' territory, or when we use our fellow creatures as commodities, the animal suffers. The Humane Society of the United States, a nonprofit organization, is devoted to making the world safe for animals through legal, educational, legislative and investigative means. The HSUS is dedicated to speaking for animals, who cannot speak for themselves. We believe that humans have a moral obligation to protect the other species with which they share the Earth. Founded in 1954, The HSUS has a constituency of more than four million persons. The HSUS is headquartered in Washington, D.C., with regional offices, an educational division, a team of investigators, legislative experts and a program staff addressing virtually every important animal protection issue.

You Can Help

You have the power to help animals. You can help animals with the choices you make every day. Think before you buy. Become a compassionate consumer by letting your purchases advertise your concern for animals. Shop for clothing and jewelry that aren't the products of cruelty. Don't buy fur, a frivolous fashion that causes unimaginable suffering to millions of animals. Do not use or buy ivory, the price of which is disappearance of elephants from the Earth. Use cosmetics and personal-care products that aren't tested on animals. A wide variety of beautiful cosmetics that do not result from cruel laboratory tests on animals is available. Eat with conscience, thereby helping to minimize the suffering of animals used for food.

Choose only tuna that is identified with a "Dolphin Safe" label. Join The Humane Society of the United States as we work to give animals their rightful place in this world. Because it's not just our world. The world belongs to the animals too.

HSUS Programs

Wildlife

We file lawsuits and conduct other action programs to save wildlife and its habitat and to protect wildlife from inhumane and cruel treatment. Also, we publish books and conduct seminars to encourage the enjoyment of wildlife and to teach people how to live compatibly with wild animals.

Companion Animals

The HSUS promotes responsible pet ownership—including the spaying or neutering of pets. Our nationwide campaign, "Until There Are None—Adopt One," encourages the public to adopt their pets exclusively from animal shelters.

Laboratory Animals

The HSUS seeks to protect those animals now being used in research from suffering and abuse and to end all unnecessary and painful experimentation.

Farm Animals

The HSUS is working with the farm community, as well as with state and federal legislators, to end cruel farming and livestock rearing practices and to promote humane sustainable agriculture.

Education

From its quarterly magazine, *HSUS News*, to its issue-oriented *Close-Up Reports*, The HSUS provides tools to help animals. The HSUS touches children too, through its educational division, the National Association for Humane and Environmental Education (NAHEE), which urges students to be kind

to animals and assists teachers with humane lesson plans.

Field Services

The HSUS maintains a network of nine regional offices, covering forty-six states, that carry out our national programs at the regional level. They also provide support to local humane organizations, animal-control agencies, officials, educators, media and the general public through legislative, investigative and educational activities.

Membership dues in The HSUS are only $10 per year. To join The Humane Society of the United States or for more information, please write us at 2100 L Street, NW, Washington, DC 20037.

The HSUS Wildlife Land Trust: Shelters without Walls— Protecting Land for Wildlife

The HSUS Wildlife Land Trust exists to protect wild animals by preserving their natural habitats and by providing them sanctuary within those habitats.

Properties placed under Wildlife Land Trust care remain undeveloped places where wildlife is perpetually protected from human exploitation of any kind.

Anyone owning undeveloped wildlife habitat anywhere in the United States who would like to have that land remain undisturbed should seriously consider placing some or all of it under the Wildlife Land Trust's protective care. Not only are animals thereafter permanently protected by the Trust but there are considerable tax benefits to the donor as well.

Properties suitable for sanctuary designation may be protected either by a transfer of title to the Trust for perpetual care or by a transfer of a legally enforceable agreement to the Trust (called a "conservation easement"). In the latter case, while landowners do not relinquish ownership, they nonetheless legally and perpetually protect their properties against future development and other consumptive uses.

Countless generations of wild animals will continue to benefit from HSUS Wildlife Land Trust–secured natural habitats because thoughtful individuals who could contribute land or otherwise support the Trust did so and continue to do so. One of these individuals could be you. If you are in a position to help but have not yet become a Trust supporter, please join this important crusade to effectively protect the imperiled habitats of wild animals. It is their planet we share, and it is they whom, in fairness, we should be protecting more and destroying less.

For more information, contact The HSUS Wildlife Land Trust at 2100 L Street, NW, Washington, DC 20037. Or call the Trust toll-free at (800) 729-SAVE.

Glossary

Alien. A non-native plant or animal species. The starling and house sparrow are *introduced*, or alien species. The term *exotic* can mean the same thing.

Arthralgia. Pain in joint.

Browse. Plant material eaten by herbivores.

Carnivore. Meat-eater.

Coterie. A social unit based on familial affinity; used to describe prairie dog groups, each of which consists of related individuals sharing a territory.

Dispersion. The movement of young animals away from the area where they were born ("maternal home range") and the associated wandering until they settle down in a permanent home range.

Ecosystem. The interaction of the living (biotic) and nonliving (abiotic) components of the environment in a particular area, such that the exchange occurs inside—not outside—the system.

Encephalitis. Inflammation of the brain.

Enzootic. When an animal disease is peculiar to a specific region.

Epizootic. A disease that attacks many animals in a region at the same time.

Extinct. No longer present; sometimes refers to a given area, but more often (and appropriately) to a line or lineage that no longer exists.

Extirpated. Removed from an area; no longer occurring in a given region.

Exudate. Fluid that has escaped from blood vessels and is deposited on tissues. High in cellular debris and protein content, this fluid usually results from inflammation.

Forb. Annual or perennial plants without woody stems and that remain above ground over winter.

Friable. Loose, easily dug—as in soil.

Genus. In taxonomy, the term applied to a closely related group of animals that shares one or more characteristics; falls between the "family" and "species" rankings.

Gestation. The period of time between conception and delivery when a mother carries young.

Herbaceous. Green leafy material that regrows annually.

Herbivore. An animal that eats only or mostly plant material.

Herd. A group of animals that live together.

Home range. The area in which an animal spends the bulk of its life.

Humane. The avoidance of inflicting pain, discomfort and harassment.

Hydrophobia. Fear of water; this term is also used as a synonym for rabies.

Inanition. Starvation; an exhausted state due to prolonged undernutrition.

Innoculum. Material that is introduced into the tissue of a living organism, usually as a disease agent or pathogenic organism.

Insectivore. Insect-eater.

Integrated Pest Management. A practice that advocates a comprehensive approach to solving problems with pest species.

Mast. Fruits or nuts eaten by wild animals. "Hard" mast usually refers to acorns or nuts, while "soft" mast usually refers to tree fruit such as cherries.

Myalgia. Pain in muscle.

Omnivore. Meat- and plant-eater.

Scat. Animal feces.

Septicemia. Disease caused by the spread of pathogenic microorganisms through the blood.

Species. A population of living organisms that shares a definable geographic area and within which all members are capable of interbreeding and producing fertile offspring.

Sylvatic. Literally means "found in the woods"; used to describe a strain of disease common to wild animals only.

Territory. An area that is defended against others of the same species; may be a part or all of a home range.

Translocation. The movement of animals from one area to another.

Zoonosis. Animal diseases transmissible to humans.

Index

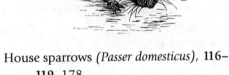

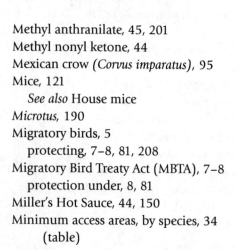

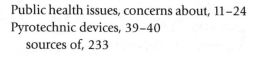

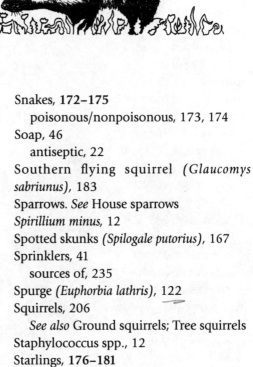

About the Authors

John Hadidian, Ph.D., is the director of the Urban/Suburban Wildlife Protection Program at The Humane Society of the United States.

Guy R. Hodge is the director of the Department of Data and Information Services.

John W. Grandy, Ph.D., is the vice president of Wildlife and Habitat Protection.